A HISTORY OF THE PULITZER PRIZE PLAYS

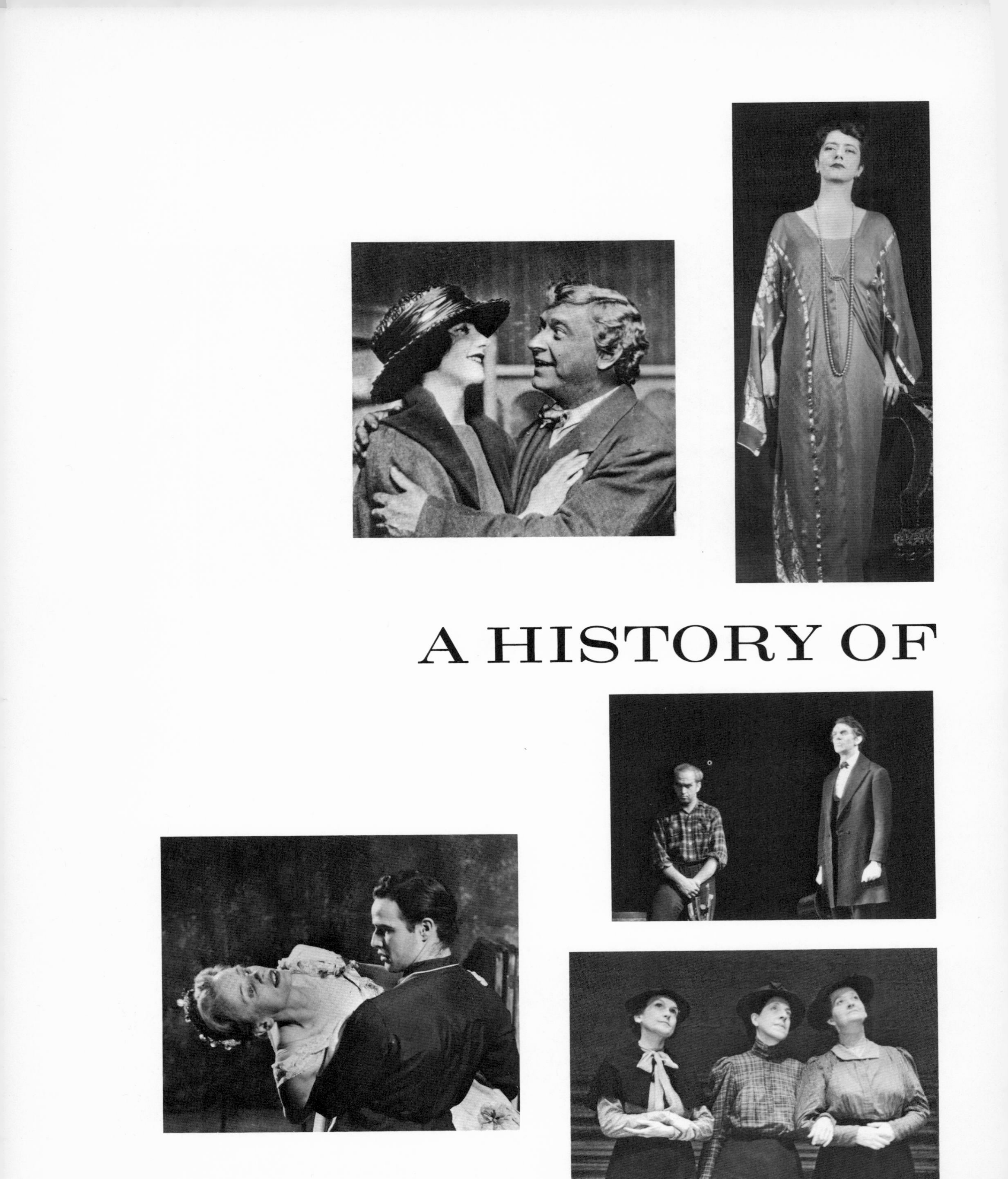

A HISTORY OF

THE PULITZER PRIZE PLAYS

by John L. Toohey

THE CITADEL PRESS New York

For John Peter Toohey

First Edition

Published by Citadel Press, Inc.
222 Park Avenue South, New York, N.Y. 10003
Published simultaneously in Canada by George J. McLeod Limited
73 Bathurst St., Toronto 2B, Ont.

Manufactured in the United States of America by The Haddon Craftsmen, Inc., Scranton, Pa.

Designed by A. Christopher Simon

Library of Congress catalog card number: 67-25654

CONTENTS

ACKNOWLEDGMENTS

Most of the research for this book was done in the Theatre Collection at the Lincoln Center Branch of the New York Public Library, where Paul Myers and his staff were enormously helpful.

Sam Pierce of the Museum of the City of New York also contributed generously of his time.

Don Freeman supplied his marvelous drawings of *Of Thee I Sing, The Time of Your Life* and *Death of a Salesman.*

Thanks also to these others who helped with pictures and/or information:

Joseph Abeles of Friedman-Abeles; Walter Alford of John Springer Associates; Howard Atlee; Edwin Bolwell of the Toronto *Globe & Mail;* Arthur Cantor; Marc Connelly; Merle Debuskey; Max Eisen; Fred Fehl; Harold Friedlander of Artcraft; Donald Gallup of the Yale University Library; Paul Green; Henry Grossman; Frances Herridge of the New York *Post;* Sol Jacobson; Tom Kilpatrick; Roy Lester of Graphic House; Howard Lindsay; Magnum Photos; Richard Maney; Armina Marshall of The Theatre Guild; Arthur Miller; Mrs. Rebecca Morehouse; James D. Proctor; Alice Regensburg of the Lynn Farnol Group; Elmer Rice; Richard Rodgers; Sheldon Secunda; and John Willis.

And thanks to Harper & Row for permission to quote from *O'Neill,* by Arthur and Barbara Gelb; to Charles Scribner's Sons for permission to quote from Robert E. Sherwood's Introductions to *Idiot's Delight* and *Abe Lincoln in Illinois;* and to Mrs. Rebecca Morehouse for permission to quote from *Matinee Tomorrow,* by Ward Morehouse, published by McGraw-Hill.

PICTURE CREDITS

Key to Abbreviations

ERC *Elmer Rice Collection,* F-A *Friedman-Abeles, Inc.,* GH *Graphic House,* JWC *John Willis Collection,* MCC *Marc Connelly Collection,* MCNY *Museum of the City of New York,* NYPL *New York Public Library,* RRC *Richard Rodgers Collection,* TGC *Theatre Guild Collection,* WAC *Walter Alford Collection,* YU *Yale University.*

1. NYPL *2-8.* MCNY *9.* NYPL *10-14.* MCNY *9.* NYPL *10-14.* MCNY *16-20.* NYPL *21-25.* YU—Abbe Studio *26.* NYPL *27.* YU—Abbe Studio *28-33.* NYPL *34-39.* MCNY *40-47.* YU—TGC *48-53.* NYPL *54.* Paul Green *55-57.* NYPL *60-67.* YU—Vandamm—TGC *68.* Theatre Guild Magazine *69.* ERC *70.* NYPL *73-74.* ERC *76.* MCC *77.* MCC—White Studio *78-84.* MCC *85.* MCC—Ben Pinchot *86-87.* MCC *88-93.* MCNY *94.* MCNY—William Auerbach-Levy *95-97.* NYPL—Vandamm *98.* Don Freeman *100-103.* NYPL—Vandamm *105.* MCNY—William Auerbach-Levy *106-111.* YU—Vandamm—TGC *112-121.* MCNY *122-129.* NYPL—Vandamm *130.* WAC—Pach Brothers *131-139.* YU—Vandamm—TGC *140.* New York Post *141-142.* NYPL—Vandamm *145.* Tom Creem *147.* NYPL—Vandamm *148.* Associated Press *149-154.* GH *156.* Mary Morris *157-165.* NYPL—Vandamm *166-169.* YU—TGC *170.* Don Freeman *172, 175.* YU—TGC *176-178.* WAC—Vandamm *180-183.* WAC—Vandamm *185.* NYPL—Vandamm *186-193.* GH *195.* NYPL—Vandamm *196-199.* Tom Kilpatrick *202.* Howard Lindsay *203-209.* GH *210.* NYPL—Vandamm *212-223.* GH *224.* Don Freeman *226-229.* GH *230.* RRC—John Swope *231.* RRC *232.* Bob Golby *233.* John Swope *234.* Bob Golby *235* (top). Bob Golby *235* (bottom). John Swope *236-239.* John Swope *240.* NYPL—Vandamm *243-247,* Fred Fehl *249.* Alfredo Valente *250-257.* YU—TGC—Zinn Arthur *258-264.* GH *266.* F-A *267.* Zinn Arthur *269-275.* F-A *276.* NYPL *277-279.* Fred Fehl *280-281.* Toronto Globe & Mail *282-283.* Fred Fehl *284* (top). JWC *284* (bottom). JWC *285.* JWC—Sy Friedman *286.* JWC *287.* JWC *288.* JWC—Arthur Cantor *289.* JWC—Gjon Mili *291.* JWC—Gjon Mili *292-313.* F-A *314-319* Sheldon Secunda *320-325.* F-A *326.* Merle Debuskey Collection *327.* Magnum Photos *328-332.* Bert Andrews, except Gilroy portrait, *p. 329,* from Max Eisen Collection *334-339.* Miss Alix Jeffry.

INTRODUCTION

A SEVENTEEN-YEAR-OLD HUNGARIAN IMMIGRANT named Joseph Pulitzer, barely able to speak English, arrived in Boston in 1865, did a wartime stint with the Union Army, and then drifted out to St. Louis, where he began a newspaper career on a German-American paper. He eventually gained control of the St. Louis *Post-Dispatch* and the New York *World*, a tight-knit little journalistic empire that made him a multimillionaire.

On April 10, 1903, Pulitzer signed an agreement with the trustees of New York's Columbia University to endow a School of Journalism, specifying that the income from $500,000 of the $2,000,000 that he was assigning to Columbia be allotted for "prizes or scholarships for the encouragement of public service, public morale, American literature and the advancement of education."

Pulitzer's will, dated April 16, 1904, spelled out in greater detail the conditions under which the Pulitzer Prizes were to be awarded. The trustees of Columbia were to be ultimately responsible for bestowing the prizes, but they were to be guided by the recommendations of an Advisory Board. The trustees were to be allowed to veto, but not to substitute choices of their own. The members of the Advisory Board, on the other hand, while expected to consider the advice of special jurors in each field, were empowered to make whatever use they chose of those juries' findings; they could accept, change, or reject them.

The thirteen members of the Advisory Board were to include the President of Columbia and a dozen assorted editors and publishers, drawn from newspapers across the nation. These board members are the true men of power, for the trustees are primarily figureheads, and the jurors have no assurance that their recommendations will be accepted.

The annual award of the Pulitzer Prize for drama is frequently a source of irritation and resentment among people who earn their living in the theatre, for they feel that this is essentially a prize given by amateurs to professionals. They often question the Advisory Board's taste; more seriously, they question its credentials. Why on earth should a random group of editors feel qualified to identify the best American play of the season, particularly when not all members of the group have always seen all of the eligible plays?

The phrase "Pulitzer Prize Play," however, has for years had magical overtones for the man in the street, who could not care less about the behind-the-scenes decisions, however arbitrary, that have led to its bestowal.

It would be misleading, in the light of the above, to suggest that a collection of the forty-two plays so far tapped for the Pulitzer Prize represents anything more than a fascinating cross-section of the past fifty years of the American theatre. This book is for the most part an index of public taste, although not all of the Pulitzer Prize plays were chosen for their popularity. *Alison's House* and *In Abraham's Bosom* set no box-offices afire.

An equally fine anthology could be compiled of plays which did *not* win the Pulitzer: *What Price Glory?, Mourning Becomes Electra, The Children's Hour, Of Mice and Men, The Show-Off, Watch on the Rhine, The Adding Machine, Awake and Sing, The Little Foxes, The Petrified Forest, Once in a Lifetime, The Glass Menagerie, Mary of Scotland, Winterset, Who's Afraid of Virginia Woolf?* and quite a few others. Some of these were necessarily eliminated because only one play is chosen each season; *Of Mice and Men*, for instance, is off the list because *Our Town* is on it, and *Mourning Becomes Electra* was shouldered aside by the bumptious *Of Thee I Sing*.

In an article published in *Theatre Annual* of 1944, Walter Prichard Eaton made the most lengthy and revealing statement ever attributed to a Pulitzer juror, most of whom have confined their public remarks to grumbling when their recommendations have been overridden by the Advisory Board.

Many of Eaton's comments on specific decisions are quoted further on in this volume. At the end of his article, after discussing the pros and cons of decisions that had often been controversial, he concluded:

"And what does all this prove? *De gustibus non est disputandum*, perhaps. That it is difficult to tell, until time has come to one's aid, what is enduring art and what is a flash in the pan. That there is a fear, sometimes, on the part of the administrators of a trust (and even the Pulitzer jurors are, in a sense, such administrators) of departing too violently from conservatism in making their judgments. That, possibly, there is a somewhat greater sense of the underlying moral responsibility of art on the part of such men as constitute the Pulitzer juries than on the part of Broadway critics. And, of course, that now and then there is just plain esthetic dumbness, as when we preferred *They Knew What They Wanted* to *What Price Glory?* But, on the whole and in recent years, matched award for award with the Critics' Circle choice, the Pulitzer Prize has not been unworthily administered. When one considers that the French Academy did not admit Molière until he had been dead a century, one might even say that the Pulitzer Prize has been awarded with some distinction.

"My own feeling is, after serving on many Pulitzer juries and taking many critical jibes on the chin, that it would have been wiser and more useful if the award had been made each year not to the author of the so-called best play, but to the new author who had shown what seemed the greatest promise of potential development in technical skill and serious purpose. We tried, perhaps unwisely, to do just that when we gave the prize to Paul Green for *In Abraham's Bosom*—unwisely because the terms of the award make no provision for such considerations. But, as matters now stand, the prize is almost sure to go to a dramatist who had already won his spurs and fought his way to an assured position in the theatre. Few, if any, men write a *best* play on the first or second try; but many a man has been unable, for want of encouragement and some financial aid, to keep on making the tries. If the critics, who must perforce see everything, could be consulted by the Pulitzer jury, or could tip off the jury when some play comes along worth a look, yet not destined for any length of run, and if the members of the play jury had as their duty not the ex-cathedra judgment of a *best* play but the encouragement of a worthy beginner, I feel that the award would then accomplish more for the American theatre. But it is too late to do anything about that now."

At any rate, here they are. For richer or for poorer, warts and all, they constitute the single most famous group of American plays written in the past fifty years: *The Pulitzer Prize Plays, 1917–1967*.

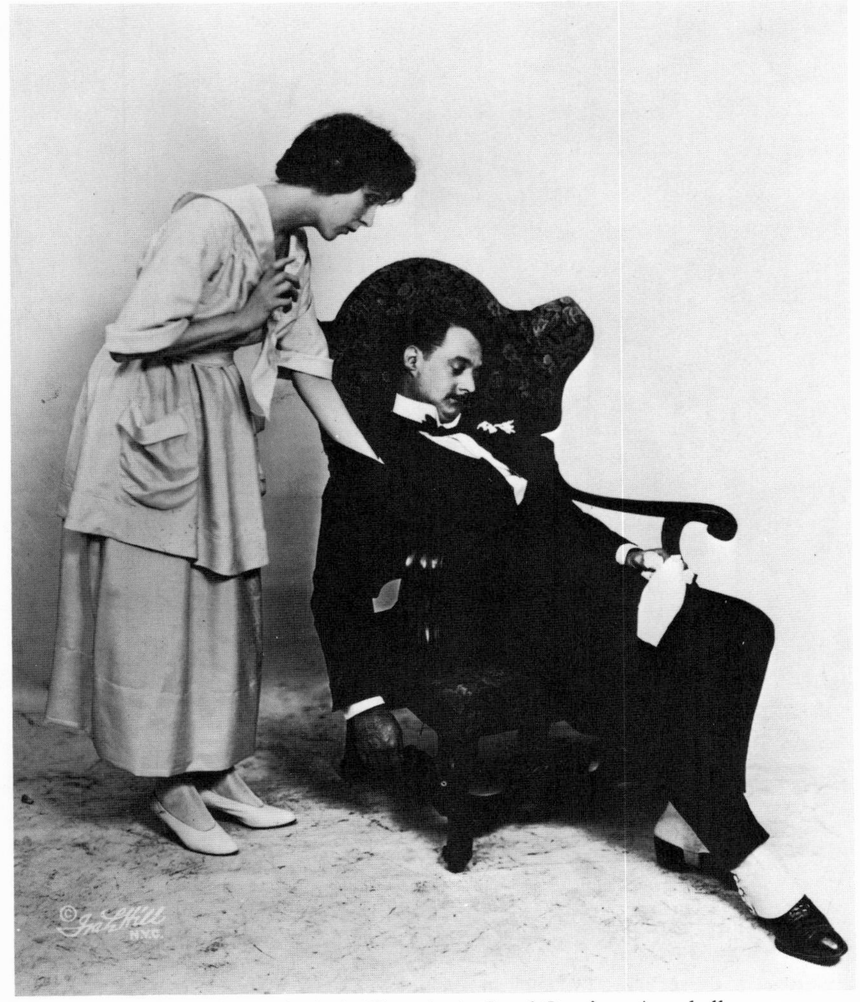

Lola Fisher and Edwin Nicander in Good Gracious Annabelle

1916-17

NO AWARD

This was the first season in which the Pulitzer Prize was to be given, but as there was no one outstanding play, Columbia obviously felt that it would be injudicious to crown a second-rater just for the sake of being able to make an award. The Advisory Board wisely held its fire.

The season's plays included Clare Kummer's *Good Gracious Annabelle* (probably the leading candidate), Winchell Smith and John E. Hazzard's *Turn to the Right*, Jules Eckert Goodman's adaptation of *The Man Who Came Back*, and Bayard Veiller's extremely successful melodrama, *The Thirteenth Chair*.

There was no commotion at the lack of an award. As yet, the general public scarcely knew that the Pulitzer Prize existed.

(Top) *Estelle Winwood, Shelly Hull*
(Bottom) *Lotus Robb, Nat C. Goodwin, Shelly Hull*

1917-18

HELEN, A FREE-THINKING YOUNG WOMAN, and Ernest, a highly respected but underpaid bacteriologist, are in love, but Helen would prefer not to marry him—she feels that marriage would give Ernest financial responsibilities that he simply could not handle, and besides, she is convinced that marriage is essentially an institution for hypocrites, entered into for convenience, kept up out of habit.

All around her Helen can see examples of bad marriages: Theodore and Mary, scraping along on his salary as a rector; Uncle Everett and Aunt Julia (she is in Reno starting divorce proceedings); John and Lucy, squabbling over money. And while Helen's sister Jean is about to marry Rex, she is doing it for money, not for love.

Ernest has a chance to study in Paris, and wants to marry Helen and take her with him. She is all for the Paris trip, but without the marriage vows, which somewhat shocks Ernest.

Helen's family is also shocked by her attitude, but nothing will change her mind, not cajolery, not even bribery. Wily old Uncle Everett, however, gets Helen and Ernest to admit aloud, in his presence, that they feel they are married "in the sight of God." Then he quickly pronounces them man and wife, under the powers granted him as a judge. Helen is furious at first, but quickly becomes resigned; after all, it would now be ridiculous to *divorce* Ernest. The newlyweds head for Paris, and to complete the happy ending, Aunt Julia returns from Reno with a change of heart.

Edmund Breese, Lotus Robb, Ernest Lawford, Estelle Winwood, Shelly Hull, Nat C. Goodwin

WHY MARRY?

THE CREDITS

A Comedy in Three Acts by Jesse Lynch Williams.
Produced by Selwyn & Co. by arrangement with Roi Cooper Megrue.
Staged by Roi Cooper Megrue.
Opened at the Astor Theatre, December 25, 1917, and ran for 120 performances.

THE CAST

Jean . . . *the host's younger sister, who has been brought up to be married and nothing else*	Lotus Robb
Cousin Theodore . . . *a clergyman and yet a human being, who believes in everything—except divorce*	Ernest Lawford
Uncle Everett . . . *a judge, who belongs to the older generation and yet understands the new—and believes in divorce*	Nat C. Goodwin

HELEN . . . *the host's other sister, whom everyone wants to marry, but who doesn't want to marry anyone*	Estelle Winwood
THE BUTLER	Richard Pitman
REX . . . *an unmarried neighbor, who has not been brought up to be anything but rich*	Harold West
LUCY . . . *the hostess, who is trying her best to be "just an old-fashioned wife" in a new-fashioned home*	Beatrice Beckley
JOHN . . . *the host, who owns the house and almost everyone in it and does not believe in divorce*	Edmund Breese
ERNEST . . . *a scientist, who believes in neither divorce nor marriage but makes a great discovery*	Shelly Hull
THE FOOTMAN	Walter Goodson

The Scene is a Week-end at a Country House Not Far Away; the Time, Saturday Afternoon, Sunday Morning and Sunday Night.

Ernest Lawford, Nat C. Goodwin, Edmund Breese, Estelle Winwood

HISTORY AND REVIEWS

"This is a comedy with brains behind it. . . ."

The announcement of the first Pulitzer Prize for drama rated only two paragraphs on an inside page of *The New York Times*; it was to take a few years for the Prize to receive national attention, or even to occasion much discussion.

The three drama jurors—Augustus Thomas, Richard Burton and Hamlin Garland—had been chosen, at Columbia University's request, by the National Institute of Arts and Letters, and it was Thomas who made the official announcement. He made it two days earlier than originally planned, for playwright Jesse Lynch Williams was about to take a trip away from New York for several months, and it was felt that he should be on hand when this first award was bestowed. The drama Prize had gone begging the year before, although the first Pulitzer Prizes in other fields had been awarded.

Why Marry? was chosen as best fitting the terms of the original citation, which was to be modified several times in years to come: "For the original American play, performed in New York, which shall best represent the educational value and power of the stage in raising the standard of good morals, good taste and good manners, $1,000.00."

Williams was 46 at the time, and was to be involved with the Pulitzer Prize in many subsequent seasons; he later served frequently as a juror, but never again wrote a play that won the honor. He had

Lotus Robb, Edmund Breese, Harold West

been a newspaperman and short story writer, and *Why Marry?* was adapted from a story he had written in 1914, *And So They Were Married*. It was the second story that he had turned into a play; in 1906 he had adapted *The Stolen Story*. It was never a big hit, but was cited as an honest job of playwriting.

Some of the notices:

Charles Darnton in the *Evening World*:

"It sounds shocking, but *Why Marry?* is simply a comedy that takes true love as a matter of course even after it has made its way to Reno. This is a comedy with brains behind it. It is the best American comedy that has found its way to the stage in years."

Alan Dale in the *American*:

"*Why Marry?*, though its theme was promising, proved to be tedious and fatiguing. Its three acts were very long. There was no suspense; there was no shock; there was really no play. The author, Jesse Lynch Williams, was well primed on the subject of marriage, and said many interesting things quite neatly, but it was all extremely vacillating, and—as in the Shaw plays—pointless. A most eventless play."

Lawrence Reamer in the *Sun*:

"*Why Marry?*, a comedy success, proves constantly amusing. No other American drama of the present year has shown such literary merit."

The Playgoer in the *Evening Sun*:

"*Why Marry?* is the best American play written in years. The brilliant comedy has dialogue quite as sparkling as the Shaw variety, accompanied by really Shavian sanity of outlook and fearlessness in truth telling. Indeed, *Why Marry?* is the happiest combination of lightness and depth that has been seen on the stage in many a season. Nat Goodwin was delicious as a witty, philosophic judge."

Unsigned in the *World*:

"The play, despite the fact that it is made up of specially manufactured conditions to bolster its author's contentions, is undeniably clever. It has an intellectual flavor that most of our native conventionally contrived comedies have not. The young idealists were impersonated by Estelle Winwood and Shelly Hull—rather more convincingly by the former than by the latter. Ernest Lawford was excellent."

Soon after the opening Williams became involved in an amiable duel with *The New York Times*. Writing in that paper on February 3, 1918, critic John Corbin said:

"Behind the scenes, Mr. Williams pulls some four hundred strings, in the manner of Tony Sarg—and his marionettes are even more marvelously lifelike—until you begin to measure up what they do against what they say, and that is too much to ask of any audience. In a word, Mr. Williams has transposed what is normally a middle-class situation, and quite serious, even tragic, into the key of society comedy with gladsome wedding bells. In the keen intelligence of his economic disquisitions and the brilliancy of his dialogue, in the vigor and humor of his characterizations, in the spirit and skill with which his characters and story are developed, *Why Marry?* rises head and shoulders above other American comedies of the sort. But as an embodiment of a normal situation in dramatic action the play is quite futile. What Ibsen put into dynamic character, the modern playwright takes out in talk. 'Katy did!' says he. 'Katy did!' But she didn't, she didn't, she didn't."

Mr. Corbin's main objection to *Why Marry?* seemed to lie in his feeling that Mr. Williams was determined to eat his cake and have it too; that the playwright let his daring young lovers profess their scorn for the technicalities of the marriage service, but that he took great care to get them married at the end of the play, even though a ruse had to be used to effect this. The *Times* gave Mr. Williams two full columns for his rebuttal, on February 10. Here is a paragraph of it:

"This climax, I submit, is not, as you imply, a playwright's sleight-of-hand trick to produce a 'happy ending.' It is the logical conclusion to all that has gone before, a result of character, conviction, and dramatic progress. These young people, these spokesmen for the scientific age, merely scrape off the slush of sentimentality, the scum of hypocrisy, from our most important institution, and get down to the eternal verities of the most important relationship in life. They do not defame marriage; they define it."

Corbin managed to have the last word, of course. In a footnote to the Williams letter, he said:

"At the last reduction, *Why Marry?* is a Katy-did comedy—eloquent in declamation against modern

Shelly Hull, Estelle Winwood, Nat C. Goodwin, Edmund Breese, Ernest Lawford, Lotus Robb

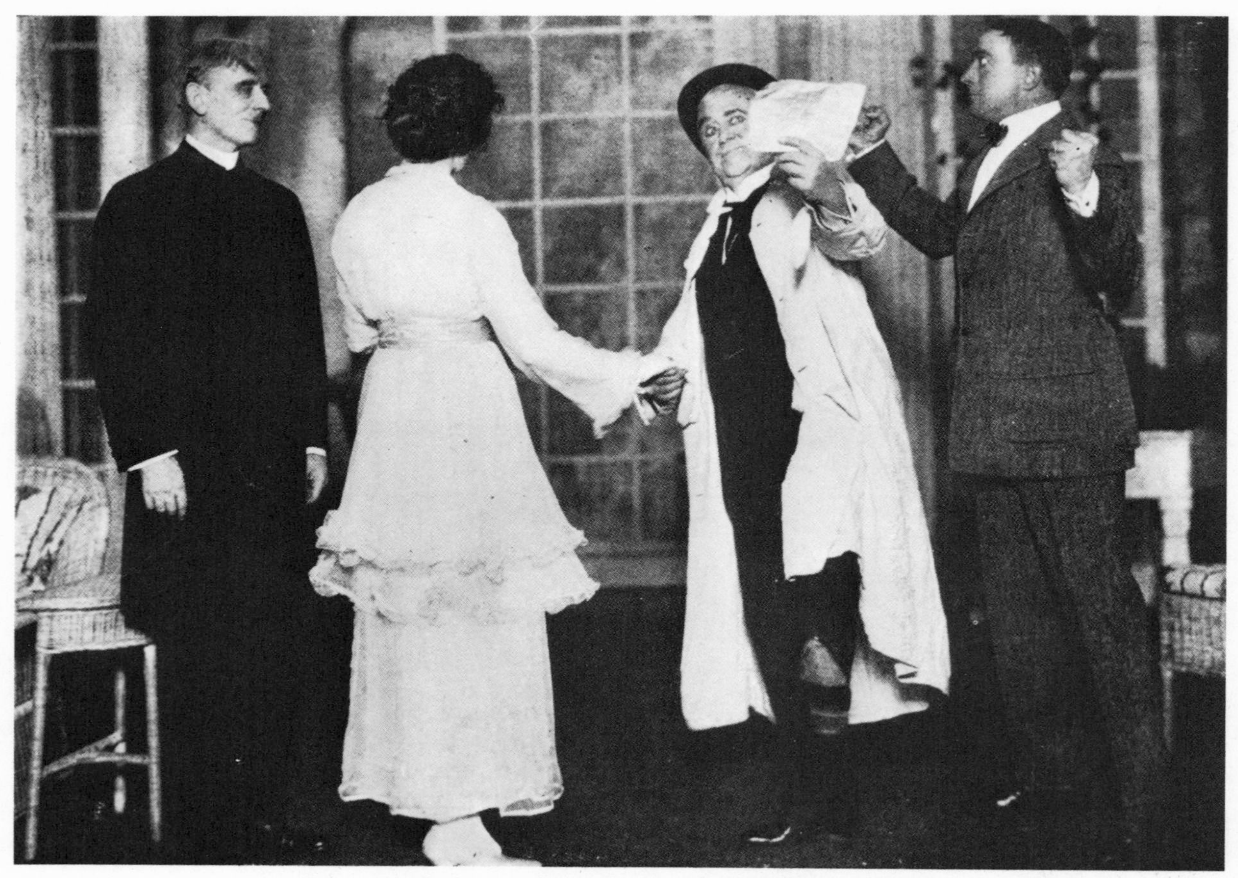

Ernest Lawford, Lotus Robb, Nat C. Goodwin, Edmund Breese

marriage, but ending in matrimony. However well this Katy meant, a legal marriage was 'put over' upon her. It was done with a dramatic shift and sleight which any playwright might be proud of, but the fact remains that Katy didn't!"

ALSO-RANS: *The Copperhead, A Tailor Made Man, Seventeen, The Country Cousin*

SUMMATION

A satisfactory decision, as there was no outstanding competition. The wartime crop of plays was pretty slim this season, and *Why Marry?,* while no world-beater, did have wit and polish, and a surprisingly sophisticated point of view for its day.

Frank Bacon as Lightnin' Bill Jones in Lightnin'

1918-19

NO AWARD

Lightnin', written by Winchell Smith and Frank Bacon, and starring Mr. Bacon as Lightnin' Bill Jones, was the biggest hit of the season, and eventually ran for an unprecedented 1,291 performances, but the Pulitzer judges apparently felt that they didn't want to give their shiny new award to a drunken old rascal, lovable or not. A quarter of a century later, however, they were to look more tolerantly on *Harvey*.

Among the other plays of the season were Austin Strong's *Three Wise Fools*, Rachel Crothers' *A Little Journey*, and Samuel Shipman and John B. Hymer's *East Is West*, with Fay Bainter teetering daintily through the proceedings as Ming Toy. Big hit though it was (680 performances), *East Is West* did not deal with an American theme, and in those days that was enough to remove it from consideration.

Eugene O'Neill, by William Zorach

1919-20

ANDREW AND ROBERT MAYO ARE BROTHERS, working the family farm together. Andrew is the true farmer, while Robert is a dreamer.

Robert, who has secretly been in love with Ruth Atkins for years, plans to sign aboard his Uncle Dick's ship and go off around the world, in order to leave Ruth to Andrew, whom he believes Ruth loves. When Ruth surprisingly admits her love for Robert, it is Andrew who leaves with Uncle Dick, while the dreamer stays home to run the farm.

Three years later, the farm has begun to show signs of mismanagement. Ruth and Robert are forever quarreling, over their child, over Robert's obsessive reading, over his lack of any practical farming skill. Andrew comes home briefly. Ruth has been desperately eager to see him, but the years have changed him—self-important, independent, he no longer feels the love for her that he had felt as a younger man.

Another five years pass. The farm is now in complete disorder. Ruth has become a sullen slattern, and Robert, dying of tuberculosis, can do little more than talk wildly about "going to the city" to make a fresh start. Andrew returns again, having lost most of his money in foolish speculations. Robert, on his deathbed, makes Andrew promise to marry Ruth. Andrew tells her that they must somehow try to help each other, but Ruth, utterly beaten down by the frustrations of the past few years, can see no hope for their future.

Mary Jeffery, Max Mitzel, Erville Alderson, George Hadden, Richard Bennett

BEYOND THE HORIZON

THE CREDITS

AN AMERICAN TRAGEDY IN THREE ACTS BY EUGENE O'NEILL.
PRODUCED BY JOHN D. WILLIAMS.
STAGED BY JOHN D. WILLIAMS, EUGENE O'NEILL, AND HOMER SAINT-GAUDENS
OPENED AT A SPECIAL MATINEE AT THE MOROSCO THEATRE, FEBRUARY 3, 1920,
AND RAN FOR 111 PERFORMANCES.

THE CAST

ROBERT MAYO	Richard Bennett
ANDREW MAYO	Edward Arnold
RUTH ATKINS	Helen MacKellar
CAPT. DICK SCOTT	Max Mitzel
MRS. KATE MAYO	Mary Jeffery
JAMES MAYO	Erville Alderson
MRS. ATKINS	Louise Closser Hale
MARY	Elfin Finn

Ben	George Hadden
Dr. Fawcett	George Riddell

ACT I

scene 1. *The Road. Sunset of a Day in Spring.*
scene 2. *The Farm House. The Same Night.*

ACT II

scene 1. *The Farm House. Noon of a Summer Day. Several Years Later.*
scene 2. *The Road. The Following Day.*

ACT III

The Farm House. Dawn of a Day in Late Fall. Five Years Later.

HISTORY AND REVIEWS

"An absorbing, significant and memorable tragedy, so full of meat that it makes most of the remaining fare seem like the merest meringue. . . ."

Eugene O'Neill had to wait until he was 31 years old for his first Broadway production, *Beyond the Horizon.* Over the previous two or three years he had steadily been building a reputation with the one-act plays that the Provincetown Players had been doing down in Greenwich Village at The Playwrights' Theatre—*Bound East for Cardiff, Fog, In the Zone, Where the Cross Is Made, The Moon of the Caribbees.* Gaunt and hollow-eyed, restless, ambitious, a man who could drink and play as hard as he could work, O'Neill blew a hot, harsh gust of life into a theatre that was in desperate need of it.

The sea held a lifelong fascination for him, and many of his early plays stemmed directly from his youthful experiences as an ordinary seaman on the square-rigged *Charles Racine* and the British tramp *Ikalis.* He knew the depravity of waterfront dives, and he knew the starlit peace of a night watch; he transmuted this knowledge, both the sweet and the sour, into raw, jagged plays that quivered with commonplace tensions.

His characters did not mesh smoothly with one another in carefully patterned relationships, but rather crashed and collided like great boulders adrift in surf. Although he could be laughably crude and sentimental, O'Neill's plays have almost no sense of humor in them, no lightness. He wrote with an axe, and much of the time he stumbled over his own feet, and he produced the greatest body of dramatic literature of any playwright of the twentieth century.

Producer John D. Williams held the script of *Beyond the Horizon* for almost two years before finally putting it on for what started as a series of special matinees, and later was expanded into a regular run. In early 1920, Williams was presenting Elmer Rice's *For the Defense* at the Morosco Theatre. Its star was the 47-year-old Richard Bennett. Quite by accident Bennett picked up a dusty copy of the O'Neill play that was pigeonholed in Williams' office, read it, and decided that he had to play the 23-year-old hero.

Bennett suggested to Williams that the bulk of the cast be recruited from *For the Defense,* and that the play be done at the Morosco itself on weekday afternoons only. It was a cheap and easy way to put a production together, and Williams fell in with the idea. O'Neill was less happy—he had wanted young John Barrymore for the leading role, and the prospect of "special matinees" sounded amateurishly unattractive—but at least it represented a Broadway production for his first full-length play, so the playwright reluctantly agreed.

Bennett, Louise Closser Hale, Mary Jeffery and George Riddell came to *Beyond the Horizon* from

For the Defense, and Edward Arnold and Helen MacKellar were recruited from the cast of another current play, *The Storm.* With makeshift settings that were cheap and tawdry, a patchwork cast, and the daunting matinee schedule, Eugene O'Neill was launched on Broadway. For thirty years, Broadway was never quite the same again.

Some of the notices:

Alexander Woollcott in *The New York Times*:

"The fare available for the New York theatregoer is immeasurably richer and more substantial because of a new play which was unfolded yesterday afternoon in the Morosco Theatre—an absorbing, significant and memorable tragedy, so full of meat that it makes most of the remaining fare seem like the merest meringue. The only reason for not calling *Beyond the Horizon* a great play is the natural gingerliness with which a reviewer uses that word. Certainly, despite a certain clumsiness and confusion in too luxurious multiplicity of scenes, the play has greatness in it, and marks O'Neill as one of our foremost playwrights. As the home-bound wanderer, Richard Bennett plays with fine eloquence, imagination and finesse."

Robert Gilbert Welsh in the *Telegram*:

"Only once or twice in the course of a crowded dramatic season does a play of such terrific force and such simple directness reward the patient theatrical chroniclers as did *Beyond the Horizon.* Eugene G. O'Neill now reveals his mastery of a larger form of dramatic construction in this three-act tragedy. *Beyond the Horizon* is a masterpiece written in a bitter, ironic strength. It is a great play—probably too great to be a popular success."

Heywood Broun in the *Tribune*:

"*Beyond the Horizon* is a significant and interesting play by a young author who does not as yet know all the tricks. Fortunately he therefore avoids many of the conventional shoddy stratagems, but at the same time there is an occasional clumsiness which mars his fine intent and achievement. Nevertheless, the play deserves a place among the noteworthy achievements of native authors. *Beyond the Horizon* is by far the best serious play which any American author has written for years."

J. Ranken Towse in the *Evening Post*:

"There can be no question that *Beyond the Horizon* is work of uncommon merit and definite ability. It is a genuine, reasonable, poignant, domestic 'American tragedy,' arising out of the conflict between circumstance and character, wholly unsensational but sufficiently dramatic, showing a sympathetic comprehension of elemental human nature and representing a realistic study of actual life. But it is not quite a masterpiece. It is somewhat shambling in construction; it is too long, and it is too uniformly and unnecessarily sombre."

Charles Darnton in the *Evening World*:

"Although Eugene O'Neill's first long play is too long and overburdened with scenes, *Beyond the Horizon* marks the advent of an American realist who promises to go far, quite as far as his Scandinavian, Russian and Irish predecessors in the theatre. One's heart aches with the pity of it all, the blind struggle against inevitable disaster, the bitter cruelty of life, for *Beyond the Horizon* is close to life. It is a real play with real people. Richard Bennett realizes the hapless dreamer with fine understanding; Louise Closser Hale does the best work of her career."

Arthur and Barbara Gelb, in *O'Neill,* go into the origin of the play's title:

"The story has been told by several of O'Neill's friends that the title for *Beyond the Horizon* was suggested by a conversation he had with a feeble-minded boy on a Provincetown beach. 'What's out there?' asked the boy, gazing out over the Atlantic. 'The horizon,' O'Neill is said to have replied. 'And what's beyond the horizon?' asked the boy."

O'Neill is also quoted directly by the Gelbs as having once written:

"I have never written anything which did not come directly from some event or impression of my own, but these things develop very differently from what you expect. For example, I intended at first in *Beyond the Horizon* to portray in a series of disconnected scenes the life of a dreamer who pursues his vision over the world, apparently without success or a completed deed in his life. At the same time, it was my intention to show at last a real accretion from his wandering and dreaming, a thing intangible but real and precious beyond compare, which he had successfully made his own. But the technical difficulty of the task proved enormous and I was led to a grimmer thing: the tragedy of the man who looks over the horizon, who longs with his whole soul to depart on the quest, but whom destiny confines to a place and a task that are not his."

The award of the Pulitzer Prize came as a complete surprise to O'Neill. Much later, the Gelbs report, he said:

"In 1920 I had honestly never heard of the Pulitzer Prize, or if I had, hadn't listened. So when a wire reached me . . . saying I had won it my reaction was a disdainful raspberry—'Oh, a damned medal! And one of those presentation ceremonies! I won't accept it!' (I have never been fond of medals or ceremonies.)

"Then a wire from my agent arrived which spoke of a thousand dollars and no medal and no

Mary Jeffery, Erville Alderson, Max Mitzel, Richard Bennett, Edward Arnold

ceremony. Well, I practically went delirious! I was broke or nearly. A thousand dollars was sure a thousand dollars! It was the most astoundingly pleasant surprise I've ever had in my life, I think."

O'Neill was justifiably proud of the success of *Beyond the Horizon*. The Gelbs quote him:

"A simon pure, uncompromising American tragedy, which a Broadway manager dared to produce on Broadway, was surely an epoch-making event, and that it actually kept going from February to the end of the season was another tremendous upset."

A few months after the Prize had been awarded, Walter Prichard Eaton, a juror that year, wrote:

"That the judges could have hesitated long over this decision is difficult to imagine, for Mr. O'Neill's drama possesses so conspicuously one merit over all competitors, the merit of a tense, driving emotional sincerity, imparting to the spectator—when he withdraws a little from the spell of the tragedy—the sense that the dramatist has been imaginatively at the mercy of his people; not manipulating them so much as being manipulated by them."

Incidentally, this odd little footnote was appended to the official announcement of the Prize:

"The Advisory Board recorded their high appreciation of *Abraham Lincoln* by John Drinkwater, and regretted that by reason of its foreign authorship this play was not eligible for consideration in connection with this award."

ALSO-RANS: *The Famous Mrs. Fair, Adam and Eva, Clarence, Déclassée*

SUMMATION

A fine decision, and a courageous one in a way, as the Pulitzer judges had been confronted with a type of art form that simply hadn't existed before. This was the first genuine tragedy that an American playwright had ever written.

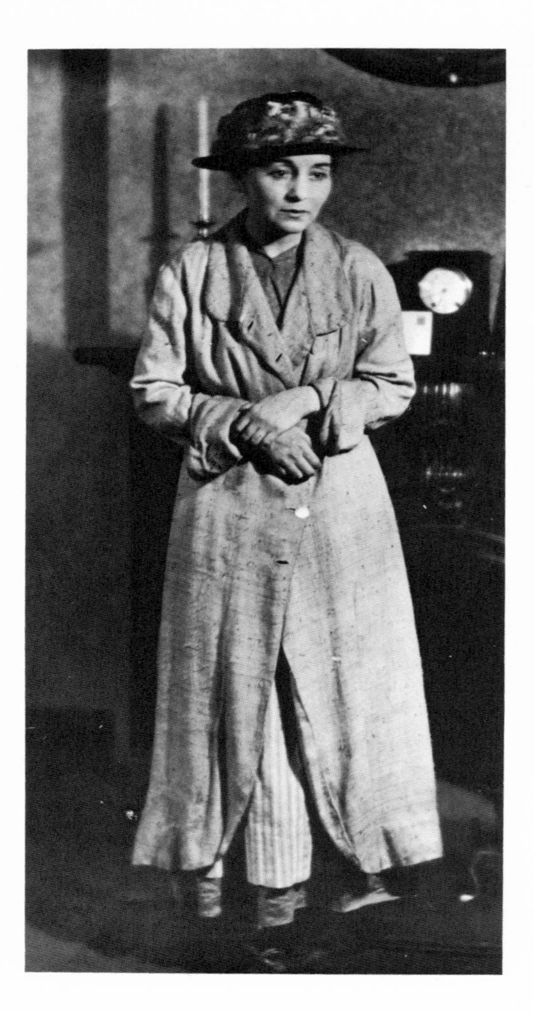

The transformation of Miss Lulu Bett, as portrayed by Carroll McComas.

1920-21

LULU BETT, A MAIDEN OF THIRTY-FOUR, is little more than a slavey in the home of Dwight Deacon, who is married to Lulu's sister, Ina. Lulu is a full-time, unsalaried maid and cook, and treats her bondage with a certain bitter humor. When Dwight's brother, Ninian, visits the house, Lulu finds romance in a most peculiar way. In what is purportedly a parlor game, she and Ninian are induced to recite the words of the marriage ceremony; the rite, they then learn, is technically binding, for Dwight Deacon's position as a judge permits him to perform marriages.

Lulu and Ninian go off on their honeymoon, but Lulu is back a week later, alone. Ninian, it seems, has confessed to the existence of another wife; he told Lulu that he had not seen or heard from her in years, and that she might very well be dead, but Lulu felt that she could hardly live with her new husband under such cloudy circumstances. For fear of a local scandal, Lulu is asked by Dwight to keep quiet about the bigamy—he would prefer the neighbors to think the newlyweds have separated merely because of incompatibility.

In the play's original ending, Ninian's first wife *is* alive, so Lulu is not officially married to him. She receives a proposal from an old admirer, Neil Cornish, but cannot agree to the marriage. She decides to leave town to think things over, and the play ends with the possibility that she may marry Neil later.

In the revised third act, Ninian returns with news that his first wife is dead, and he and Lulu have a happy reconciliation.

William E. Holden, Catherine Calhoun Doucet, Brigham Royce, Carroll McComas, Lois Shore, Louise Closser Hale, Beth Varden

MISS LULU BETT

THE CREDITS

A Comedy in Three Acts by Zona Gale.
Produced and Staged by Brock Pemberton.
Opened at the Belmont Theatre, December 27, 1920, and ran for 176 performances.

THE CAST

Monona Deacon	Lois Shore
Dwight Herbert Deacon	William E. Holden
Ina Deacon	Catherine Calhoun Doucet
Lulu Bett	Carroll McComas
Bobby Larkin	Jack Bohn
Mrs. Bett	Louise Closser Hale
Diana Deacon	Beth Varden
Neil Cornish	Willard Robertson
Ninian Deacon	Brigham Royce

ACT I

SCENE 1. *The Deacons' Dining Room.*
SCENE 2. *The Same. Ten Days Later.*

ACT II

SCENE 1. *The Deacons' Front Porch. A Month Later.*
SCENE 2. *The Same. The Following Evening.*
SCENE 3. *The Same. A Week Later.*

ACT III

Cornish's Music Store.

TIME: *The Present.* PLACE: *The Middle-class.*

Louise Closser Hale, Jack Bohn, Catherine Calhoun Doucet, William E. Holden, Beth Varden, Carroll McComas

HISTORY AND REVIEWS

"A homely and bitter piece of genuine American realism. . . ."

Miss Lulu Bett was the only play in history that ever opened at Sing-Sing.

David Belasco, the white-haired, ministerial-collared showman, had just presented the prison with something known as the "Belasco Stage." According to a handout distributed at its unveiling, "This stage is collapsable [*sic*] and portable and is as perfect a piece of stagecraftsmanship as considerations of quick and easy erection and dismounting will admit."

Belasco had originally planned to take his own production of *Call the Doctor* up to Ossining from the Empire Theatre, and *Miss Lulu Bett* was a last-minute substitute. It previewed at Sing-Sing on December 26, 1920 (a wife-murderer and a bigamist were among those pressed into service as stagehands), and then opened on Broadway the following night.

There were four other openings in New York on December 27, an indication of the way the theatre was thriving in those days. *Miss Lulu Bett's* opposition included *Her Family Tree*, Fritz Lieber in *Hamlet*, *Where the Lark Sings*, and a double bill at the Provincetown Playhouse, Eugene O'Neill's *Diff'rent* and Lawrence Vail's *What D'You Want?* Mr. O'Neill went on to larger things; Mr. Vail had a brief taste of reflected glory ten years later when Kaufman and Hart used his name for the character of the melancholy Broadway playwright in *Once in a Lifetime*, a role played by Mr. Kaufman himself.

Miss Lulu Bett was based on Zona Gale's best-selling novel of the same name, and Miss Gale did the dramatization herself, in a swift eight days. Born in Wisconsin, Miss Gale first turned her hand to writing short stories, then in 1906 wrote a book called *Romance Island*. Perhaps her best-known work was a collection of sketches about a place named Friendship Village, in a series of books variously titled *The Loves of Pelleas and Ettarre*, *When I Was a Little Girl* and *Christmas*.

Miss Lulu Bett was the first adaptation to win the Prize, in violation of the terms of the Pulitzer citation, which specified that the award was to go to an "original American play." The judges probably felt that since Miss Gale had adapted her own novel, the originality of the play was not in question. They were to wait almost ten years (until *The Green Pastures*, in 1929–30) before giving the Prize to another adaptation.

Some of the notices:

Alan Dale in the *American*:

"Miss Zona Gale's dramatization of her own novel was chiefly interesting by reason of a set of clever, amusing, almost Dickensonian family characterizations. Miss Lulu Bett herself was perhaps the least interesting character in this admirable gallery. Miss Lulu Bett was strained, a trifle false, and somewhat difficult to assimilate. And she demanded sympathy. Oh, she was a heroine. An Ibsen finish to a Dickensonian fabric is quite odd, not to say grotesque, and the end of *Miss Lulu Bett* suggested this. Not that it mattered. The plot of the play was, for me, utterly negligible, not to say foolish; the characters were delectable."

Unsigned in the *Herald*:

"All of Miss Gale's amusing satire and her truthful observation of American middle life were in the play, just as they had been in the novel. But they were projected through a medium to which they had not been adjusted."

Heywood Broun in the *Tribune*:

"*Miss Lulu Bett* is not quite a good play, but it is of the stuff of which great plays are made. Although often crude and sometimes tedious the play is a living thing. With the exception of Frank Craven no other American dramatist has loomed up so promisingly as Zona Gale as a national champion to be set up against St. John Ervine, perhaps the most adroit of living British realists. The most exacting role falls to Carroll McComas; she does exceedingly well."

Alexander Woollcott in *The New York Times*:

"In the play called *Miss Lulu Bett* there are a good many sources of genuine pleasure for those who are both familiar with and fond of the book. What impression it would make on that *tabula rasa* which must be counted upon as the average playgoer's mind, it is not possible to say with any assurance. One can only guess, and the guess would be that the stray visitor to the Belmont would find there a rather dull and flabby play, one somewhat sleazily put together by a playwright who has but slight sense of dramatic values and no instinct at all for the idiom of the theatre. Carroll McComas is an excellent actress and no mistake; her achievement last evening was extraordinary."

Charles Darnton in the *Evening World*:

"Zona Gale has not lived in vain in a small town, for she has caught its people, their talk and manners perfectly in *Miss Lulu Bett*. Miss Gale is a true Main Street realist. It's a scandalous thing to say, but the whole town is likely to fall in love with and want to marry *Miss Lulu Bett*."

William E. Holden, Catherine Calhoun Doucet, Brigham Royce, Carroll McComas, Louise Closser Hale

William E. Holden, Carroll McComas, Catherine Calhoun Doucet

Kenneth MacGowan in the *Globe and Commercial Advertiser*:

"A homely and bitter piece of genuine American realism, too well acted to be altogether pleasant entertainment and not suspensive enough to mitigate truth with excitement."

Francis Hackett in *The New Republic*:

"Miss Gale has done authentically what perhaps only a feminist, and certainly what only an artist can do. She has shown, in perfect American terms, the serious comedy of an emancipation."

Robert C. Benchley in *Life*:

"*Miss Lulu Bett* is great because of its pitiless fidelity to everyday people and everyday life, and because of this very fidelity it sometimes seems dull. But the glory of it is that Miss Gale has made it seem dull because she knows better, and it takes an artist to be dull on purpose."

A week after its Broadway opening, *Miss Lulu Bett* had a brand-new third act. (Said one wag: "Now they can change the title to *Miss Lulu Better*.") Originally, Lulu had been left free to decide her own future, an ambiguous ending looked upon as "artistic." However, the play's young producer, Brock Pemberton, and Miss Gale allegedly received "hundreds of letters" from people who felt that the play ended in a disappointing manner. These cheated theatregoers wanted Lulu to get her man, so Miss Gale obligingly saw that she did. The setting of the rewritten act was switched from Cornish's piano store to the Deacons' front porch. Ninian, Lulu's old flame, disencumbered at last of a marriage he had never really wanted, returned for a routine final embrace, and at the new end of the play he and Lulu were obviously ready to walk down life's happy highway together. This may not have been artistic, but it seemed much more satisfying from a box-office point of view.

On February 19, 1921, Miss Gale wrote an explanation in the *Literary Review* of the startling change she had made in her play:

"*Miss Lulu Bett*, as a play, has an ending which is technically known as 'happy.' In the book Lulu's first marriage proves invalid and she marries another man. In the play such a consummation was impossible. Lulu could not marry two men in the space of an evening, no matter how vehemently the program announced that time had elapsed. Two marriages in the interval of two and a half hours would have been, one critic observed, almost bigamous."

ALSO-RANS: *The First Year, The Emperor Jones, The Bad Man, Nice People*

SUMMATION

A poor decision, as Frank Craven's *The First Year* was one of the funniest and most perceptive domestic comedies of the decade. O'Neill's *The Emperor Jones* was somewhat less than a full-length play.

Carroll McComas, Louise Closser Hale

George Marion, Pauline Lord

1921-22

CHRIS CHRISTOPHERSON, the middle-aged captain of a coal barge, sits in Johnny-the-Priest's waterfront saloon and anxiously awaits the arrival of his daughter, Anna, whom he has not seen since she was a child of five, fifteen years earlier. When Anna appears, wan and tired after a stay in the hospital, it is obvious from her dress and demeanor that she is a prostitute, but drunken old Chris, lost in the joy of seeing his daughter again, does not realize what she has become. He insists that she come live with him on his barge.

After spending ten days on the barge, Anna is vigorous and healthy, and is beginning to put her sordid past out of her mind. The barge picks up a shipwrecked sailor, who has been drifting in a lifeboat for days. He is Mat Burke, a rough, tough, simple-minded Irishman who promptly falls in love with Anna.

Chris is horrified by this budding romance, feeling that no daughter of his should ever think of marrying a sailor. He even pulls a knife on Mat, but is disarmed by the younger man. Mat proposes to Anna; she says that she loves him, but cannot marry him. When he tries to bully her into it, she becomes furious, and blurts out the truth about her unsavory past. Broken-hearted, Mat storms ashore to get drunk, but comes back two days later, haggard, unshaven and willing to take Anna on almost any terms.

Anna is made to swear on a crucifix that Mat is the only man she has ever truly loved, and they plan to marry the next day. After the ceremony, Mat and Chris will ship out on the same freighter, while Anna waits for them at home. As the play ends, Anna and Mat are facing the future with desperate hope, while Chris is gloomily muttering about "dat ole davil sea" and her tricks.

George Marion

Pauline Lord

ANNA CHRISTIE

THE CREDITS

A Drama in Four Acts by Eugene O'Neill.
Produced and Staged by Arthur Hopkins.
Opened at the Vanderbilt Theatre, November 2, 1921, and ran for 177 performances.

THE CAST

Johnny-the-Priest	James C. Mack
First Longshoreman	G. O. Taylor
Second Longshoreman	John Hanley
A Postman	William Augustin
Chris Christopherson	George Marion
Marthy Owen	Eugenie Blair
Anna Christopherson	Pauline Lord
Mat Burke	Frank Shannon
Johnson	Ole Anderson
Three Sailors	Messrs. Reilly, Hansen and Kennedy

ACT I

Johnny-the-Priest's Saloon Near the Waterfront, New York City.

ACT II

The Barge, SIMEON WINTHROP, *at Anchor in the Harbor of Provincetown, Mass., Ten Days Later.*

ACTS III and IV

Cabin of the Barge, at Dock in Boston, a Week Later.

Pauline Lord, James C. Mack, Eugenie Blair

HISTORY AND REVIEWS

"A rich and salty play that grips the attention with the rise of the first curtain and holds it fiercely to the end. . . ."

By November of 1921, when *Anna Christie* opened in New York, Eugene O'Neill had already been accepted as the most dynamic force in the American theatre, and the new play added substantially to his formidable reputation. *The Emperor Jones* had opened a year earlier, and that impressionistic study of a terrified Negro's disintegration had been a triumph; Heywood Broun had written in the *Tribune*, "Eugene O'Neill's *The Emperor Jones* seems to us just about the most interesting play which has yet come from the most promising playwright in America."

O'Neill had a great deal of trouble with *Anna Christie.* He wrote a first version under the title of *Chris Christopherson,* a rather gentle (for O'Neill) play about a nice young girl whose father didn't want her to marry a sailor. *Chris Christopherson* was tried out in Atlantic City and Philadelphia in the spring of 1920, with a new English actress named Lynn Fontanne as Anna. It failed, and was withdrawn for extensive revisions.

Frank Shannon

By the time O'Neill finished rewriting, Anna had been transformed into a prostitute, making the play much more muscular. The genteel Miss Fontanne faded out of the picture (she could never have convinced an audience that she was a waterfront floozy), and was replaced by Pauline Lord, then 31 and at the peak of her powers. In those days, and for some years to come, Miss Lord shared with Laurette Taylor a sort of quicksilver vulnerability that enriched every role she played, and she made a superb Anna.

The first act of *Anna Christie* is laid in Johnny-the-Priest's saloon, on the New York waterfront. It is modeled after a real-life saloon on Fulton Street, Jimmy-the-Priest's, where O'Neill spent many a nickel for a shot of throat-searing bar whiskey in his sailoring days. Years later O'Neill was to use the same seedy bar as the setting for *The Iceman Cometh.*

"Gorki's *Night's Lodging* was an ice cream parlor in comparison," O'Neill once said, as quoted by the Gelbs in *O'Neill.*

Johnny-the-Priest himself is meticulously described by O'Neill in *Anna Christie's* opening scene:

"With his pale, thin, clean-shaven face, mild blue eyes and white hair, a cassock would seem more suited to him than the apron he wears. Neither his voice nor his general manner dispels this illusion which has made him a personage of the waterfront. They are soft and bland. But beneath all his mildness one senses the man behind the mask—cynical, callous, hard as nails."

O'Neill blew hot and cold about many of his plays, and *Anna Christie* was no exception. At one point he happily identified it as being among his "finest" works, but years later, in a letter to Malcolm Cowley, he scornfully said: "I never liked it so well as some of my other plays. In telling the story I deliberately employed all the Broadway tricks which I had learned in my stage training."

Some of the notices:

Alexander Woollcott in *The New York Times*:

"That most gifted and interesting actress, Pauline Lord, gives a telling performance in a rich and salty play that grips the attention with the rise of the first curtain and holds it fiercely to the end. *Anna Christie* might be described as a work which towers above most of the plays in town, but which falls short of the stature and the perfection reached by Eugene O'Neill in some of his earlier work. The earlier work had established him as the nearest thing to a genius America has yet produced in the way of a playwright, and, though this *Anna Christie* of his has less directness and more dross and

In its first version, subsequently completely rewritten. Anna Christie *was called* Chris Christopherson. *Emmett Corrigan played old Chris, and young Lynn Fontanne made an implausibly radiant Anna.*

more moments of weak violence than any of its forerunners, it is, nevertheless, a play written with that abundant imagination, that fresh and venturesome mind and that sure instinct for the theatre which set this young author apart—apart from a lot of funny little holiday workers in cardboard and tinsel."

Percy Hammond in the *Tribune*:

"If the gloomy trademark of Eugene O'Neill's depressing product has kept you hitherto away from his plays, disregard it for an hour or two and go to see *Anna Christie*. The promise thus suggested is not that you will have a gay time in the observation of that drama, but that its veracious picture of some interesting characters in interesting circumstances will appeal to your intelligence, while its 'meaning' will not in the least irritate you. Is there better acting in New York than that of Miss Pauline Lord as the weary ex-prostitute; or that of Mr. George Marion, as her pitiable old parent? Perhaps there is, but you will find none more satisfactory."

J. Ranken Towse in the *Evening Post*:

"There are one or two things that can be said about this play without hesitation. In the first place it has passages of indisputable dramatic power, if not of the highest kind, and in the second it is a remarkable work for a young man, but something that falls a good way short of a masterpiece. The notion of a possible happy ending, after all the fiery fury, thunder and rain of the third act is almost inconceivable. But Mr. O'Neill, by means of methods which in their obvious theatricality and unreasonableness can only be called, in an artistic sense, unscrupulous, contrives to reach it, and moreover, is bold enough to discredit his tragedy by ending upon a comic note. Laughter at such a moment may have been appropriate, but it was a little sad. It marked the disastrous, as well as unexpected, finish of a maimed play."

Burns Mantle in the *Mail*:

"For sheer realism, stripped to its ugly vitals, *Anna Christie* is the finest piece of writing Eugene O'Neill has done. It is another of the O'Neill plays that swings uncertainly between moments of superb drama and somber stretches of an eloquent inactivity. Whether the art of *Anna Christie* be rejected because of its ugliness, or its ugliness be accepted as art, the thrill of its playing will long be the boast of those who see it."

Kenneth MacGowan in the *Globe and Commercial Advertiser*:

"*Anna Christie* is a play of power, humor and understanding that searches its portion of life as no American drama has yet done. A production notable in vision, in writing and in acting."

Audiences had an unfortunate habit of bursting into laughter near the end of the play, during the scene in which Anna swears on the crucifix that she will ever after live the good life. O'Neill was inevitably stubborn about scenes of this nature, in which he had overreached himself with unintentionally ludicrous effect—he would refuse to rewrite them, and would simply glower at audiences' silly laughter.

The ending of the play, with its clear implication that poor battered Anna was somehow going to be able to make a success of her marriage to Mat Burke, managed to irritate a number of people, among them John Mason Brown, then writing for the Louisville *Courier-Journal*. He said:

"Here is a young author for the first time giving in to the demands of the professional theatre and giving in at the cost of probability and reality. His artistic concession to popular tastes at the final curtain is a curiously hybrid thing."

O'Neill professed to be mystified by these charges; he had never thought that *Anna Christie* had a happy ending. Writing in *The New York Times* of December 18, 1921, the playwright commented:

"A kiss in the last act, a word about marriage, and the audience grows blind and deaf to what follows. No one hears old Chris when he makes his gloomy, foreboding comment on the new set of coincidences, which to him reveal the old devil sea—fate—up to her old tricks again."

Pauline Lord, George Marion

ALSO-RANS: *Dulcy, Six-Cylinder Love, To the Ladies, The Hero, The Hairy Ape*

SUMMATION

A good choice, for the featherweight *Dulcy* was no match for this bruiser. *The Hairy Ape*, another powerful O'Neill play, was not particularly well received by the critics.

Phyllis Povah

1922-23

THE MEMBERS OF THE JORDAN FAMILY have gathered at their Maine homestead to wait for old Mother Jordan to die, and to share, they hope, in her estate. They are a cold and unattractive crew: stolid Henry, spinsterish Ella, gossipy Sadie, and their assorted spouses and children. The only Jordan with real blood in his veins is the youngest brother, Ben, and he is a ne'er-do-well fugitive from justice, with an arson charge hanging over him. His appearance at the homestead startles his family, who are even more surprised when they discover that it is Jane Crosby who has sent the money enabling him to come. Jane, a plain girl of twenty-four, is a distant relative who has been taking care of Mother Jordan.

When the will is read, it turns out that Jane has been left the entire estate, with only token bequests going to the others. Ben is still faced with jail, but Jane agrees to go bail for him, if he will in turn agree to work the farm for her for the next few months, until his trial comes up. She has secretly loved him for years, although he has never paid the slightest attention to her. Ben reluctantly agrees to the proposal, although it smacks to him of "slavery."

Two months later, under Jane's guidance, Ben has changed his ways, and now that he has achieved a measure of responsibility Jane is prepared to deed the homestead over to him and go on her way. Ben belatedly realizes, however, that he loves and needs her, and as the play ends they are planning to be married, an eventuality that Mother Jordan had foreseen in an informal letter she had left with her will.

Robert Ames, Edna May Oliver, Phyllis Povah

ICEBOUND

THE CREDITS

A Drama in Three Acts by Owen Davis.
Produced by Sam H. Harris.
Staged by Sam Forrest.
Opened at the Sam H. Harris Theatre, February 10, 1923, and ran for 171 performances.

THE CAST

Emma Jordan	Lotta Linthicum
Henry Jordan	John Westley
Nettie Jordan	Boots Wooster
Ella Jordan	Frances Neilson
Sadie Fellows	Eva Condon
Orin Fellows	Andrew J. Lawlor, Jr.
Doctor Curtis	Lawrence Eddinger
Jane Crosby	Phyllis Povah
Judge Bradford	Willard Robertson

BEN JORDAN	Robert Ames
HANNAH	Edna May Oliver
JIM JAY	Charles Henderson

ACT I

The Parlor of the Jordan Homestead.

ACT II

The Sitting Room.

ACT III

The Parlor Again.

HISTORY AND REVIEWS

"Perhaps it ought to be called a bit of grim genre painting, rather than drama, drawn with a bold hand and sharply etched with the acids of biting satire. . . ."

Owen Davis was 46 when *Icebound* opened, a playwright with a long string of lurid melodramas to his credit: *The Confessions of a Wife, Bertha the Sewing Machine Girl, Nellie the Beautiful Cloak Model, Chinatown Charlie,* and literally dozens of others. Davis once said that a melodrama's title represented fifty percent of its chances for success, and then gave a brief formula for the construction of a proper thriller:

ACT I. Start the trouble.

ACT II. Here things look bad. The lady, having left home, is quite at the mercy of the villain.

ACT III. The lady is saved by the help of the stage carpenter. (The big scenic and mechanical effects were always in Act III.)

ACT IV. The lovers are united and the villains are punished.

These Davis melodramas were full of lines like: "You may strike me, Harold Halverton, but there is a God that will protect a woman's honor." Davis' most famous line, curiously innocent in its sheer nuttiness, was written for *Nellie the Beautiful Cloak Model.* In the course of the play the villain had thrown Nellie under a descending elevator, had later hurled her off the Brooklyn Bridge, and had finally bound her to the railroad tracks in front of an oncoming train. Resourceful Nellie managed to wriggle out of these various predicaments, but finally was trapped once more by the villain, this time in her bedroom. As she cowered, he said plaintively:

"Why do you fear me, Nellie?"

By 1921 Davis was sick of melodramas (he had once had as many as seventeen running simultaneously), and turned to serious drama with *The Detour*, which he was always to regard as his favorite play. *Icebound* was in the same realistic vein, and in a program note he explained his reasons for writing it:

"With the production of *The Detour* about a year ago, I managed to secure some measure of success in drawing a simple picture of life as it is lived on a Long Island farm; encouraged by this, I am now turning toward my own people, the people of Northern New England, whose folklore, up to the present time, has been quite neglected in our theatre. I mean, of course, that few serious attempts have been made in the direction of a genre comedy of this locality. Here I have at least tried to draw a true picture of these people, and I am of their blood, born of generations of Northern Maine, small-town folk, and brought up among them. In my memory of them is little of the 'Rube' caricature of the conventional theatre, they are neither buffoons nor sentimentalists, and, at least, neither their faults nor their virtues are borrowed from the melting pot but are the direct result of their own heritage and environment."

Some of the notices:

Unsigned in *The New York Times*:

"A fine performance and an unusually good play come together in *Icebound*, a New England character study which represents one more attempt on the part of the penitent Owen Davis to lift himself out of his past. It is a grim and nearly relentless play of the New England and the New Englanders that Owen Davis knows. The performance is excellent. In particular, Robert Ames and Phyllis Povah do splendid work as the family black sheep and the instrument of his redemption."

Alan Dale in the *American*:

"It was grimly American; it was only occasionally theatrical; it was filled to the brim with typically American characters; it was eminently colloquial, and—as far as its staging went—Moscow hasn't so much on Sam Forrest. Mr. Forrest really triumphed. Every detail of that icebound Jordan homestead was most conscientiously shown."

James Craig in the *Evening Mail*:

"Perhaps it ought to be called a bit of grim genre painting, rather than drama, drawn with a bold hand and sharply etched with the acids of biting satire. The theme is the decay of an old New England family, as icebound in emotions as the landscape outside and as bleak in human qualities as Maine hills in midwinter. With extraordinary skill dramatist and producer maintained a uniform, somber tone throughout the three acts. In fact, they seemed to keep their limitations so well in mind that they purposely avoided any lightening of the shades. The result was a play that was always intense, sometimes gripping, although nothing in particular ever seemed to happen."

Phyllis Povah, Lawrence Eddinger

Heywood Broun in the *World*:

"*Icebound* belongs in the class of plays which are set down as 'promising.' It is a mixture of things fine and things shoddy. It seems to us that a good deal which is theatrical and implausible lies in the scheme of the comedy. Mr. Davis has recourse to the device of writing about two young people who are in love with each other and don't find it out until just before the final curtain. This stratagem may have sound theatrical foundation but it seldom convinces us. Our observation is that among mortals the tendency is rather for any two people to think themselves in love some six months before it happens."

Percy Hammond in the *Tribune*:

"*Icebound* is a rather honest slice of life; not so good, we surmise, as Mr. Davis' unsuccessful *The Detour*; but far, far more intelligent than the average Broadway entertainment. A good new play."

Burns Mantle in the *Daily News*:

"*Icebound* is good, honest character drama. The key of it is monotonous, and the action frequently sluggish. But only the restless and the theatre-worn will notice this. These Maine folks are unlovely and hard, but they are also human enough to be recognizable."

Robert C. Benchley in *Life*:

"It isn't until you have left the theatre that you realize that *Icebound* isn't really much of an opus. It is just a fairly ordinary tale of New England village life."

The Playgoer in the *Sun*:

"A vivid and biting study of a New England family. *Icebound* is written in Owen Davis' newest and best style, and, in spite of its title, will thaw the theatregoer into moisture and good humor."

Davis went on to a long and honorable career as a serious playwright, and by the time he died in 1956, at the age of 82, he had dramatized such novels as *The Great Gatsby, The Good Earth* and *Ethan Frome*. Every now and then, perhaps, he may have let himself think wistfully of the three plots that he had once told George Middleton he could always fall back on: the Sheriff Against the Outlaws, the Prodigal Son story, and the story of the Magdalene. But never again did he go back to the old melodramas; they had long since outlived their theatrical usefulness. Nellie and Bertha and their colorful woes belonged to a gentler, more credulous age.

ALSO-RANS: *The Adding Machine, You and I, The Torchbearers, The Fool, Why Not?*

SUMMATION

A questionable decision, if an understandable one, for in the early 1920's the Pulitzer trustees would have had to have been equipped with a high degree of theatrical sophistication to understand and endorse Elmer Rice's expressionistic *The Adding Machine*, a much more permanent contribution to the American theatre than *Icebound*. *The Torchbearers* was an extremely funny comedy about amateur theatricals, but too lightweight for consideration.

Robert Ames

Augustin Duncan

1923-24

THE SCENE OF THE PLAY is Matt Hunt's home in the Kentucky mountains. Rufe Pryor, a young religious fanatic, has been doing odd jobs for the Hunts, and is desperate when Sid Hunt returns from World War I; with Sid back, Rufe will no longer be needed. Neither will he be able to continue his pathetically futile courting of Sid's girl, Jude Lowry.

Rufe, covering all his machinations with a coating of religious fervor, subtly stirs up trouble between Sid and Andy Lowry, Jude's brother. He gets Andy drunk and taunts him with reminders of the ancient Hunt/Lowry feud, suggesting that Andy is a coward to let Sid live, when an unfair number of Lowrys had been killed so many years ago. Inflamed, Andy does indeed try to shoot Sid as they are riding in the woods, but succeeds only in putting a bullet hole through his hat.

The rest of the male Hunts, under the mistaken impression that Sid has actually been killed, set off through the woods to the Lowry cabin to avenge him. Sid staggers back home, finds where his kinfolk have gone, and rushes to the nearest telephone, trying to head off a pointless massacre. The phone happens to be directly under a bridge, and Rufe, willing to try anything, blows up a dam in order to have the flood waters sweep Sid away. Sid escapes, however, and by the play's end the Hunts and the Lowrys are friends once more, Rufe's villainy having been exposed.

In the original ending, Rufe is trapped alone in the cabin by the very flood he is responsible for; this was subsequently revised, and in the rewritten final scene old Dad Hunt arranges matters so that Rufe is permitted to escape, against the wishes of Matt and Sid, who are all for killing him.

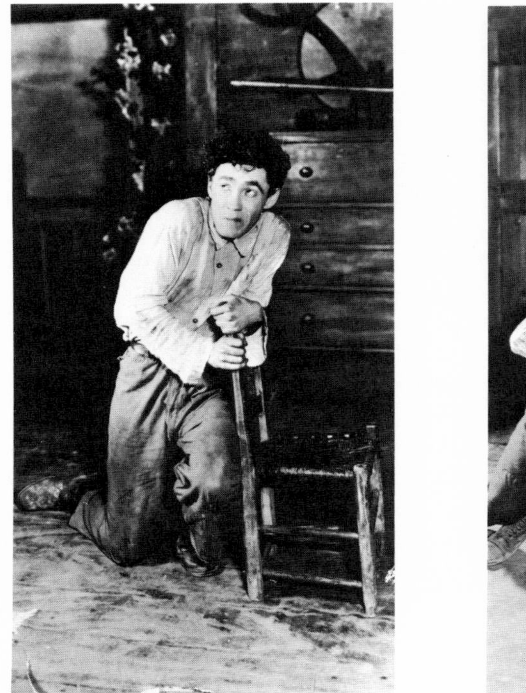

(Left) *John F. Hamilton*
(Right) *Glenn Anders, John F. Hamilton*

HELL BENT FER HEAVEN

THE CREDITS

A Play in Three Acts by Hatcher Hughes.
Produced by Marc Klaw, Inc.
Staged by Augustin Duncan.
Opened with a Special Matinee at the Klaw Theatre, January 4, 1924. Moved to Frazee Theatre four weeks later for a regular engagement, and ran for 122 performances.

THE CAST

David Hunt	Augustin Duncan
Meg Hunt	Clara Blandick
Sid Hunt	George Abbott
Rufe Pryor	John F. Hamilton
Matt Hunt	Burke Clarke
Andy Lowry	Glenn Anders
Jude Lowry	Margaret Borough

The Three Acts of the Play Occur in the Hunt Home in the Blue Ridge Mountains Between 4 p.m. and 9 p.m. of a Midsummer Day.

HISTORY AND REVIEWS

"Our recommendation is supposed to be secret. How did Dr. Brander Matthews find out what it was? What right did he have to interfere in the matter. . . ."

The selection of Professor Hatcher Hughes' *Hell Bent fer Heaven* over George Kelly's *The Show-Off* was responsible for the first of the messy controversies that were to plague the Pulitzer Prize drama awards down through the years. There had been questionable decisions before this one—the credentials of *Miss Lulu Bett* and *Icebound* were debatable—but in the case of *Hell Bent fer Heaven* the unpleasant charge of favoritism was publicly raised, tarnishing an award that could otherwise have been fairly reasonably justified.

Hatcher Hughes was 40 when *Hell Bent fer Heaven* was produced, and was a member of the Columbia University faculty. Back in 1911 he had taken graduate work in drama under Professor Brander Matthews, and the following year had become Matthews' assistant. As Matthews was directly responsible for seeing that *Hell Bent fer Heaven* received the Prize against the wishes of the three jurors, William Lyon Phelps, Clayton Hamilton and Owen Johnson, who had recommended *The Show-Off*, there were quite a few eyebrows raised.

Burke Clarke, Glenn Anders, Margaret Borough, Augustin Duncan

In a first informal vote, Johnson plumped for *The Show-Off*, listing no second choice; Phelps (who had not even seen *Hell Bent fer Heaven*) listed *The Changelings* first, with *The Show-Off* second; Hamilton rated *Hell Bent fer Heaven* first, and *The Show-Off* second. Johnson and Hamilton finally agreed that *The Show-Off* was their choice, and Phelps told them that he was willing to accept their judgment.

The jurors had no idea that they had been reversed until they saw the announcement of the *Hell Bent fer Heaven* award in the newspapers. It turned out that Professor Matthews, after getting wind of the proposed award to *The Show-Off*, had immediately written an impassioned letter to Nicholas Murray Butler, setting forth his arguments in favor of the play written by his old assistant. Dr. Butler, President of Columbia University, had passed the Matthews letter on to the Pulitzer Advisory Board, and the Board had decided that the arguments were valid ones.

Owen Johnson got hopping mad about the whole thing, and gave *The New York Times* a fine, angry telephone interview as soon as the award was announced:

"Our recommendation is supposed to be secret," said Mr. Johnson. "How did Dr. Brander Matthews find out what it was? What right did he have to interfere in the matter, especially to interest himself in behalf of a member of the Columbia faculty who was a junior in his own department? The value of the Pulitzer award is greatly impaired by the overshadowing influence of Columbia University, especially when it is exercised to give the award to a member of its own teaching staff. Professor Phelps and myself feel we were treated with gross discourtesy in this matter, and we will never serve on a Pulitzer jury again. We do not dispute the power of the Advisory Board to overrule our verdict, but in a delicate case like this, where there is interference at Columbia in favor of a Columbia man, we feel that an explanation certainly should have been made to us."

Margaret Borough, Glenn Anders, George Abbott

Johnson, true to his word, never again served as a juror, but it turned out that he had been speaking prematurely for Professor Phelps; ten years later, in the season of 1934–35, Phelps was to return to the jury, just in time to help shepherd *The Old Maid* to its peculiar victory over *The Children's Hour*.

An anonymous member of the Advisory Board had this to say about Johnson's comments:

"The members of the Advisory Board are free to accept or reject the recommendations of juries. We have done so quite a number of times before. When the issue was raised this time, I went to both plays and so did other members of the Advisory Board. We were also strongly influenced by Dr. Brander Matthews and by the reasons which he gave in favor of *Hell Bent fer Heaven*."

Some of the notices:

James Craig in the *Mail*:

"*Hell Bent fer Heaven* falls short of being a good play. There seems overmuch preparation for what finally takes place. You feel that when you had got all set for a tornado you encountered only a thunderstorm. Augustin Duncan gives a marvelously fine characterization of the part of the grandfather, and George Abbott, whom we have seen heretofore in comedy cowboy roles, has more than justified the selection of him for the leading 'straight' part, the hero of the tale."

Heywood Broun in the *Evening World*:

"The best thing the theatre of these parts has done for itself in a long time was to rescue Hatcher Hughes' *Hell Bent fer Heaven* from the irritations and inconveniences of matinee performances and provide it with a playhouse all to itself. Very few plays have ever had the robustness to survive the special matinee. *Beyond the Horizon* did it, and a few others. Mr. Hughes hasn't done a perfect job on his second comedy, but he has done some perfect things in it."

Alexander Woollcott in the *Sun*:

"A capitally acted and intensely interesting comedy of the Blue Ridge mountains. *Hell Bent fer Heaven* is a kind of American *John Ferguson*, of which the central figure is a cowering, writhing, sickly fellow. A timid, unhappy youth, shoved into the corner by his burlier neighbors and made wretched by the fact that the very girl he would love to fondle is all for a soldier lad of quite another stripe, he turns poisonous. With feminine guile and an utter malignancy he sets household against household, and loosens the waters of destruction. But he does it all in the name of the God he has, like most mortals, created in his own image—his own hideous image."

John Corbin in *The New York Times*:

"One of the most original and vividly colored pieces in the contemporary drama. In its major structure the play is at times uncertain. In the last act especially, there is apparent indecision and ineffective repetition. But these are minor flaws in comparison with the high originality and truth of the characters and the absorbing interest of the action."

M. A. G. in the *Tribune*:

"Religious fanaticism is thrillingly dealt with in *Hell Bent fer Heaven*. Rufe Pryor, somewhat tainted with idiocy, but intensely pious, is the Christian dervish of a tiny community in the Blue Ridge mountains. Every act he performs—and each is for his own ends—he performs because God wills it. If this splendidly interesting play has any salient weakness, it is that it depends so utterly on the able characterization of this mountain Tartuffe, although it contains an almost melodramatic plot. The acting honors of the production—and they are no mean honors—must go to John F. Hamilton as the fanatic, Rufe."

Alan Dale in the *American*:

"This melodrama by Hatcher Hughes has some strength, all of which does not materialize, owing to faulty construction. The characters talk too much, and one of them prays too much, and in the last act they all sit around and chat until it is time to go home. The second act, however, is a good act."

L. W. in the *Morning World*:

"*Hell Bent fer Heaven* deserves to take rank with the best American comedy. An extraordinary play, rich, poetic, and with more thrills than *The Bat*."

Burns Mantle in the *Daily News*:

"A darned good melodrama. John F. Hamilton is amazingly good, helped by the skillful writing and direction of the part. *Hell Bent fer Heaven* is first class entertainment."

Unsigned in the *Herald*:

"A play of undeniable power is capturing attention, despite the need for condensation and a curiously flabby last act in which this comedy of the Kentucky mountains ran downhill."

The Pulitzer Prize was a posthumous one—it was awarded on May 11, and *Hell Bent fer Heaven* had closed the night before.

Augustin Duncan, Burke Clarke, John F. Hamilton, Margaret Borough, George Abbott, Clara Blandick

ALSO-RANS: *The Show-Off, The Changelings, Tarnish, Sun-Up*

SUMMATION

While *The Show-Off* obviously had the clearest title to the prize, *Hell Bent fer Heaven* was itself an honest, well-written play, and had the question of log-rolling not been a factor, there would probably have been comparatively little fuss about this decision. Under the circumstances, however, the choice was a very poor one. Columbia gets a black mark for its lack of common sense; why didn't the Advisory Board, or Drs. Matthews and Butler, anticipate the comments that people were bound to make?

(Right) *Pauline Lord, Richard Bennett, Glenn Anders*

(Below) *Richard Bennett, Pauline Lord*

1924-25

TONY PATUCCI, the prosperous, middle-aged owner of a vineyard in California's Napa Valley, takes a trip to San Francisco, sees Amy, a waitress, and falls in love with her. Upon his return to the vineyard he conducts a long-range courtship by mail, with Joe, his handsome assistant, writing the letters for him. Tony finally sends Amy a photograph, purportedly of himself, but actually of Joe, and it is this picture which helps her make up her mind to come to the Valley.

On the day of Amy's arrival at the vineyard, Tony nervously drinks a great deal of wine, then sets off in his Ford to pick her up at the station. Amy arrives, alone; nobody has met her. When she first meets Joe, she naturally believes him to be her intended husband, but then Tony is carried into the room, both legs broken in an auto accident. He will have to stay in bed for at least six months

Tony's pathetic deception is exposed. Angry and heartsick at the trick that has been played on her, Amy is all for going back to San Francisco, but then decides that she will still keep her bargain, and go through with the marriage to Tony. After the ceremony, with Tony in bed in another room, Joe and

Glenn Anders, Richard Bennett, Pauline Lord

THEY KNEW WHAT THEY WANTED

Amy are left alone. They are drawn to each other physically, out of loneliness and frustration rather than love, and Joe seduces her.

Three months later, Amy realizes that she is pregnant. Joe is the only possible father. They are not in love, for their intimacy began and ended with that one quick embrace. Indeed, by now Amy has come to love Tony, because of his warmth and kindness, and she despises herself for the effect her unfaithfulness is bound to have on him.

Amy and Joe, both desperate, plan to go to San Francisco together, but before they leave Amy must tell Tony the truth. Tony is at first crushed, then hysterically enraged; he attempts to shoot Joe, but the younger man manages to get the gun away from him. Then Tony has second thoughts. Joe and Amy do not love one another; they could have no possible decent life together. Let Amy stay at the vineyard and have her baby; Tony will raise it as his own child. The implication is clear that Tony and Amy will piece together a successful, loving marriage.

Richard Bennett, playwright Sidney Howard, Pauline Lord, Glenn Anders

THE CREDITS

A Comedy in Three Acts by Sidney Howard.
Produced by The Theatre Guild.
Staged by Philip Moeller.
Opened at the Garrick Theatre, November 24, 1924, and ran for 414 performances.

THE CAST

Joe	Glenn Anders
Father McKee	Charles Kennedy
Ah Gee	Allen Atwell
Tony	Richard Bennett
The R.F.D.	Robert Cook
Amy	Pauline Lord
Angelo	Hardwick Nevin
Giorgio	Jacob Zollinger
The Doctor	Charles Tazewell
First Italian Mother	Frances Hyde
Her Daughter	Antoinette Bizzoco
Second Italian Mother	Peggy Conway
Her Son	Thomas Scherman

Farm Hands: The Misses Cosette Faustine, Helen Fowble, Dorothy Greene, Audrey Thal, Eleanor Mish; the Messrs. Alvah Bessie, Edward Hogan, Peter Marsters, Sanford Meisner, Arthur Sircom, Ernest Thompson, Angelo de Palma, Michael Zito.

SCENE: *Tony's Farmhouse in the Napa Valley, California.*

ACT I

Morning, in Early Summer.

ACT II

Evening, Same Day.

ACT III

Three Months Later.

HISTORY AND REVIEWS

"A winning little idyl of the California vineyards, none the less fond and sunny for the thumbprint of reality that is on it. . . ."

In his Preface to the published edition of *They Knew What They Wanted* (Doubleday, Page & Co., 1925), playwright Sidney Howard wrote:

"Of the story of this play, I have this to say. It has been generously related to the legend of Paolo and Francesca, to the dirtiest anecdotes of the Gallic pornographica, and to its superb contemporary of the New York theatre, Eugene O'Neill's *Desire Under the Elms.* On that last score, Mr. O'Neill and I can readily, as they say, 'get together' and agree that no two plays could possibly bear less resemblance to each other than this simple comedy of mine and his glorious tragedy of New England farmers and their Puritan philosophy. Of the second alleged source and kinship I cannot speak with authority because I am not sure that I know all the dirtiest French anecdotes. The first relationship I hotly deny.

"The story of this play, in its noblest form, served Richard Wagner as the libretto for the greatest of all romantic operas. It is shamelessly, consciously, and even proudly derived from the legend of Tristram and Yseult, and the difference between the legend of Tristram and Yseult and that of Paolo and Francesca is simply that the Italian wronged husband killed everybody in sight while his northern counterpart forgave everybody—which amounts to the monumental difference between a bad temper and tolerance."

In *They Knew What They Wanted* Howard was writing about an area he knew well; as a boy he had lived in California's Napa Valley, working on a fruit ranch. Years later, in an interview in the *World*, he spoke of the Valley:

"The low hills and wide valleys north of San Francisco Bay, behind the venerable (for California) walls and thoroughfares of Vallejo, grow grapes for wine and support as vivid and genial a community of Latins as this melting pot of the nations has yet failed to melt. Other crops than grapes grow there, but the spell of Bacchus is over all the land. It was here I found the characters for *They Knew What They Wanted.*"

Howard had served in World War I, first as an ambulance driver and then as a flier, and came into the theatre after a few years of newspaper reporting. *They Knew What They Wanted* was his first Broadway hit, after three earlier short-run plays—*Swords, The Kingdom of Sancho Panza* and *Bewitched*—that had given no indication whatsoever of the brilliant future he was to have as a playwright. *They Knew What They Wanted* was the first of a string of excellent plays that included *Ned McCobb's Daughter, The Silver Cord, The Late Christopher Bean, Dodsworth* and *Yellow Jack.* He died at 44, in 1939, on his Massachusetts farm, crushed in a tractor accident.

The Howard play was outspoken in its language; the playwright had been determined to set down the true speech of the vineyard workers, so *They Knew What They Wanted* was freely salted with profanity. Profanity was very big on the Broadway stage that season, as *What Price Glory?* also had its full share of taboo words.

It was the gaminess of *What Price Glory?*'s dialogue (much rougher than the talk in *They Knew What They Wanted*) which probably cost the famous war play the Pulitzer Prize. Hamlin Garland, one of the jurors, refused outright to vote for *What Price Glory?*. Clayton Hamilton and Jesse Lynch Williams were the other two jurors, and Hamilton said later:

"In deference to Mr. Garland, who was fifteen years older than Mr. Williams and twenty-five years older than myself, we offered to agree upon Sidney Howard's *They Knew What They Wanted*."

Howard himself once said (*Stage Magazine*, February, 1935) that he considered *What Price Glory?* to be "the great American play," so his emotions must have been strangely mixed when his own play nosed it out for the Pulitzer.

Some of the notices:

Alan Dale in the *American*:

"A peach of a play, rich with characterization, candor and novel twists was offered by the Theatre Guild at the Garrick Theatre last night. *They Knew What They Wanted* was not only charmingly written, with humor and with enough of the indelicate colloquialisms of today to set its brand, but it was beautifully staged, and matchlessly acted. Pauline Lord gave a perfectly gorgeous performance."

Percy Hammond in the *Herald Tribune*:

"An excellent tale, told with a fine veracity by the author, the actors and the director. Such hard punches as it bestows are softened by the mellow four-ounce gloves of humor and sentiment. *They Knew What They Wanted* is a mature and sophisticated comedy. At this hurried moment I am inclined to tip my hat to Mr. Bennett as the most competent actor of the Western Hemisphere."

Burns Mantle in the *Daily News*:

"There is little waste in this drama, and it is pretty certain to pick any auditor up and carry him along in the swiftly rushing current of its story. It has the advantage of telling a believable story and it is wonderfully acted."

Gilbert W. Gabriel in the *Telegram*:

"*They Knew What They Wanted* is a winning little idyl of the California vineyards, none the less fond and sunny for the thumbprint of reality that is on it. Sidney Howard is down to the shirtsleeves, Ford cars and spaghetti joint waitresses of the generation which gave him understanding. He is in a section of America which evidently smiled so warmly on his knee pants days that he cannot help smiling back. He cannot help turning it into a happy, lovable play. There is no more beaming evening ahead of you than this."

Heywood Broun in the *World*:

"*They Knew What They Wanted* is a soul-rousing play out of American life. Comedy and tragedy struggle for the soul of this story, and it is no weak-kneed concession that comedy plunges through. Rather the dramatist has caught and set down the toughness of human fibre and the fine drive of it. It is a beautiful cast which the Theatre Guild has assembled for the play. Pauline Lord gives the finest performance I have ever seen. Richard Bennett is magnificent, and there is fine work by Glenn Anders and Charles Tazewell. *They Knew What They Wanted* belongs among the best of all American comedies."

Alexander Woollcott in the *Evening Sun*:

"*They Knew What They Wanted* is a true, living, salty comedy . . . a colorful piece cut from the genuine fabric of American life. It is one of those comedies which move uneasy on the edge of tragedy."

A lone dissent from E. W. Osborn in the *Evening World*:

"Mr. Howard has woven a play neither tense nor deeply moving in its interest. There are frequent moments when it seems to halt and balance, like a man in doubt teetering on his heels."

Richard Bennett left the play's cast in June of 1926, and was replaced by Leo Carillo. The following month Bennett wrote one of the oddest letters imaginable to Percy Hammond, who printed it in his *Herald Tribune* column. It was odd on two counts: (a) actors are rarely capable of irony; (b) actors never, under any circumstances, complain about good notices:

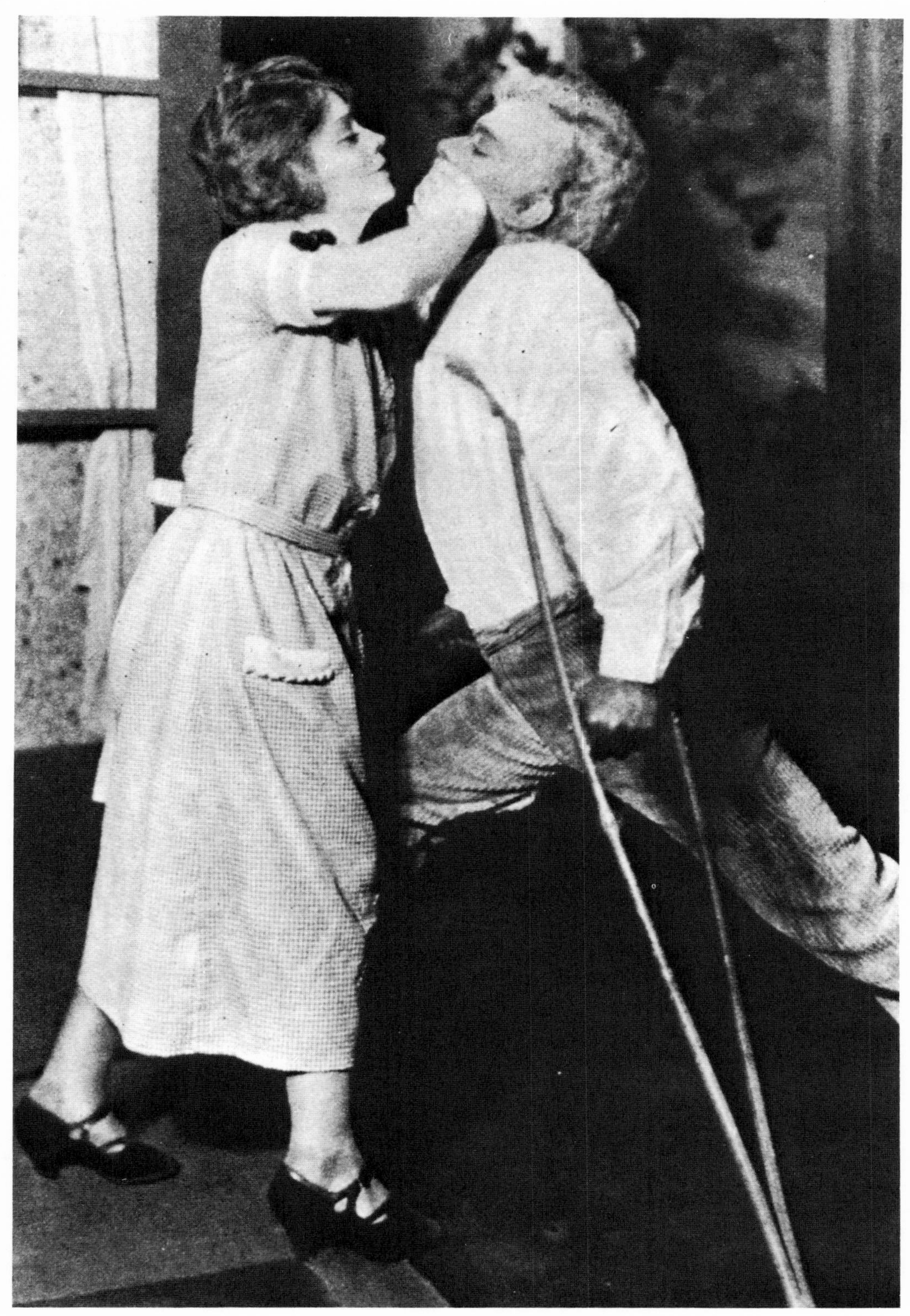

Pauline Lord, Richard Bennett

My Dear Sir:

Eight months ago over your signature you wrote that my performance in *They Knew What They Wanted* indicated that I was the best actor of the Western Hemisphere. Since that time I have been wondering by what right you hand down your lofty decisions.

Stark Young, a contemporary critic of yours, being a dramatist, an actor and a stage director, possesses the qualifications essential to the distribution of well-grounded opinions. When he wrote of my characterization of 'Tony' that it was "too professional" I knew that he was right. As a result of my confidence in his unfavorable estimate, I made my performance more amateurish and improved it by adding numerous overtones, nuances and rhythms. Thanks to Mr. Young's helpful instruction, the role, which on the first night was but a professional outline, was later filled with shades and distinctions, subtle, perhaps, but always amateurish and artistic. Many of the author's most meaningful speeches I spoke meaninglessly, thus increasing the character's similarity to nature.

Destructive critics like Mr. Young, my dear sir, are of great value in telling the actors how to act. The constructive reviewing that you indulge in, especially as it concerns me, is worse than useless. I do not doubt you think me a great actor, but I wish that hereafter you would, if possible, abstain from saying so.

Yours truly,
Richard Bennett

ALSO-RANS: *What Price Glory?, Desire Under the Elms, Processional, Minick, The Youngest, Dancing Mothers*

SUMMATION

This was not one of the better decisions. As honest and touching a play as *They Knew What They Wanted* was, the prize should have gone to *What Price Glory?*, and would probably have done so but for the pure accident of Hamlin Garland's seniority. Walter Prichard Eaton (not a juror in 1924–25, although he speaks as if he had been), said in *Theatre Annual* in 1944: "I now freely admit that our recommendation of *They Knew What They Wanted*, when we might (and should) have recommended *What Price Glory?*, was a boner. I may add that the play jury gave long consideration to its recommendation that year, and finally saw the Howard play as a more lasting contribution than *What Price Glory?*, which we decided was topical."

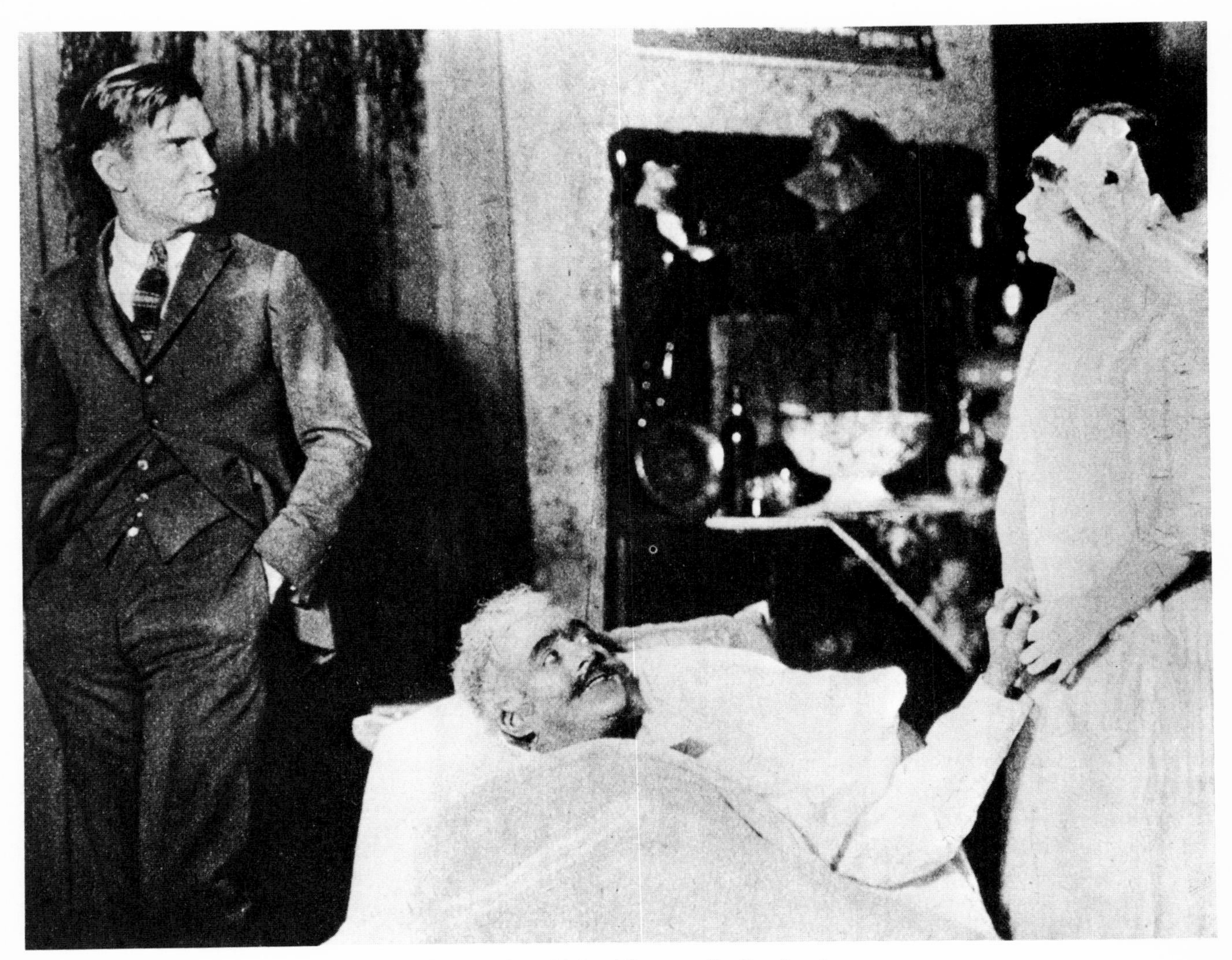

Glenn Anders, Richard Bennett, Pauline Lord

Charles Trowbridge, Chrystal Herne

1925-26

HARRIET CRAIG'S pride in her well-kept house is overdeveloped to the extent of mania; the house is her whole life, and she cannot tolerate a single scratch on a piece of furniture, or the smell of cigarette smoke in the living room.

During the two years of her marriage she has been subtly undermining the position of her husband, Walter Craig, in their home; she has succeeded in cutting off all of their relationships with friends, finding her own peculiar happiness in the lonely, antiseptic order that she has imposed upon her surroundings. Walter, blind to Harriet's flaws, continues to love her.

Miss Austen, Walter's aunt, who has been living with them, sees Harriet for what she is, and bluntly tells her off. Walter, meanwhile, becomes innocently involved in a local scandal concerning a murder and a suicide at a friend's house where he had recently been paying a call. In her desperation to keep her husband's name out of the newspapers, Harriet unwittingly reveals to Walter the real reasons for her anxiety—she is not truly worried about him, but about her own threatened position.

His eyes open at last, Walter symbolically breaks with Harriet by smoking a forbidden cigarette in the living room, and by deliberately smashing one of her prized ornaments. Finally, he moves out of the house, along with his aunt. At the play's end Harriet is alone in her immaculate house, forlornly wandering from room to room, a bunch of roses in her arms. The petals are falling unnoticed on the spotless floor.

Mary Gildea, Josephine Williams, Chrystal Herne, Charles Trowbridge, Anne Sutherland, Miss Herne again, Josephine Hull

CRAIG'S WIFE

THE CREDITS

A Drama in Three Acts by George Kelly.
Produced by Rosalie Stewart.
Staged by George Kelly.
Opened at the Morosco Theatre, October 12, 1925, and ran for 289 performances.

THE CAST

Miss Austen	Anne Sutherland
Mrs. Harold	Josephine Williams
Mazie	Mary Gildea
Harriet Craig	Chrystal Herne
Ethel Landreth	Eleanor Mish
Walter Craig	Charles Trowbridge
Mrs. Frazier	Josephine Hull
Billy Birkmire	Arling Alcine

Josephine Williams, Mary Gildea, Chrystal Herne

JOSEPH CATELLE	Arthur Shaw
HARRY	J. A. Curtis
EUGENE FREDERICKS	Nelan Jaap

SCENE: *A Room in Craig's House.*

ACT I

A Friday Evening in June. About 6 o'clock.

ACT II

Ten Minutes Later.

ACT III

The Following Morning. About 8:30.

HISTORY AND REVIEWS

"A hard-driving drama, a domestic tragedy without pistols or blows but one that is superlatively engrossing and impressive."

Over a period of three years, 1923–24–25, playwright George Kelly wrote three successive Broadway hits: *The Torchbearers, The Show-Off,* and *Craig's Wife*. He kept on writing plays for the next two decades—*Daisy Mayme, Maggie the Magnificent, Behold the Bridegroom, Reflected Glory*—with varying degrees of success, but he never truly lived up to the vast promise of those golden years in the Twenties. Kelly's niece, Grace, Princess of Monaco, has long been the most celebrated member of the Kelly family; hardly anybody now, alas, remembers much about her Uncle George.

George Kelly began his theatrical career as an actor, one good enough to play the title role in a road company of *The Virginian*. Soon he was in vaudeville, already the province of his brother Walter, who for years toured the country as the "Virginia Judge." George acted in his own sketches: *Smarty's Party, The Flattering Word,* and one called *Poor Aubrey,* which proved so successful that he expanded it into a full-length play, *The Show-Off*.

Many Broadway observers felt that *Craig's Wife* was awarded the Pulitzer Prize because the more deserving *The Show-Off* had not been awarded it two years earlier, that the committee was making belated restitution for a bad blunder. If so, the situation was most unfair both to Kelly himself and to all of the other playwrights represented on Broadway during the *Craig's Wife* season. The *Telegram* commented:

"*The Wisdom Tooth* is not only better written, with a touch of beauty utterly lacking in *Craig's Wife*, and having a far greater power to stimulate and reflect on American life, but it has a much wider appeal. Perhaps Marc Connelly will be attended to next year, when he will be granted the prize for a play not so good as his current one, and overshadowed by other successes. The only way out of this situation seems to be for authors who feel they had well fortified claims to the prize to keep an extra play on hand, ready to be cast out as bait the following season. The Pulitzer Prize committee seems to be just about a year behind in their wash."

Walter Prichard Eaton, a Pulitzer juror that season, felt differently about the matter, and explained his position many years later in the 1944 *Theatre Annual*:

"In the matter of the *Craig's Wife* award, it seems to me that no apologies are called for. Kelly's *The Show-Off* is as dated now as the slang it is written in, but *Craig's Wife* is still in the active repertoire of our theatre—meaning by our theatre, the hundreds of acting groups all over the country. *The Butter and Egg Man* was a trivial farce comedy with nothing behind it; *The Wisdom Tooth*, though a play with much charm, never came across in the theatre; *The Great God Brown* was an interesting experiment, but bewildering and fumbling. *Craig's Wife* was, actually, a rather clever award, as time has proved."

Kelly was a great advocate of surface realism, which infuriated some of his critics; Mary McCarthy, summing up his career in the *Partisan Review* in 1947, commented acidly that "the real heroes and heroines of his plays are glasses of water, pocketbooks, telephones, and after-dinner coffee cups." But, at his best, Kelly *could* see the forest, so perhaps he should be forgiven his meticulous reportage on the trees.

Here Kelly talks about *Craig's Wife* in a *World* interview:

"Everybody knows several Mrs. Craigs. I've seen hundreds of them. The woman in the play is a composite. I've seen such a woman put her arms around her husband's shoulders, ask him to do something he doesn't in the least want to do, and wink over his protests at me. I think that Mrs. Craig is the modern woman. She is less than the truth as I have seen it many times. People always refuse to believe in the theatre the reality as they hear and see it in their every-day lives. Give them the reality as strong as it is and they will not listen or look."

Craig's Wife was Kelly's first serious play, although there had certainly been a few horrifying undertones lurking under the maniacal banter of *The Show-Off's* Aubrey Piper. The heroine of the title was a humorless monster, all the more terrifying because of her ordinariness. Kelly drew her so vividly that audiences hated her; actual cheers used to go up when her long-suffering husband finally rebelled.

Some of the notices:

Alexander Woollcott in the *World*:

"*Craig's Wife* is a thorough, unsmiling, patiently detailed and profoundly interesting dramatic portrait of a woman whom every playgoer will recognize with something like a start and yet whose prototype has never before appeared in any book or play that has passed my way. Chrystal Herne's performance is a brilliant achievement."

Frank Vreeland in the *Telegram*:

"Staged by the author himself, and played by Chrystal Herne and a competent cast with the quiet rustle of actuality, the play is at times attenuated and given to pauses, and yet it presents curiously vivid peeps into the keyhole of many a home."

J. Brooks Atkinson in *The New York Times*:

"Nothing is more imperative than a quiet, dispassionate view of George Kelly's new drama, *Craig's Wife*, which was acted somewhat sententiously at the Morosco Theatre last evening. Mr. Kelly has written an earnest study of character which he seems to confuse with the problem play. If he has not built his play with perfect skill, he has observed his subject matter accurately and transcribed it honestly in terms of the theatre."

Alan Dale in the *American*:

"Mr. Kelly's case as made out last night in *Craig's Wife* appears to be somewhat exceptional and entirely exaggerated. The wife being such an odious character, suspicious, friendless, hating company in her own home, dreading any gaiety, loathing dust, how came it that the dear downtrodden husband didn't guess at it until Auntie told him? It was all rather sordidly horrid."

Gilbert W. Gabriel in the *Evening Sun*:

"A minor problem swells to major size in *Craig's Wife*. An unloved husband leaves his home behind him, a steely wife achieves a desolate triumph, and a shrewd, tense, provocative household drama works itself out to honest conclusion."

Burns Mantle in the *Daily News*:

"*Craig's Wife* is an inspiringly observant piece of writing, as superbly polished a sample of stage fiction as any season has produced. But I seriously question the extent of its appeal. It reveals a bitter truthfulness, a biting irony, a searching analysis of feminine character that in all probability is too devastating to prove popular."

Richard Garrick in the *Journal*:

" 'Great' is a word that should be handled with the utmost circumspection, but due thought makes

Charles Trowbridge, Anne Sutherland, Josephine Hull

it imperative that the adjective be applied to *Craig's Wife*. A hard-driving drama, a domestic tragedy without pistols or blows but one that is superlatively engrossing and impressive. Mr. Kelly emerges from the ranks of able mirthmakers into the company of America's leading dramatists."

Robert Coleman, in the *Mirror*, called it "one of the finest plays ever written by an American." John Anderson, in the *Evening Post*, said: "*Craig's Wife* is both hot and cold. But it should be seen; if you don't like it, it will be a fine subject for an argument."

More than twenty years after its original opening, *Craig's Wife* was still working its old spell on audiences. Writing in the *Saturday Review*, John Mason Brown had this to say about the 1947 revival:

"It is not often in a theatre that a match thrown on the floor, a cigarette lighted in a living room, or a man hurling his wife's most prized vase into the fireplace can cause an audience to cheer and applaud as if the Marines had just landed or Desperate Desmond been foiled. Yet this is what still happens at every performance of Mr. Kelly's play. Doubtless it will keep on happening whenever it is revived in the future."

Chrystal Herne, Charles Trowbridge

ALSO-RANS: *The Wisdom Tooth, The Enemy, Outside Looking In, The Butter and Egg Man, The Great God Brown, Lucky Sam McCarver*

SUMMATION

A solid play, and a solid choice. *The Wisdom Tooth* was probably the closest competitor, but the judges had never crowned a fantasy, and weren't about to do so just yet. *The Great God Brown* was inferior O'Neill.

Playright Paul Green

(Opposite Page) *Abbie Mitchell, Julius Bledsoe, Rose McClendon*

1926-27

ABRAHAM MCCRANIE is a powerful, intelligent young man, half black, half white, the illegitimate son of the owner of the turpentine plantation upon which he works. Abraham is determined to educate himself and his fellow workers, a plan sneered at by his white half-brother, Lonnie. A fight between the brothers is broken up by their father, Colonel McCranie, who then cruelly whips Abraham.

Abraham and his wife, Goldie, have a child, and Colonel McCranie gives them a cottage and twenty-five acres of land. The Colonel appoints Abraham as the local schoolteacher, but his pupils refuse to study. This so enrages Abraham that he beats one of them almost to death, and as a result his teaching job is taken away from him.

Fifteen years later, Abraham and Goldie are still together; they now have a worthless son, Douglas, who is thrashed by Abraham when he will make no attempt to take a regular job. The McCranies, now living in a slum section of a city, plan to move back to the country. Abraham is still determined to educate the ignorant workers.

Three years later, in the same drab countryside where the play began, Abraham is desperately trying to get his school going again. Douglas, by now a petty crook, is in jail.

Abraham attempts to make a speech at his new school building, but is shouted down by the local whites. As he staggers home, bloody from a beating that the whites have given him, he meets Lonnie, who is now the owner of the plantation. Lonnie taunts his half-brother with a charge of neglecting his duties as a farmer, and tells him that his land is going to be taken away from him again. Abraham kills Lonnie, and then is himself killed by a lynch mob.

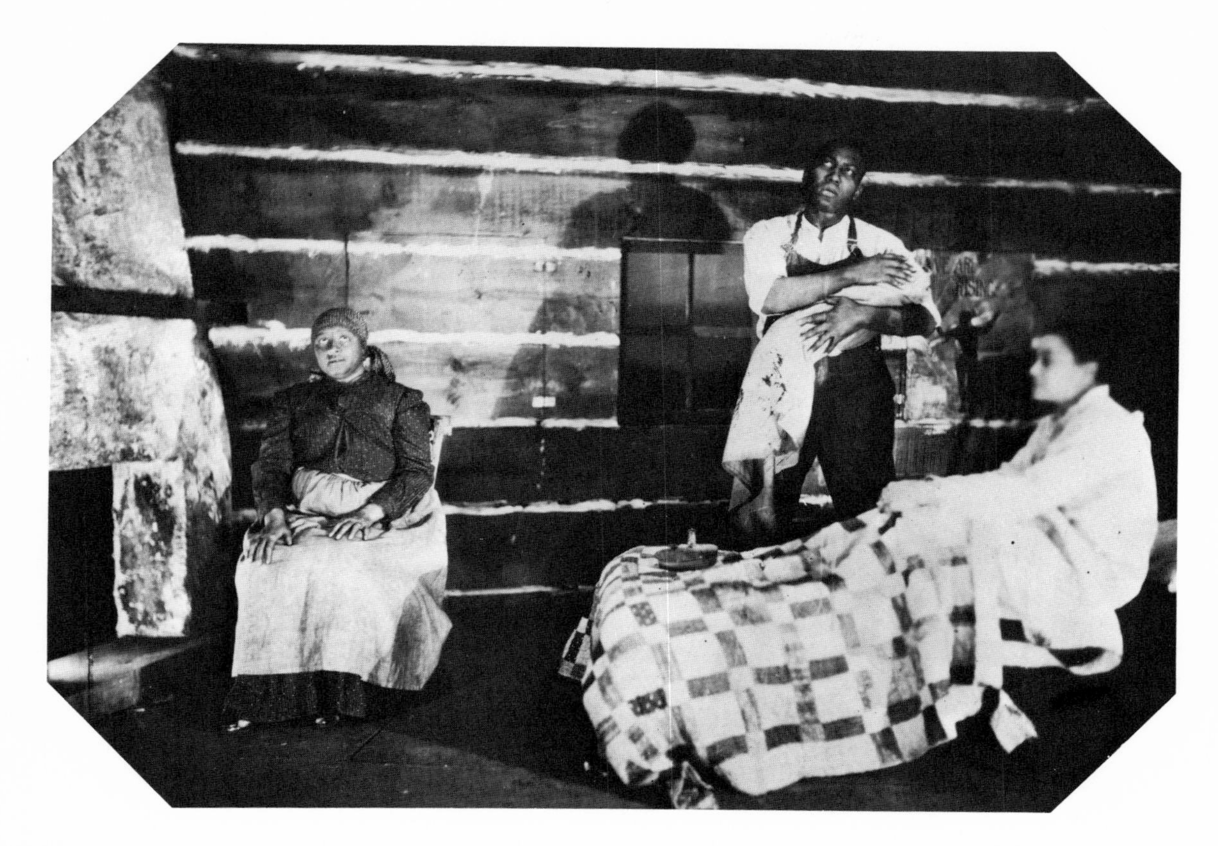

IN ABRAHAM'S BOSOM

THE CREDITS

THE BIOGRAPHY OF A NEGRO IN SEVEN SCENES BY PAUL GREEN.
PRODUCED BY THE PROVINCETOWN PLAYERS.
STAGED BY JASPER DEETER.
OPENED AT THE PROVINCETOWN THEATRE, DECEMBER 30, 1926, AND RAN FOR 123 PERFORMANCES.

THE CAST

BUD GASKINS	Frank Wilson
LIJE HUNNEYCUTT	Thomas Mosley
PUNY AVERY	James Dunmore
ABRAHAM MCCRANIE	Julius Bledsoe
COLONEL MCCRANIE	L. Rufus Hill
LONNIE MCCRANIE	H. Ben Smith
GOLDIE MCALLISTER	Rose McClendon
MUH MACK	Abbie Mitchell
DOUGLAS MCCRANIE	R. J. Huey
EDDIE WILLIAMS	Melvin Greene
LANIE HORTON	Armithine Lattimer
NEILLY MCNEILL	Stanley Greene

Seven Scenes in and near the Turpentine Woods of Eastern North Carolina, 1885–1909.

SCENE 1. *The Turpentine Woods of Eastern North Carolina, the Summer of 1885.*

SCENE 2. *In Abraham McCranie's Cabin, Spring, Three Years Later.*

SCENE 3. *The School House, Winter of the Same Year.*

SCENE 4. *A House in Durham, Winter, Eighteen Years Later.*

SCENE 5. *Same as Scene 2, an Autumn Evening, Three Years Later.*

SCENE 6. *On a Road, Near the School House, an Hour Later.*

SCENE 7. *Same as Scene 5, About Thirty Minutes Later.*

HISTORY AND REVIEWS

"A tragedy so charged with primitive emotion and the terrible longing of the human spirit that the Provincetown's narrow walls could scarce contain its fury. . . ."

In December of 1926 the Provincetown Players were almost bankrupt. In one way or another, however, the organization managed to scrape together $1,500, the bare minimum needed to produce an angry new play by a young playwright named Paul Green. Money was so tight that nobody connected with the production—actors, stagehands, director, playwright—received any sum at all from it during the first few weeks of the run.

The play was called *In Abraham's Bosom*, and its author had already made a reputation with his one-act plays; two volumes of them, *The Lonesome Road* and *The Lord's Will*, had been published in 1925. *In Abraham's Bosom* had itself first been written as a one-acter, which subsequently was combined with another short play, *Your Fiery Furnace*, to make the long play that the Provincetown Players presented in New York.

Paul Green was 32 when *In Abraham's Bosom* was produced, and a professor at the University of North Carolina. For all his education and sophistication, he remained essentially a country boy, uneasy in the bustle of Manhattan, and after the opening performance of his play he made a modest curtain speech saying that he was surprised that "a play from the provinces could please a New York audience so well." He later went on to write *The Lost Colony*, a pageant produced annually at Roanoke, N.C., since 1937, and *The Common Glory*, an annual fixture at Williamsburg since 1947. His Broadway contributions were to include *The House of Connelly*, the book for Kurt Weill's *Johnny Johnson*, and a collaboration with Richard Wright on the dramatization of Wright's famous novel, *Native Son.*

Green told of the genesis of *In Abraham's Bosom* in a long letter to Ward Morehouse, printed in Morehouse's *Matinee Tomorrow* (McGraw-Hill, 1949):

"It was many, many years ago. I was a little boy come to the neighboring town of Angier on a bright day to get a load of fertilizer for our farm. I wanted to see the train come in. I stood by the little shack of a station waiting along with several others, among them an old Confederate soldier leaning on his walking stick, for the train to put in its appearance. Soon it showed its round black moon of a locomotive end around the bend. It puffed and wheezed along toward us and finally drew in with a rusty squealing of its brakes. It was an old wood-burner, and the climb into town had been tough. The en-

Thomas Mosley, James Dunmore, Rose McClendon, Julius Bledsoe, Frank Wilson

gineer piled out of the cab, grease-marked outside and full of spleen and frustration inside. He began to work on the old locomotive, squirting grease here and there into its aged joints. I looked down the track and spilling out of the Jim Crow car—there were only four in all, a white car, a Negro car, a freight car and a caboose—spilling out was a swarm of little Negro school girls all dressed in their pink and white and blue picnic garments and with ribbons in their hair. Also there was a sprinkling of young Negro boys all ironed and pressed and scrubbed clean by their mamas for this great day. At the head of them was a tall yellow Negro man wearing gold-rimmed glasses and with a wide expanse of white slick-ironed shirt front and wing collar, and big black bolster tie. The little Negro children twittered and chirped in the sunny air, looking about them, happy as only children can be happy. They were on their way to Durham, North Carolina, on what was called in the springy parlance of those days a 'skursion.' The big yellow man was the teacher and he was taking the children on this jaunt as a wind-up for his year's school teaching. He came strolling forward, toward us and toward the irate and working engineer. He felt good. He was expansive. The world was sitting to his hand.

" 'Good mawning, gentlemen,' he said graciously to us. The old Confederate soldier blinked up at him, continued leaning on his stick, said nothing. I, a little boy, naturally said nothing. But I was already in my heart admiring this gracious, this genial, this successful and respectable representative of the Negro race.

" 'What time do the train get to Durhams, sir?' the Negro teacher asked of the engineer.

" 'None of your damned business,' called the engineer behind him, still bent over one of the drivers with his oil can. Then he looked around. He straightened spasmodically up and glared at the colored man.

"The Negro had already taken a shocked and rebuffed step backward.

" 'Sorry, suh, sorry,' he said, and he was beginning to bob his head up and down a bit, bending his body at the waist.

" 'Take off your hat,' the engineer suddenly squealed. Off it came in the culprit's hand. The little children down at the other end of the train began to see something was wrong, and in the blink of my eye I saw them begin to huddle together a little closer as if some fearful threat were beginning to be felt in the air.

" 'Take off your specs,' the engineer snapped.

" 'But I ain't done nothing, white folks, ain't done nothing,' said the colored man, and he backed away a couple of more steps.

" 'Don't white-folks me!' the engineer shouted. He flung the oil can behind him, snatched the walking stick from under the old Confederate soldier's resting hand and quick as lightning struck the Negro teacher a terrific wham across the face. Before the engineer pulled the stick away the blood had already rushed out and stained its splintered wood.

"A little babble of shrieks and moanings rose from the school children, and like a gang of pursued goats they bounded up the steps of the Jim Crow car and inside to safety. The old Confederate soldier had almost fallen on his face when his support was jerked away. He righted himself with spread-out legs; the engineer handed his walking stick back to him. The old soldier took it and resumed his resting without a word. I couldn't look at the dreadful stick. I couldn't look at the colored man. I shivered as if some bitter freezing chill had overspread the world. A low whimpering moaning sound came from the Negro school teacher. And what did he say? What was his accusation there for a moment in time and space? He simply said, 'Lawd, white folks, you done ruined my shirt.'

" 'All aboard!' yelled the engineer. He climbed hastily into his cab, pulled the whistle cord a couple of times. The Negro school teacher turned, still holding his big white handkerchief, now dyeing itself all over crimson, against his face. . . .

"Yes, that was a sort of anecdote. Years later when trying to speak a word for the Negro people, the scene haunted me and I sat down and wrote the story of a school teacher who tried desperately to help his people and failed. It wasn't a Confederate veteran's walking stick that laid my hero low. It was something more up-to-date and final—a shotgun. The school teacher of that spring morning long ago still lives—now a very old man. A bad scar still shows on his face, running from his forehead down across his chin. And there must be a scar in his heart too. There is in mine, and always will be."

Some of the notices:

George Goldsmith in the *Herald Tribune*:

"*In Abraham's Bosom* is a tragedy so charged with primitive emotion and the terrible longing of the human spirit that the Provincetown's narrow walls could scarce contain its fury. It is, as I said, a tragedy, authentic, sincere, and at moments profoundly moving. It is also a tract. I wonder, only, if it is a play. There is in this conflict of man and his environment, I venture to suggest, a far finer piece for the theatre than Mr. Green has wrought. Despite its pathos and strength, the play is often preachy, repetitious and faulty in construction."

Percy Hammond in the *Herald Tribune* (the newspaper ran a second notice after the play had moved uptown to the Garrick Theatre):

"It is a sad play, so well written and so well acted that even the near-Southerners who applaud 'Dixie' the loudest may be urged to tears. Too long, too deliberate and too much concerned with emphasizing its propaganda, it eventually becomes a little tiresome to the average playgoer. It would be a finer play perhaps if it were a bit disciplined."

R. S. in the *Evening World*:

"Newcomer Paul Green is an artist, not in the making, but made. The scenery is enchantingly native, and the play is so real that it is a bit painful at times, especially when two whippings and a murder occur."

A. S. in the *Morning World*:

"*In Abraham's Bosom* is the first full-length drama of Paul Green, whose one-act plays have won various prizes in little theatre tournaments. In its compassionate study of the struggles and defeats of the aspiring Negro it confirms these verdicts of the author's literary distinction, a distinction which only occasionally fails to meet the test of the footlights. Professor Green has put into his picture a searching and passionate sympathy for all those who seek to help humanity in spite of itself; unfortunately he has also reproduced much of the tedium of this experience with a detailed fidelity which only the magic of sustained emotion could make good stagecraft. The results are isolated moments of true tragedy and interminable stretches which even the excellent cast could not uphold."

Unsigned in the *Post*:

"Almost always *In Abraham's Bosom* is poetry, ringing with the true accents of the naive, superstitious, singing and cursing Negro folk of North Carolina. Almost never is it a drama in the sense that its literary values have been drawn taut, all the water squeezed out, all the action galvanized into dramatic life."

Thomas Van Dycke in the *Telegraph*:

"After writing a first act of great power and beauty, Green has let his matter and message dwindle away until the rest of the evening is just so much boredom. All in all, it seems a pity that one has to label this play a failure in the artistic sense (for it surely will be from a commercial viewpoint) for it had more than the elements of a fine play."

Writing about the 1926–27 award in 1944's *Theatre Annual*, juror Walter Prichard Eaton said:

"Our choice lay between *The Silver Cord* and the new play by young Green, his first play to reach New York, although it only reached the Provincetown Playhouse. Because this play came up out of the soil of the South, and with a passionate sincerity tried to say something important about the Negro problem, and because it seemed to us that the prize, if given to Green, might be a great encouragement to regional American drama, we recommended *In Abraham's Bosom*. We knew we would be criticized, but I still think we did right."

ALSO-RANS: *The Silver Cord, Broadway, Saturday's Children, The Road to Rome*

SUMMATION

This was an excellent, unorthodox decision. *In Abraham's Bosom* was not as well-made as *The Silver Cord*, not as gaudily theatrical as *Broadway*, not as close to standard American life as *Saturday's Children*. But this "pure and inevitable tragedy," as Carl Carmer called it, was both honest and well written, and had a great deal to say. Its selection did credit to the Advisory Board.

Lynn Fontanne

(Opposite Page, Left) *Earle Larimore, Lynn Fontanne* (Right) *Lynn Fontanne, John J. Burns, Glenn Anders*

1927-28

THE NINE ACTS OF *Strange Interlude* make it the longest play ever presented professionally in America, comparable in length only to O'Neill's other giant, *Mourning Becomes Electra.*

The play covers a time span of some twenty-five years. Nina Leeds is the chief character, and the action revolves around her relationships with three men: Charles Marsden, Sam Evans and Dr. Edmund Darrell.

Marsden is fussy and old-maidish, a non-romantic friend of long standing, and it is the boyish Evans whom Nina marries, following a nervous breakdown suffered after the wartime loss of her fiancé. Nina's anguish over his death has led her into promiscuity, and the marriage is an attempted "cure." Nina becomes pregnant by Evans, but is then informed by Evans' mother of a history of family insanity. The mother advises Nina to have an abortion, and then to have a child by another man, keeping this unorthodox arrangement secret from Sam, of course.

Nina enlists Dr. Darrell's aid in the project; he enters it on a purely businesslike basis, but soon he and Nina fall in love. Nina becomes pregnant again, by Darrell, and when the baby is born she allows Evans to think he is the father. Darrell is tempted to tell Evans the truth, but cannot bring himself to do so. Darrell and Nina continue their affair for years, while the child grows up.

Nina eventually blurts out the truth concerning her son to Marsden, but he is the only one she tells; when Evans dies of a heart attack, he dies believing the boy to be his own. Darrell proposes to Nina after Evans' death, but Nina will have none of him now, and settles for marrying the sexless, adoring Marsden.

STRANGE INTERLUDE

THE CREDITS

A PLAY IN NINE ACTS BY EUGENE O'NEILL.
PRODUCED BY THE THEATRE GUILD.
STAGED BY PHILIP MOELLER.
OPENED AT THE JOHN GOLDEN THEATRE, JANUARY 30, 1928, AND RAN FOR 426 PERFORMANCES.

THE CAST

CHARLES MARSDEN	Tom Powers
PROFESSOR LEEDS	Philip Leigh
NINA LEEDS	Lynn Fontanne
SAM EVANS	Earle Larimore
EDMUND DARRELL	Glenn Anders
MRS. AMOS EVANS	Helen Westley
GORDON EVANS, AS A BOY	Charles Walters
MADELINE ARNOLD	Ethel Westley
GORDON EVANS, AS A MAN	John J. Burns

Harry Bannister, Ralph Morgan, Pauline Lord (Road Company)

ACT I

Library of the Leeds' Home in a Small University Town of New England.

ACT II

The Same.

ACT III

Dining Room of the Evans' Homestead in Northern New York.

ACT IV

The Library.

ACT V

Sitting Room of a Small House at the Seashore.

ACT VI

The Same.

ACT VII

Sitting Room of the Evans' Apartment on Park Avenue.

ACT VIII

Section of Afterdeck on the Evans' Cruiser.

ACT IX

A Terrace on the Evans' Estate on Long Island.

HISTORY AND REVIEWS

"It builds up to such savagery of plot, such analytic slaying of its several people, that its last acts are soaked, strewn battlefields. . . ."

Eugene O'Neill's *Strange Interlude* was a nine-act giant of a play, so long that its audiences had to be given the first "dinner break" in theatre history; the curtain went up at 5:15 P.M., there was a recess from 7:40 to 9 P.M., and then the proceedings went on (and on) until 11 o'clock.

In addition to its inordinate length, *Strange Interlude* made constant use of "asides" in which its characters' secret thoughts were verbalized. Arthur and Barbara Gelb, in *O'Neill*, note that these mental comments posed a very tricky problem for director Philip Moeller. At first he was going to have them spoken in one particular zone of the stage, then thought that he might experiment with special lighting effects whenever the characters began to think aloud. Finally he decided to immobilize the actor who was soliloquizing; it sounds awkward, but, in theatre argot, it "worked." Audiences accepted the device, caught up as they were in the headlong rush of the cataract that O'Neill had poured so prodigally onto the stage.

Strange Interlude was the first Eugene O'Neill drama to be acquired by The Theatre Guild, although *Marco Millions*, which the Guild bought somewhat later, actually beat *Interlude* to Broadway by three weeks. Guild director Lawrence Langner had been friendly with O'Neill for ten years, ever since 1917, and had made a series of futile efforts to produce several of his plays, notably *Anna Christie*. When *Strange Interlude* came along, Langner did not intend to be frustrated again.

"If we fail to do this great experiment," he wrote to his fellow members on the Board of Directors, "if we lack the courage and the vision, then we should forever hang our heads in shame, for we will have lost one of the greatest opportunities in our history."

Langner was the play's great champion at the Guild. Many of that organization's directors felt lukewarm about it; one of them, indeed, suggested that it could be enormously improved (and shortened, certainly) by cutting out all of the asides! Langner bridled, the pruner retreated, and the asides stayed in.

The unpredictable Alexander Woollcott, fervently pro-O'Neill in the days of *Beyond the Horizon* and *Anna Christie*, was loaned an advance copy of the *Strange Interlude* script by one of its actors, and hated the play on sight. He wrote a waspish article for *Vanity Fair*, and through a mistake in timing (not attributable to Woollcott) the piece was published a few days before the play's Broadway opening. Woollcott was then the critic for the *World*, and Herbert Bayard Swope, the paper's editor, felt that the magazine story disqualified him as an opening night reviewer for *Strange Interlude*. Swope sidelined Woollcott, and assigned Dudley Nichols to do the review. Ironically, Nichols wrote a rave notice.

Some of the notices:

Gilbert W. Gabriel in the *Sun*:

"*Strange Interlude* is inescapably O'Neill. It has the hugeness of mills of the gods. It builds up to such savagery of plot, such analytic slaying of its several people, that its last acts are soaked, strewn battlefields. But when one has done with *Strange Interlude* one has lived with it and its people a long, long while, completely, timelessly, as long as one lives with one's own secret self. And one has lived deep in the coils of a scheme of constant fascination, an enthralling and greatly affecting theme carried to furthest possible honesty and irony, to occasionally breath-taking beauty. It is a venture magnificent and a milestone to cleave the skyline of the future."

Dudley Nichols in the *World*:

"It needs all the restraint a reporter can muster not to stamp the occasion without a second thought the most important event in the present era of the American theatre. This play marks the top of O'Neill's career. It would seem that he has not only written a great American play, but the great American novel as well. The drama mounts to a peak of tragic power and strange beauty in the sixth act. In this scene O'Neill seems to gather all of mankind and all of woman."

J. Brooks Atkinson in *The New York Times*:

"Written by our foremost dramatist, acted intelligently by a notable troupe of actors, directed intel-

Glenn Anders, Lynn Fontanne, Tom Powers, Earle Larimore

ligently by Philip Moeller and sponsored by the Theatre Guild, *Strange Interlude* commands the respectful interest of the enthusiastic playgoer to whom experiment is never dull. All this one can earnestly report without believing that *Strange Interlude* is distinguished as a play or that Mr. O'Neill's combination of the novel and drama techniques is a permanent addition to the theatre. Mr. O'Neill does not illuminate his theme with pity or interpret its significance. Regarded purely as a story, *Strange Interlude* appears, at least to this observer, to lack dramatic distinction and originality. Mr. O'Neill has restored the 'aside' without giving it an entirely new meaning. He has not, one suspects, always used it wisely. Lynn Fontanne and Earle Larimore play with admirable distinction and resourcefulness. One cannot speak too highly of their skill."

George Jean Nathan, in the *American Mercury*, said that O'Neill had written "the finest, the profoundest drama of his entire career." Stark Young called the play "an overwhelming milestone in the American theatre—it stretches the range of modern English drama to a wide, rich new limit." Robert Littell in the *Evening Post* identified it as "the greatest of American plays." But harsher voices were raised, too. Here is Alan Dale in the *American*:

" 'What a sordid mess!' cried one of the characters kneaded into the nausea bondesic dough presented with pomp, pretentiousness and absurd pose at the John Golden Theatre yesterday and labelled *Strange Interlude*. What a sordid mess! It was, indeed. What a Parisian playwright would toss off in three hours as a French farce Mr. O'Neill, loudly acclaimed as our premier dramatist, laboriously offered as an American tragedy. What the Parisian playwright would laughingly produce as a somewhat ribald bit of a smoking-room story, Mr. O'Neill, with sobs and tears and arch-Pecksniffian outbursts of lovely protestation, set down as a New England study of hidden depths."

Alexander Woollcott fired a week-late salvo in the *World*:

"Neither the really brilliant resourcefulness with which the unhampered Theatre Guild brought

Lynn Fontanne, Helen Westley

Strange Interlude to life, nor the novelty of the archaic technique O'Neill had resurrected for the writing of it, served to conceal, even for the fleeting hours of the performance, what often seemed to me the naive and tasteless pomposity of its speech and the fearful pretentiousness of its heavily furrowed brow. Indeed, I thought that the net result of all the patient and austere effort that went into *Strange Interlude* was a resonant emptiness. I came away from it feeling as if I had spent a good many years with a chance assemblage of clothing-store dummies, each neatly ticketed with a firmly lettered placard, each all too visibly bewigged, and each of them spouting all too unmistakably the words of the ventriloquial O'Neill himself."

Woollcott, no man to forgive and forget, used his *World* column to print the following letter from Ben Hecht, after the Pulitzer Prize had been awarded:

"There is so thick an air of middle-class awe gathered around *Strange Interlude*, that when I attended the play, which was the day after it had been walloped with the Pulitzer Prize, I knew myself in the presence of a Masterpiece. The first function of a Masterpiece, alas, is to turn the otherwise honest and simple moujiks who haunt the Broadway box-offices into a rabble of literary bounders. *Strange Interlude* offers a series of psychological lantern slides so pompously drawn, and yet so Brisbanish in their content, that the theatregoer experiences the flattering glow of understanding (for once in his life, at least) something very highfalutin'."

Glenn Anders, Charles Walters, Judith Anderson (after she had replaced Miss Fontanne as Nina)

Glenn Anders, Charles Walters, Lynn Fontanne

Strange Interlude made national headlines when the Mayor of Boston refused to let the show play his city. Unwilling to be denied a chance at the rich Boston market, the Guild managed to book a theatre in suburban Quincy. Thomas J. McGrath, Mayor of Quincy, issued this statement:

"The full significance of the whole controversy over *Strange Interlude* is the downright public distaste of prejudgments. However sincere some people may be in their dislike of certain literature and plays the great majority is determined that censorship shall be sparingly exercised. The great majority of last night's audience had not seen the play or even read the book, and so had been swayed somewhat by the claim that the story was simply a well done piece of pornographic literature. Last night's demonstration dispelled all misconceptions and doubts."

There was even more significance to that Quincy engagement than Mayor McGrath could have dreamed of. Across the street from the Quincy theatre was a restaurant that had just been taken over by a new management. Business boomed at intermission time, because of the play's unorthodox dinner break, and so mightily did the little restaurant prosper that its owner began thinking of opening a branch, or perhaps even a couple of branches. The owner was Howard Johnson.

Tom Powers, Lynn Fontanne

ALSO-RANS: *Coquette, The Royal Family, Porgy, Paris Bound, Behold the Bridegroom*

SUMMATION

A good choice, and an inevitable one, as the competition was not very powerful. The poignant *Porgy* was doomed to be lost in the shuffle; O'Neill's enormous play, whatever its flaws, utterly dominated the season.

Artist Peggy Bacon caught *Street Scene's* atmosphere in this drawing.

1928-29

THE SETTING IS A DINGY New York side street. A brownstone house dominates the scene, and it is its occupants with whom the play chiefly deals: the Maurrants, on the second floor; the Kaplans and the Fiorentinos, on the ground floor; and up above, the Hildebrands and the Buchanans.

While the play is spiced with typical vignettes of city life—gossiping neighbors, roller-skating children, an eviction, an imminent birth—there are two major plot lines woven through the highly realistic clatter and clamor. One involves a doomed romance between young Rose Maurrant and Sam Kaplan. The other, which gives the play its most melodramatic moments, is concerned with the elder Maurrants.

Anna Maurrant, an attractive woman in early middle age, is unhappy in her marriage to Frank, a sullen, violent stagehand. Anna begins a surreptitious love affair with Steve Sankey, a milkman; Frank comes home unexpectedly, drunk and furious, surprises Steve in the Maurrant apartment with Anna, and kills them both.

Frank escapes for a few hours, but is then captured by the police. They drag him onstage, bloody and disheveled, and he says a last sad goodbye to Rose. She is now determined to take her little brother Willie and go away from the block forever, and will not listen to Sam's pleas that they "belong to each other." People should belong only to themselves, Rose feels; had her father and mother led self-fulfilling lives, the tragedy might never have occurred.

As Rose leaves the house for the last time, a new couple appears, making plans to move into the now vacant Maurrant apartment. The scars have already started to heal, and life will go on pretty much as usual.

Horace Braham (Seated on curb), *Anna Kostant, John M. Qualen, Leo Bulgakov, Robert Kelly, George Humbert, Mary Servoss, Eleanor Wesselhoeft, Beulah Bondi*

STREET SCENE

THE CREDITS

A PLAY IN THREE ACTS BY ELMER RICE.
PRODUCED BY WILLIAM A. BRADY, LTD.
STAGED BY ELMER RICE.
OPENED AT THE PLAYHOUSE, JANUARY 10, 1929, AND RAN FOR 601 PERFORMANCES.

THE CAST

ABRAHAM KAPLAN	Leo Bulgakov
GRETA FIORENTINO	Eleanor Wesselhoeft
EMMA JONES	Beulah Bondi
OLGA OLSEN	Hilda Bruce
WILLIE MAURRANT	Russell Griffin
ANNA MAURRANT	Mary Servoss
DANIEL BUCHANAN	Conway Washburne
FRANK MAURRANT	Robert Kelly
GEORGE JONES	T. H. Manning
STEVE SANKEY	Joseph Baird

Erin O'Brien-Moore

Agnes Cushing	Jane Corcoran
Carl Olsen	John M. Qualen
Shirley Kaplan	Anna Kostant
Filippo Fiorentino	George Humbert
Alice Simpson	Emily Hamill
Laura Hildebrand	Frederica Going
Mary Hildebrand	Eileen Smith
Charlie Hildebrand	Alexander Lewis
Samuel Kaplan	Horace Braham
Rose Maurrant	Erin O'Brien-Moore
Harry Easter	Glenn Coulter
Mae Jones	Millicent Green
Dick McGann	Joseph Lee
Vincent Jones	Matthew McHugh
Dr. John Wilson	John Crump
Officer Harry Murphy	Edward Downes
A Milkman	Ralph Willard
A Letter-Carrier	Herbert Lindholm
An Ice-Man	Samuel S. Bonnell
Two College Girls	Rose Lerner Astrid Alwynn
A Music Student	Mary Emerson
Marshall James Henry	Ellsworth Jones
Fred Cullen	Jean Sidney

An Old-Clothes Man	Joe Cogert
An Interne	Samuel S. Bonnell
An Ambulance Driver	Anthony Pawley
A Furniture Mover	Ed. A. McHugh
Two Nurse-Maids	Astrid Alwynn Nelly Neil
Policemen	Carl C. Milter John Kelly Anthony Pawley
Two Apartment Hunters	Frances F. Golden Otto Frederick

Passers-by: Ruth Randolph, Elizabeth Goodyear, Josephine Coghlan, Emily Hamill, Jean Sidney, Samuel S. Bonnell, Robert Mack, John Cambridge, Carl C. Milter, Anthony Pawley, Herbert Lindholm, Ed. A. McHugh, Ralph Willard, Otto Frederick, Benn Trivers.

scene: *There is One Setting, the Exterior of a "Walk-up" Apartment House, in a Mean Quarter of New York.*

HISTORY AND REVIEWS

"From the very beginning I conceived the house as the real protagonist of the drama. . . ."

Street Scene came very close to never being produced at all; its author, 35-year-old Elmer Rice, had the disheartening experience of having it rejected by half a dozen top Broadway producers. The Theatre Guild, Winthrop Ames, David Belasco, Arthur Hopkins, Jed Harris and Sam H. Harris all passed up the chance to present this unusual "slice of life" play, perhaps intimidated by its giant setting and swarming cast of characters. *Street Scene* was finally picked up by William A. Brady, a derby-hatted, cigar-smoking showman who at 66 was in the sunset of a gaudy career.

Elmer Rice had had his first Broadway hit back in 1914, at the age of 21, when as Elmer L. Reizenstein he had written the sensationally successful *On Trial.* In 1923 he had written *The Adding Machine*, widely hailed as an important expressionistic play, but good for only a six-week Broadway run. His fortunes were low when *Street Scene* went into rehearsal, and, to make matters worse, Brady's whole family (his wife, Grace George; his daughter, Alice Brady; and his son, William Brady Jr.) were loudly vocal in their disapproval of the whole venture.

Brady himself was a notorious tightwad, but shortly before *Street Scene* opened he obviously began to feel hopeful about its prospects, for he invested an extra $700 to put a thin coat of cement over the wooden platform that served as a sidewalk in the setting. The cement made the clatter of the play's roller-skating children sound quite authentic. Rice was overwhelmed.

"This was the first genuine compliment the play had received," he said later.

On February 24, 1929, a few weeks after the opening, Rice wrote in *The New York Times*:

"*Street Scene* had a rather curious beginning. Some four or five years ago I wrote—largely for my own entertainment and as an exercise in technique—a play without words. (It was called *The Sidewalks of New York*, that phrase being at the time still relatively unhackneyed.) I included only such situations as did not require speech—situations, that is, in which the action spoke for itself. The play consisted of about fifteen scenes—some realistic, some stylized, some fantastic, some symbolical—dealing with various aspects of New York life. One episode in this wordless play represented the awakening of a 'brownstone front' in the early morning hours. There was neither plot nor situation. One merely saw the house shaking off its sleep and beginning to go about the business of the day. The late homecomers, the janitor, the tradespeople, the weary doctor, the passers-by, the workmen, the music pupil—all were there; the substance, in short, of the first ten minutes of the second act of *Street Scene*. It seemed to me at the time I wrote this scene that it contained the germ of a full-length play."

Rice returned to America in the fall of 1927 after three years in Europe, and was so vividly impressed with the vitality of the New York scene that his old idea came back. He began working on it in November, and had it finished by February of 1928, but another full year went by before *Street Scene* finally opened on Broadway.

Street Scene's single setting, a stretch of city street with a brownstone front as its centerpiece (Rice, Brady and designer Jo Mielziner chose an actual house at 25 West 65th St. and duplicated it as literally as possible) was one of the most elaborate ever seen on Broadway. Writing in *Theatre Arts* in May of 1929, Rice said:

"From the very beginning—before the play was written even—I conceived the house as the real protagonist of the drama, a brooding presence, which not only literally dominated the scene, but which integrated and gave a kind of dramatic unity to the sprawling and unrelated lives of the multitudinous characters, and lent to the whole whatever 'meaning' it may have."

When *Street Scene* went into rehearsal George Cukor was its director; he lasted four days. Rouben Mamoulian was offered the job, but never even showed up at the theatre. Rice, who had never before directed professionally (he subsequently staged all of his own plays), took over in desperation. As much traffic cop as director, he had to organize the movements of more than sixty people on four different levels of playing space, and had to synchronize the action with a wild variety of offstage noises—the rumble of traffic, gunshots, steamboat whistles, the rasping of a violin during a music lesson, the wailing of a baby.

Some of the notices:

J. Brooks Atkinson in *The New York Times*:

"Still unwilling to write a conventional play according to the safe, stereotyped forms, Elmer Rice contents himself with writing an honest one in *Street Scene*. *Street Scene's* story is slight and unoriginal, yet it manages to be generally interesting, frequently amusing, and extraordinarily authentic. Mr. Rice has observed and transcribed his material perfectly. Never did the phantasmagoria of street episodes seem so lacking in sketchy types and so packed with fully delineated character."

Gilbert W. Gabriel in the *American*:

"Plot upon plot, episodic, runaway, hastily snatching at the possibilities of drama, yet somehow interlocking into one tremendously fascinating piece of processionary playdom, where the city street is both hero and villain, agonist, antagonist, chorus and all. The setting is amazingly solid, literal, explicit —an old-fashioned stone apartment house, steps, windows, curbs, janitor's cellar, scaffoldings. The veracity of it rolls you down and runs you over like a moving van."

John Anderson in the *Journal*:

"Out of the clutter and racket and brownstone complacency of any New York side street Elmer Rice has wrought *Street Scene*. It is a play which builds engrossing trivialities into a drama that is rich and compelling. Call it photographic if you like; call it the baldest sort of realism, it remains, nevertheless, tremendously effective and deeply moving."

Burns Mantle in the *Daily News*:

"*Street Scene* is as photographic as a play can be. It is human as it is sordid. The detail is vivid. The acting vibrant. It is a good show, but I don't believe they can sell it."

Robert Littell in the *Evening Post*:

"Elmer Rice's generous, juicy and enormously interesting slice of New York life is something to stand up and cheer for. Made of the simplest human ingredients, it is strikingly original, amusing, moving and exciting; it is admirably acted, and staged with such skill that one does not know whether Mr. Rice ought to take most bows as director or as author."

Richard Lockridge in the *Sun*:

"Through no other play now current does life run more surely. Through *Street Scene*, indeed, life not so much runs as pours. Here is an illusion of reality so perfect that to call it an illusion is to belie. Here is a play poignant, immediate, contemporary—a play of this city, of this moment."

Playwright Elmer Rice poses in the original stage set.

The only off-key note in this chorus of hallelujahs was sounded by St. John Ervine, over from England to do a guest stint as critic for the *World*. Said Mr. Ervine:

"I thought to myself as I watched Mr. Elmer Rice's three-act play *Street Scene* being performed at The Playhouse that we were being offered an exhibition of pointless realism. There on the stage was a garbage can, an actual and veritable garbage can, and I felt that if Mr. Rice had had his way the entire contents of the can would have been shown to us too. I am unable to regard *Street Scene* as a great play or even as a moderately good one. It is, in fact, a very poor play which obtains effect by the addition of details that are entirely irrelevant to the story."

The 1928–29 season was the one in which the original Pulitzer Prize citation was truncated. It still read: "For the original American play, performed in New York, which shall best represent the educational value and power of the stage," but the final phrase, "in raising the standard of good morals, good taste and good manners," was dropped. Clayton Hamilton, one of the jurors, commented on the change:

"You can't get up on the stage and cry about manners and morals today and by doing so expect to raise the standards of the American people. Any good play is a moral play, and the only immoral play is a poor play."

Percy Hammond, the critic of the *Herald Tribune*, took a slightly different view. In a piece written after the award had been made, he said:

"I like *Street Scene*, which is Broadway show-business at its best. I like it, as you do, more than Mr. Pulitzer would were he here to see it. Something tells me he would add some codicils to his will, leaving *Street Scene* without a nickel. His executors, however, are of a kind that disapprove his mouldy

standards, and they put the crown on *Street Scene*. I believe that they are justified in thus upsetting the Founder's last will and testament, and probating it according to the better and easier Broadway laws."

The award to *Street Scene* was a popular one, stirring up little or no animosity in any quarter. So unaccustomed was the calm that prevailed that Whitney Bolton was moved to write in the *Telegraph*:

"It is a sad case, this jealousy in the theatre. It turns the Pulitzer award from a chaste and coveted prize into a form of itching powder which, dusted annually on the necks of the boys, sets them plumb crazy. Mr. Rice may consider his victory as doubly an achievement, since he not only is garlanded as the author of a fine play, but is the first playwright in years to win the prize without arousing some bitter comment."

Alexander Woollcott had the last word.

"Personally," said Woollcott, "I would never have believed it possible that so fine a play could be written by anyone named Elmer."

ALSO-RANS: *Holiday, The Front Page, Gypsy, Machinal, Exceeding Small, Gods of the Lightning*

SUMMATION

An excellent choice. *Holiday* was a silk-smooth, witty play, but *Street Scene* was much meatier. *The Front Page* never pretended to be anything more than a crackling, first-rate melodrama.

Robert Kelly, gun in hand, holds off a curious crowd after his murder of his wife's lover.

Playwright Marc Connelly

1929-30

THE GREEN PASTURES, a deeply reverent fable, is a loving look at the Old Testament through the eyes of the old-fashioned Southern Negro. In its American productions it has always been played by an all-Negro cast. Negro spirituals, sung by the Hall Johnson Choir in the original production, were threaded through the entire play.

The Green Pastures opens at a Sunday school in Louisiana, during a lesson on the Creation. Then the scene quickly switches to the fanciful Heaven that the preacher has just been describing. A fish fry is in progress, and The Lord himself pays the picnickers a visit. He performs a number of miracles, and creates the earth. Then He creates Adam and Eve, in His own image.

Things quickly turn sour on The Lord's new planet, and when He walks the earth as a natural man He finds little but mockery and sin. He orders Noah to build an ark, and instructs him to people it with animals, two by two. Noah rides out the subsequent flood with the aid of a "kag of likker."

Richard B. Harrison, Tutt Whitney

The King of Babylon (Jay Mondaaye) surrounded by various Babylonian cuties

THE GREEN PASTURES

Shortly afterwards The Lord appears to Moses in the burning bush, and commissions him to free His people from Pharaoh's bondage and lead them into Canaan. Moses successfully tricks Pharaoh and reaches the Promised Land, but he has broken the Tablets, and may not himself enter Canaan. The Lord gently guides the old man to Heaven.

Sin becomes rampant again on Earth, this time in Babylon, and The Lord, vastly displeased with His people, abandons them for many years, returning only when the Romans threaten Jerusalem. In a quiet talk with a soldier, Hezdrel, He hears that the old wrathful God of Moses has been replaced in the affections of the faithful by the God of Hosea, a merciful God. Hezdrel says that he and his followers have found their way to this new God through suffering. The Lord returns to Heaven, realizing that He too must suffer if mankind is to find final salvation. As the play ends The Lord, in Heaven, is looking somberly down toward Earth, where Jesus Christ is toiling toward Calvary with a heavy cross.

Noah (Tutt Whitney) on his Ark, just before the Flood

THE CREDITS

A FABLE IN TWO PARTS BY MARC CONNELLY.
The Green Pastures was suggested by Roark Bradford's
Southern Sketches, *Ol' Man Adam an' His Chillun.*
PRODUCED BY LAURENCE RIVERS, INC. (ROWLAND STEBBINS.)
STAGED BY MARC CONNELLY.
OPENED AT THE MANSFIELD THEATRE, FEBRUARY 26, 1930, AND RAN FOR 640 PERFORMANCES.

THE CAST

MR. DESHEE	Charles H. Moore
MYRTLE	Alicia Escamilla
FIRST BOY	Jazzlips Richardson, Jr.
SECOND BOY	Howard Washington
THIRD BOY	Reginald Blythwood
RANDOLPH	Joe Byrd
A COOK	Frances Smith
CUSTARD MAKER	Homer Tutt
FIRST MAMMY ANGEL	Anna Mae Fritz
A STOUT ANGEL	Josephine Byrd

Assorted angels enjoy a celestial fish fry.

A Slender Angel	Edna Thrower
Archangel	J. A. Shipp
Gabriel	Wesley Hill
The Lord	Richard B. Harrison
Choir Leader	McKinley Reeves
Adam	Daniel L. Haynes
Eve	Inez Richardson Wilson
Cain	Lou Vernon
Cain's Girl	Dorothy Randolph
Zeba	Edna M. Harris
Cain the Sixth	James Fuller
Boy Gambler	Louis Kelsey
First Gambler	Collington Hayes
Second Gambler	Ivan Sharp
Voice in Shanty	Josephine Byrd
Noah	Tutt Whitney
Noah's Wife	Susie Sutton
Shem	Milton J. Williams
First Woman	Dinks Thomas
Second Woman	Anna Mae Fritz
Third Woman	Geneva Blythwood

First Man	Emory Richardson
Flatfoot	Freddie Archibald
Ham	J. Homer Tutt
Japheth	Stanleigh Morrell
First Cleaner	Josephine Byrd
Second Cleaner	Florence Fields
Abraham	J. A. Shipp
Isaac	Charles H. Moore
Jacob	Edgar Burks
Moses	Alonzo Fenderson
Zipporah	Mercedes Gilbert
Aaron	McKinley Reeves
A Candidate Magician	Reginald Fenderson
Pharaoh	George Randol
The General	Walt McClane
First Wizard	Emory Richardson
Head Magician	Arthur Porter
Joshua	Stanleigh Morrell
First Scout	Ivan Sharp
Master of Ceremonies	Billy Cumby
King of Babylon	Jay Mondaaye
Prophet	Ivan Sharp
High Priest	J. Homer Tutt
The King's Favorites	Leona Winkler
	Florence Lee
	Constance Van Dyke
	Mary Ella Hart
	Inez Persand
Officer	Emory Richardson
Hezdrel	Daniel L. Haynes
Another Officer	Stanleigh Morrell

Mr. Deshee (Charles H. Moore) and his Sunday School class

PART I

SCENE 1. *Sunday School.*
SCENE 2. *A Fish Fry.*
SCENE 3. *A Garden.*
SCENE 4. *A Roadside.*
SCENE 5. *A Private Office.*
SCENE 6. *A Private Office.*
SCENE 7. *Another Roadside.*
SCENE 8. *A House.*
SCENE 9. *A Hillside.*
SCENE 10. *A Mountain Top.*

PART II

SCENE 1. *A Private Office.*
SCENE 2. *Mouth of a Cave.*
SCENE 3. *Throne Room.*
SCENE 4. *Foot of a Mountain.*
SCENE 5. *A Cabaret.*
SCENE 6. *A Private Office.*
SCENE 7. *Outside a Temple.*
SCENE 8. *Another Fish Fry.*

Wesley Hill as Gabriel

HISTORY AND REVIEWS

"Gangway! Gangway for de Lawd God Jehovah!"

The Green Pastures contained the greatest entrance line ever written. The setting was a bustling fish fry, in a Negro heaven. The Angel Gabriel strode onstage, massive and self-assured, and shouted:

"Gangway! Gangway for de Lawd God Jehovah!"

Onto the stage, with sweet and solemn dignity, stepped Richard B. Harrison, the son of fugitive slaves, one-time bellhop, newsboy and railroad worker. Harrison was sixty-six years old, and had never acted professionally before. He was wearing a flat black hat and a dark swallowtail coat, and in his courtly bearing he exuded gentle, controlled power and sheer goodness. This was the Old Testament God of the Southern Negro in the living flesh, and the fate of *The Green Pastures* hung upon Harrison's instantaneous and unquestioned acceptance by the audience. Accepted he was, with a warmth that verged on reverence. A most remarkable theatrical gamble had paid off.

The Green Pastures was based on Roark Bradford's *Ol' Man Adam an' His Chillun*, a series of short stories which retold the Old Testament in the homely terms that an old Negro preacher might have used. In the stories God was a sort of glorified preacher, a much brasher and commoner figure than the one who later emerged in the play. He presided over a workaday heaven, one in which Gabriel could polish his doomsday trumpet and wistfully ask for permission to blow it, in which hungry angels socialized at fish fries, and housemaid angels wore gingham aprons on their wings. When He walked the earth as a natural man, it was logical enough that God should have stern words with Noah over an extra "kag of likker" for the ark, or that the Babylonians should mock Him with an orgy that was a caricature of Harlem debauchery.

Playwright Marc Connelly wrote the following program note:

"*The Green Pastures* is an attempt to present certain aspects of a living religion in the terms of its believers. The religion is that of thousands of Negroes in the deep South. With terrific spiritual hunger and the greatest humility these untutored black Christians—many of whom cannot even read the book

At Pharaoh's court, Aaron (McKinley Reeves) shows Pharaoh (George Randol) a trick walking stick that is about to turn into a snake

which is the treasure house of their faith—have adapted the contents of the Bible to the consistencies of their everyday lives.

"Unburdened by the differences of more educated theologians they accept the Old Testament as a chronicle of wonders which happened to people like themselves in vague but actual places and of rules of conduct, true acceptance of which will lead them to a tangible, three-dimensional Heaven. In this Heaven, if one has been born in a district where fish fries are popular, the angels do have magnificent fish fries through an eternity somewhat resembling a series of earthly holidays. The Lord Jehovah will be the promised comforter, a just but compassionate patriarch, the summation of all the virtues His follower has observed in the human beings about him. The Lord may look like the reverend Mr. Du Bois, as our Sunday School teacher speculates in the play, or He may resemble another believer's own grandfather. In any event, His face will have an earthly familiarity to the one who has come for his reward."

Connelly, not quite 40 years old when he wrote *The Green Pastures*, had started off as a reporter on the *Pittsburgh Sun*, then had come to New York to collaborate with George S. Kaufman on *Dulcy*, *Merton of the Movies* and *Beggar on Horseback*, and to write *The Wisdom Tooth* as a solo effort. In *The Green Pastures* he was dealing with material so fanciful and so far removed from ordinary Broadway fare that the project seemed to verge on lunacy. After *The Green Pastures* opened it was easy enough to see how marvelously right Connelly had been in his judgment, but before the verdict came in there were few on Broadway who would have given a nickel for the play's chances of commercial success.

True, there had been plays with Negro casts before—*In Abraham's Bosom*, *Porgy*—but *The Green Pastures* ran much greater risks. It had to capture and hold a mood that quivered just this side of irreverence. Although *The Green Pastures* was full of laughter, a laugh or two in the wrong places could have destroyed it. No wrong laughs ever shattered the mood.

Some of the notices:

J. Brooks Atkinson in *The New York Times*:

"From almost any point of view, *The Green Pastures* is a play of surpassing beauty. As comedy, fantasy, folklore, religion, poetry, theatre—it hardly matters which. For occasionally there comes a time when those names hardly matter in comparison with the sublime beauty of the complete impression. And Marc Connelly has lifted his fable of the Lord walking on the earth to those exalted heights where utter simplicity in religious conception produces a play of great emotional depth and spiritual exaltation—in fact the divine comedy of the modern theatre. The beauty of the writing, the humility of the performance put the theatre to its highest use. Richard B. Harrison plays the Lord with the mute grandeur of complete simplicity. You believe in him implicitly. In fact, you believe in the entire play; it is belief incarnadined. Such things are truer than the truth."

Robert Littell in the *World*:

"*The Green Pastures* is simply and briefly one of the finest things that the theatre of our generation has seen. Take that as tribute from one who forgot time, space and deadlines, and sat through it until the final curtain. It will move you to tears, and make you gasp with the simple beauty of the Old Testament pageantry. I am too shaken by it to more than blurt out that *The Green Pastures* has done something which has never been done before."

Gilbert W. Gabriel in the *American*:

"This devout fantasy is the most fortunate and affecting play of the year. *The Green Pastures* merits a respect, a passionate affection and admiration which, you'll find, have nothing to do with its Pulitzer Prize possibilities, or its box-office metal. It is too endearing a play to be soiled with stale hoorays."

Arthur Ruhl in the *Herald Tribune*:

"The whole entertainment is something that may be smiled at as entertainment by a more or less sophisticated and patronizing white audience. But it is strange and impressive how much of the supernatural burden of the story—the real spiritual hunger and steadfast faith of these groping souls—is carried over the footlights by the simplest and most unaffected means."

A lone dissent came from John Mason Brown in the *Evening Post*:

"In spite of the bravery of Mr. Connelly's attempt, he has fallen short of his goal. Admirable as

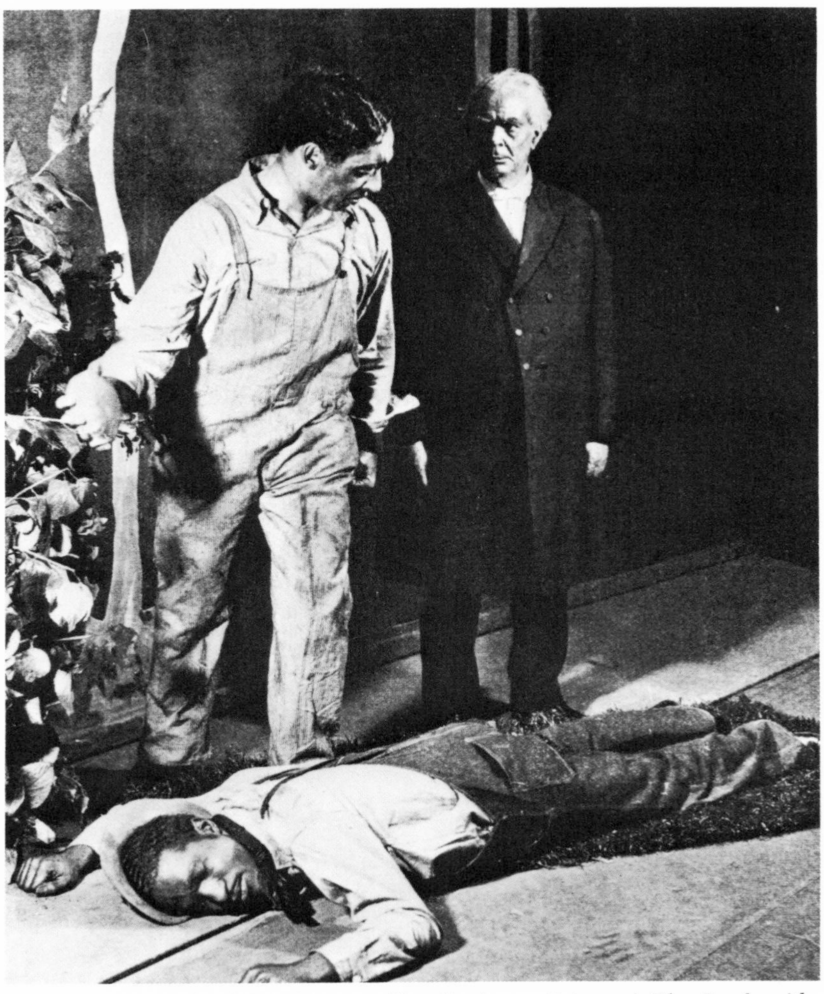

Lou Vernon, Richard B. Harrison (Standing), *as Cain and The Lord, with unidentified extra playing the dead Abel*

the whole intention of *The Green Pastures* is, and worthwhile as are most of its features, it somehow fails to click in its entirety."

After its year-and-a-half run on Broadway, *The Green Pastures* took to the road for the first of five tours. There had been some doubts about how it would be received in Southern states, but they were quickly banished. A story in *The New York Times* of October 22, 1933, said:

"*The Green Pastures* is treated with even more reverence by theatre audiences in the South than in the East and North, where the play has been considered primarily a comedy. Said the editor of the Greensboro, S.C., *Daily News*: 'Southern audiences take their religion, the religion of their Negroes, seriously, reverently. There was in the theatre last night what one might term a holy atmosphere; a tribute of silence far more effective than thunderous applause. Southerners do not applaud in church, and *The Green Pastures* seemed strangely like church.' "

During the entire series of tours, covering the better part of five years, Harrison never missed a performance. Serene and content, he felt that he had managed to achieve his life's goal, and backstage he was the same patriarchal figure who so awed audiences. His fellow actors admired and respected him, and also borrowed money from him frequently; The Lord had a reputation for being a very easy touch.

The Green Pastures duplicated its American success in countries across the world, but translating this peculiarly American play sometimes produced strange side effects. In Stockholm, where it opened as *Guds Grona Angar*, the pickaninnies curtseyed in the time-honored fashion of Swedish children. Too, the Swedish audiences sat in gloomy silence at the humorous scene in which Noah pleaded for "two kags of likker" to take with him on the ark. Every Swede was restricted to a rigid allowance of four liters of alcoholic beverages per householder each month, with no exceptions. Who was this Noah, to ask for more than his share?

Wesley Hill, the play's original Gabriel, was killed in an automobile accident during the Broadway run, and Hill's successor in the role died too, not long afterward. When Harrison himself died in March of 1935, Alexander Woollcott recalled the deceased pair of Gabriels, and wrote, in the *Ladies' Home Journal*:

"On the night of Harrison's funeral I had a notion that these two must have been hanging around the Golden Gates—waiting, waiting. And at last I seemed to hear them calling up those streets of right orient pearl, in voices joyous and exultant, 'Gangway! Gangway for Richard Berry Harrison!' "

Richard B. Harrison as The Lord

ALSO-RANS: *The Criminal Code, The Last Mile, June Moon, Rebound, Hotel Universe*

SUMMATION

An obvious choice; no other play of the season could conceivably have beaten out *The Green Pastures*, once the committee had decided that it could in conscience give the prize to an adaptation (*Miss Lulu Bett*, in 1920–21, had been an adaptation, but of the playwright's own novel). Walter Prichard Eaton reminisced in 1944, in *Theatre Annual*: "Before recommending *The Green Pastures*, which was based on Roark Bradford's stories, we consulted Mr. Pulitzer's son, who said: 'Does it add something original, making the work a new and perhaps larger thing, as Shakespeare added to the stories he took?' We said we thought it did. 'Then give it the prize,' said he."

Tutt Whitney

Richard B. Harrison, J. A. Shipp, Charles H. Moore, Edgar Burks

Playwright Susan Glaspell and Eva Le Gallienne

1930-31

IT IS THE LAST DAY of the nineteenth century. At the old Stanhope homestead, in Iowa, all of the books and papers are being catalogued and packed, as the house is being sold.

It soon becomes apparent that the most vital personality in the house is that of Alison Stanhope, even though she has been dead for eighteen years. Shy, introspective Alison was a poetess, and her posthumously published poems have given her a world-wide reputation. Most of the members of her family, however, would prefer that the memory of Alison be allowed to die. Kind-hearted Alison, so gentle and understanding in her relationships with her nieces and nephews, had immured herself in her room for the last years of her life; in love with a married man, she had chosen isolation rather than the scandal of a fulfilled affair.

Young Elsa Stanhope comes home to spend one last day at the old house. Her father, Alison's brother, is the only person who can find it in his heart to welcome her, for Elsa is the family black sheep, living openly with a married man who has deserted his wife and children for her.

A mysterious fire breaks out upstairs in Alison's old room; it had been set by addled old Aunt Agatha, who was futilely attempting to burn some papers. Before a heart attack takes her off, Aunt Agatha gives the papers to Elsa. They are more poems by Alison, the existence of which was not even suspected, and many of them deal frankly with her great lost love. Elsa's father is all for burning them, to avoid raking up an old scandal, but Elsa finally convinces him that their beauty must be preserved for the whole world to cherish, at whatever cost in pride to the immediate family.

Josephine Hutchinson

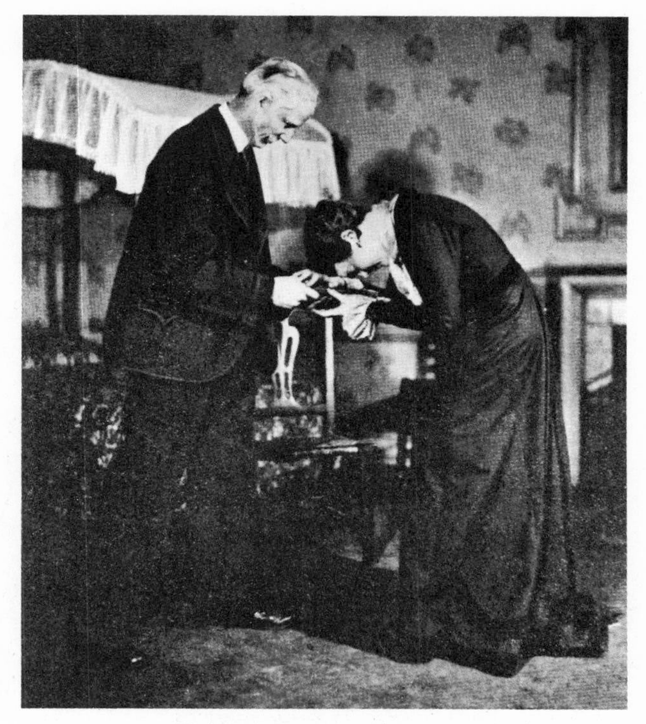

Walter Beck, Eva Le Gallienne

ALISON'S HOUSE

THE CREDITS

A Drama in Three Acts by Susan Glaspell.
Produced by the Civic Repertory Company.
Staged by Eva Le Gallienne.

Opened at the Civic Repertory Theatre, December 1, 1930. Through April, 1931, played in repertory once or twice a week. After winning the Prize, opened a continuous engagement at the Ritz Theatre on May 11, running for two weeks. Total performances, 41.

THE CAST

Ann Leslie	Florida Friebus
Jennie	Leona Roberts
Richard Knowles	Robert Ross
Ted Stanhope	Herbert Shapiro
Louise	Josephine Hutchinson
John Stanhope	Walter Beck
Eben	Donald Cameron

ELSA	Eva Le Gallienne
MISS AGATHA	Alma Kruger
HODGES	Howard da Silva
MRS. HODGES	Mary Ward

ACTS I and II

Library of the Old Stanhope Homestead in Iowa, on the Mississippi.

ACT III

Alison's Room.

HISTORY AND REVIEWS

"As the play slowly uncoiled itself in drab and sluggish motions, I joined my dissatisfied confreres in wondering by what processes the judges had reached their verdict. . . ."

Susan Glaspell's *Alison's House* was the rankest outsider ever to win the Pulitzer Prize, even exceeding *The Old Maid* in this respect. Nobody gave *Alison's House* a chance; indeed, one rival producer had been so sure that his own entry would win that he ordered a fresh set of posters printed, trumpeting the expected victory. After *Alison's House* sneaked under the wire, the posters became a collector's item to rank with the *Chicago Tribune's* celebrated DEWEY DEFEATS TRUMAN headline.

Alison's House opened quite inconspicuously in December, down on 14th Street, as part of Eva Le Gallienne's Civic Repertory season. It played one or two performances a week until the Pulitzer decision was announced, at which time the play was moved up to Broadway for a regular run that lasted for only two weeks.

Authoress Susan Glaspell had made her principal reputation as a novelist and short story writer, although she had had some theatrical experience; she was one of the founders of the Provincetown Playhouse, and in 1917 had collaborated with her husband, George Cram Cook, on a play called *Suppressed Desires*, a satire on that new fad, psychoanalysis. Another Glaspell play, *The Inheritors*, had been in Miss Le Gallienne's repertory in 1928–29.

Miss Glaspell's inspiration for *Alison's House* was drawn from the story of Emily Dickinson, the superb American poetess who died virtually unknown in 1886. Miss Dickinson had written in secret, for the most part, and the vast majority of her poems were not published until 1924, almost four decades after her death.

Some of the notices:

Robert Garland in the *Telegram*:

"To tell the truth, *Alison's House* is not the play it should have been. Somewhere, there is stirring drama in the life and death and resurrection of Miss Emily Dickinson. But Susan Glaspell has not managed to find where the life, the death and the resurrection are. The Miss Dickinson of Miss Glaspell's play is no resurrected ghost to dominate an evening's entertainment. Instead, she is a poetical prig who is dead but will not lie down. 'Well-meaning' is a more or less unpleasant phrase, but *Alison's House* remains well-meaning."

J. Brooks Atkinson in *The New York Times*:

"*Alison's House* is, for the most part, a disappointingly elusive play. Miss Glaspell's drama is full of ideas and perceptions. The loyalty of family, the imprisonment of genius, the brutal heedlessness of outside world, the new expression of the same genius in the next generation are obviously the ideas on which the drama revolves. But the theatre needs more concrete evidence than *Alison's House* supplies. Although *Alison's House* discusses an interesting theme it has not been sufficiently translated out of ideas into the theatre."

Robert Littell in the *Morning World*:

"How closely *Alison's House* follows the facts of Emily Dickinson's life I am unable to tell you. It is a play that makes one want to know those facts. It is also a play that often seems more like a labor of love than a play. It is charming, too long, and in spite of its attempt to create an intense atmosphere of nostalgic memory, a little empty."

Richard Lockridge in the *Evening Sun*:

"Susan Glaspell's *Alison's House* is a play which gropes in the darkness like the searcher in a game of blind man's buff, and the production which was given it last evening by the Civic Repertory Theatre does, much of the time, little enough to guide it. It wanders from its path and clutches wildly in odd corners, it fastens on the most unlikely objects and brings them forward with triumph as ill-concealed as it is ill-advised. Yet it is more to the point—to almost any point one can think of—than any of a dozen shrewder plays; it stumbles often into an illumination too rarely seen in the theatre or elsewhere. The play sadly needs, and misses, a directing tyrant—one with a large and heavy hand, grasping a large blue pencil. As it now stands it requires both patience and tolerance. But it repays them both."

John Mason Brown in the *Evening Post*:

"Unfortunately, as Miss Glaspell has written her play one gets but occasional glimpses of the Alison who dominates its action. She is talked about incessantly, but neither she nor the people who speak of her are drawn with a skill that creates complete illusion or carries conviction. Too often Miss Glaspell writes murkily, obscuring her own intentions, employing ponderous sentences and pompous phrases that are devoid of life. Too often, also, her attempts at comedy are woefully sad; heavy, guileless interludes which dispel whatever magic or poignancy certain of her scenes possess."

As might have been expected, there were quite a number of post-Prize comments in the press. Here is Percy Hammond in the *Herald Tribune*:

"The grumbles of the drama critics over the award of the Pulitzer Prize to *Alison's House* have been tempered with a seemly tolerance. Though discontented with the decision of the Triumvirate, the scribes have recorded it as a mystery rather than an injustice. I saw *Alison's House* last night for the first time, Mr. Shubert having brought it from faraway 14th Street to the Ritz, a point within a reasonable distance of the *Herald Tribune* printing presses. As the play slowly uncoiled itself in drab and sluggish motions, I joined my dissatisfied confreres in wondering by what processes the judges reached their verdict. *Alison's House* is a dull and melancholy story. The Civic Repertory cast is onerously sincere; Miss Le Gallienne herself is subtle, and, if one may be forgiven for saying so, expert."

J. Brooks Atkinson in the *Sunday Times*:

"Every few years the drama committee for the Pulitzer Prize sows one wild oat, and sows it with bravado. Miss Glaspell is one of our most gifted writers, particularly of novels, and *Alison's House* is a play with a respectable theme. But to select it as the best play of the season shows how meagerly the

Eva Le Gallienne

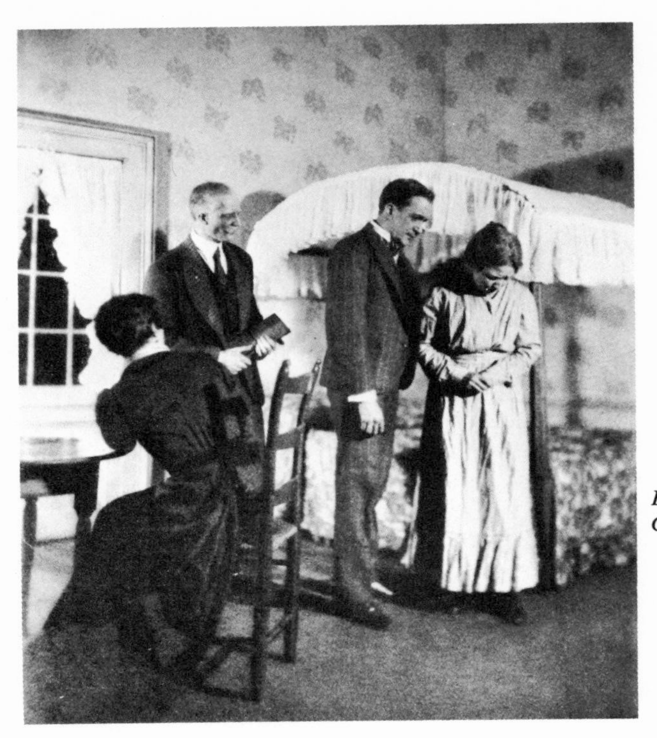

Eva Le Gallienne, Walter Beck, Donald Cameron, Leona Roberts

committee esteems the current American drama and the annual prize it helps bestow. Every few years the drama committee insists upon publishing its ignorance. *Alison's House* is a play of flat statements—of assertions, of sentimentally literary flourishes and of perfunctory characterizations. No matter how earnestly the characters talk, in a strangely stereotyped prose, the image of Alison never appears for an instant. Prize committees are always unpopular and under suspicion. But sometimes the drama committee for the Pulitzer Prize goes out of its way to make its glory hollow."

Richard Lockridge in the *Evening Sun*:

"It seems to me that it must have been with some idea of giving art a helping hand that the Messrs. Hamilton, Strong and Eaton crowned *Alison's House* as the best of all American plays produced in New York this season. They must have felt that it would be well to reward the obvious artistic integrity and high purpose of Miss Le Gallienne and Miss Glaspell; to establish that in a world of noise and gaudy sham, they were on the side of good intentions. They determined to give art a boost, forgetting that there is a difference between a boost and a crown, and that, in any event, this particular crown was somewhat large. A particular annoyance with this theory about art—this contention that art is too weak, too precious, to stand alone—and the suspicion that it was a theory which entered into the committee's deliberations, join to accentuate the vigor of my dissent from the award. It seems to me a bad award, on a purely comparative basis, and a mischievous award on any other. It is difficult to believe that men of the critical acumen of those who serve on the committee can really think *Alison's House*, all other things aside, a better play than, for example, *Once in a Lifetime* or *Tomorrow and Tomorrow*, to name but two of the four or five which might be set above it."

Walter Prichard Eaton, a juror, said, in the 1944 *Theatre Annual*:

"By recommending *Alison's House* we brought down on our heads immediate scorn. But its only real competitors among native plays were *Elizabeth the Queen* and Barry's *Tomorrow and Tomorrow*, the latter not a serious competitor. The choice, really, was between a play acted with great acclaim by Lunt and Fontanne in the older fashion of romantic verse drama, and a play acted down on 14th Street by Miss Le Gallienne's struggling Civic Repertory Company which plumbed the deep American love of home and family still existing outside the confines of New York cubbyhole apartments, and which also brought the strange story of Emily Dickinson to dramatic life. Again I have no apologies for this choice. *Alison's House* somewhat bored the critics in New York (it always bored them to have to go down to 14th Street, anyhow), but it was acted for a long time by many theatre groups throughout the country, and in a production I saw only three years ago (1941), it was still a moving and provocative play which deserved a recognition Broadway refused."

ALSO-RANS: *Elizabeth the Queen, Once in a Lifetime, Tomorrow and Tomorrow, Green Grow the Lilacs, Five Star Final*

SUMMATION

Despite Mr. Eaton's comments, this has to be rated as a dreadful decision, one in which sentiment for the underdog was allowed to carry the day at the expense of many worthier plays. Had the judges been looking for a play more strictly American in tone than *Elizabeth the Queen*, they need have looked no further than *Once in a Lifetime*, the first collaboration of George S. Kaufman and Moss Hart, and a stinging, timely satire on Hollywood.

Eva Le Gallienne

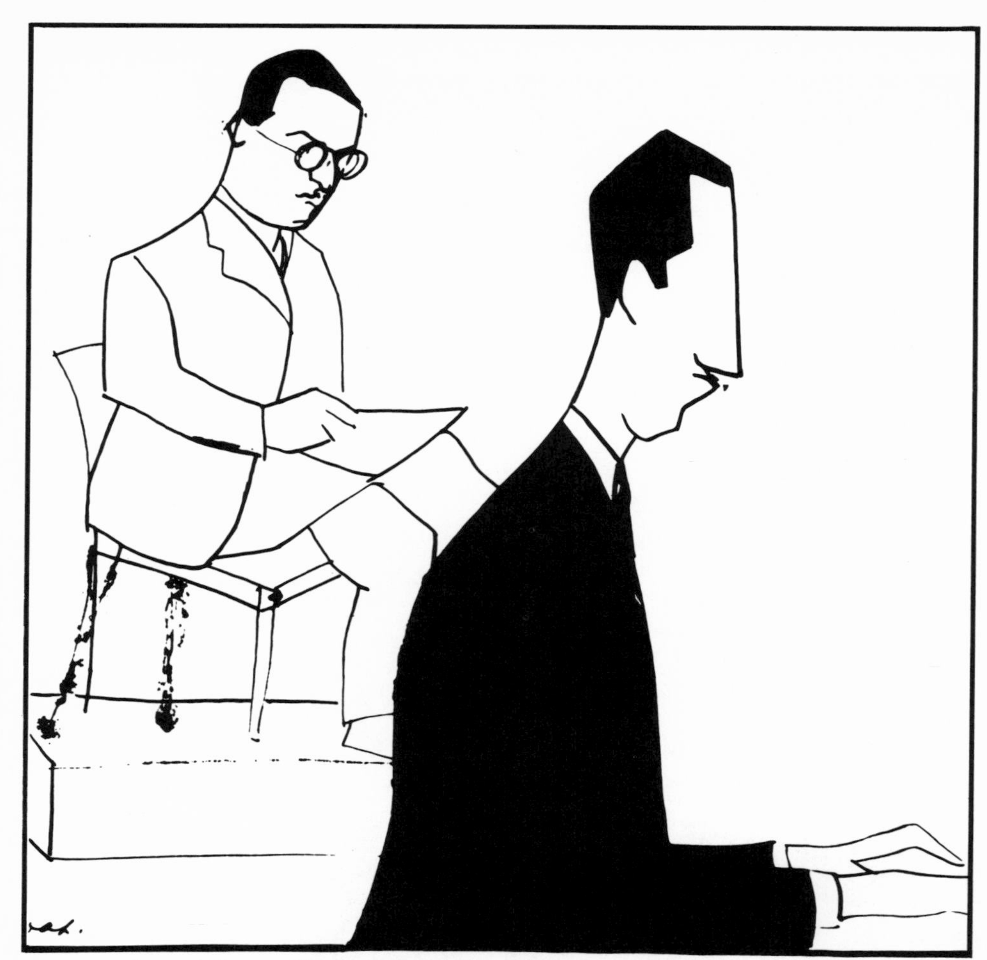

Ira and George Gershwin, caught in caricature by William Auerbach-Levy

(Opposite Page) *Dudley Clements, Harold Moffet, Victor Moore, Edward H. Robins, William Gaxton, Sam Mann, George E. Mack*

1931-32

JOHN P. WINTERGREEN, candidate for President of the United States, needs a proper All-American First Lady, so a national beauty contest is held. It is won by a striking blonde, Diana Devereaux, but Wintergreen perversely falls in love with a pretty little secretary, Mary Turner, whose chief attribute is her ability to make superb corn muffins. Wintergreen jilts Diana, and with Mary at his side is swept into the White House on a platform that does little but extol Love.

Swept along with him is his Vice-President, a lovable, bumbling incompetent named Alexander Throttlebottom, who has not even been able to join the Public Library because "you need two friends."

After John and Mary have been established in Washington for a while, grave trouble arises. It turns out that Diana Devereaux is a direct (if illegitimate) descendant of Napoleon, and the French Ambassador is furious at this affront to his nation's honor. The Ambassador demands that Wintergreen be impeached, and the Supreme Court is in the very process of doing so when Mary rushes dramatically onto the scene. She announces that she is going to have a baby—or, as the chorus gleefully puts it, "Posterity Is Just Around the Corner."

It's well known that the Supreme Court has never yet impeached an expectant father; Wintergreen is saved, and Diana and the French Ambassador retire in discomfiture. As a final fillip, Mary has twins, and Love is triumphant as the curtain falls.

Some of the songs: "Wintergreen for President"; "Who Cares?"; "Love is Sweeping the Country"; "Jilted"; "Of Thee I Sing, Baby"; "Because"; and "She's the Illegitimate Daughter of an Illegitimate Son of an Illegitimate Nephew of Napoleon."

OF THEE I SING

THE CREDITS

A Musical Comedy in Two Acts by George S. Kaufman and Morrie Ryskind.
Music by George Gershwin. Lyrics by Ira Gershwin.
Produced by Sam H. Harris.
Staged by George S. Kaufman.
Opened at the Music Box Theatre, December 26, 1931, and ran for 441 performances.

THE CAST

Louis Lippman	Sam Mann
Francis X. Gilhooley	Harold Moffet
Maid	Vivian Barry
Matthew Arnold Fulton	Dudley Clements
Senator Robert E. Lyons	George E. Mack
Senator Carver Jones	Edward H. Robins
Alexander Throttlebottom	Victor Moore
John P. Wintergreen	William Gaxton
Sam Jenkins	George Murphy

DIANA DEVEREAUX	Grace Brinkley
MARY TURNER	Lois Moran
MISS BENSON	June O'Dea
VLADIMIR VIDOVITCH	Tom Draak
YUSSEF YUSSEVITCH	Sulo Hevonpaa
THE CHIEF JUSTICE	Ralph Riggs
SCRUBWOMAN	Leslie Bingham
THE FRENCH AMBASSADOR	Florenz Ames
SENATE CLERK	Martin Leroy
GUIDE	Ralph Riggs

PHOTOGRAPHERS, POLICEMEN, SUPREME COURT JUSTICES, SECRETARIES, SIGHT-SEERS, NEWSPAPERMEN, SENATORS, FLUNKIES, GUESTS, ETC.:

The Misses Ruth Adams, Olgene Foster, Peggy Greene, Yvonne Gray, Billie Seward, Grenna Sloan, Adele Smith, Jessica Worth, Kathleen Ayres, Bobbie Brodsley, Martha Carroll, Mary Carroll, Ann Ecklund, Virginia Franck, Dorothy Graves, Georgette Lampsi, Terry Lawlor, Lillian Lorray, Martha Maggard, Mary Mascher, Anita Pam, Barbara Smith, Baun Sturtz, Peggy Thomas, Patricia Whitney.

The Messrs. Robert Burton, Ray Clark, Charles Conklin, Frank Erickson, Jack Fago, Frank Gagen, Hazzard Newberry, Jack Ray, Bruce Barclay, Tom Curley, Leon Dunar, Michael Forbes, David Lawrence, Charles McClelland, Richard Neely, John McCahill.

THE JACK LINTON BAND: Jack Linton, Dave Allman, Charles Bennett, Walter Hinger, Milton Hollander, Frank Miller, Pete Shance, Jake Vander Meulen.

William Gaxton

Presidential candidate John P. Wintergreen (William Gaxton), his wife (Lois Moran) at his side, addresses a rally at Madison Square Garden.

ACT I

SCENE 1. *Main Street.*
SCENE 2. *A Hotel Room.*
SCENE 3. *Atlantic City.*
SCENE 4. *Madison Square Garden.*
SCENE 5. *Election Night.*
SCENE 6. *Washington.*

ACT II

SCENE 1. *The White House.*
SCENE 2. *The Capitol.*
SCENE 3. *The Senate.*
SCENE 4. *Again the White House.*
SCENE 5. *The Yellow Room.*

HISTORY AND REVIEWS

"We first-nighters were in at the liberation of musical comedy from twaddle and treacle and garden-party truck. . . ."

Of Thee I Sing, a fine firecracker of a musical that kidded the pants off everything from the sorry state of the Vice-Presidency to motherhood, astounded and delighted almost everybody when it won the Pulitzer Prize. The victory was remarkable on many counts. For one thing, it was the first time that a song-and-dance show had won; not even *Show Boat*, five years earlier, had been able to crack that barrier. Too, *Of Thee I Sing* triumphed over absolutely top-drawer competitors, including Eugene O'Neill's monumental trilogy, *Mourning Becomes Electra*. Had O'Neill not already won the prize on three previous occasions, it almost surely would have gone to him, but such speculations did little to tarnish the great win for *Of Thee I Sing*.

So off beat was their choice that the members of the Pulitzer Prize committee felt called upon to make an official explanation:

"This award may seem unusual, but the play is unusual. Not only is it coherent and well knit enough to class as a play, aside from the music, but it is a biting and true satire on American politics and the public attitude toward them. Its effect on the stage promises to be very considerable, because musical plays are always popular and by injecting genuine satire and point into them a very large public is reached. The spirit and style of the play are topical and popular, but, of course, the work is all the more spontaneous for that, and has a freshness and vitality which are both unusual and admirable. The play is genuine, and it is felt the prize could not serve a better purpose than to recognize such work."

Walter Prichard Eaton, one of the jurors, commented on the 1931–32 award a few years later:

"We had to choose," he said, "the Lord help us, from *Mourning Becomes Electra*, *Reunion in Vienna*, *The House of Connelly* and a musical comedy, *Of Thee I Sing*. We gave the award to the musical comedy, expecting another critical blast upon our heads. But the critics were either stunned or pleased, I can't say which—perhaps a little of both. At any rate, I like to feel that the award to that musical comedy had something to do with the subsequent increase of intelligence in the better librettos. I like to fancy, even, that it helped a tiny bit in making *Oklahoma!* possible."

George S. Kaufman, co-author with Morrie Ryskind of the *Of Thee I Sing* libretto, had already been

Caricaturist Don Freeman finds the Justices of the Supreme Court getting into their robes in the incongruous hurly-burly of backstage activity.

Victor Moore

a leading figure in the American theatre for a decade, collaborating with Marc Connelly on *Dulcy*, *To the Ladies*, *Merton of the Movies* and *Beggar on Horseback*, with Edna Ferber on *Minick* and *The Royal Family*, with Ring Lardner on *June Moon*, with young Moss Hart on *Once in a Lifetime* just the season before, and with Mr. Ryskind himself on such musicals as *The Cocoanuts*, *Animal Crackers* and *Strike Up the Band*. Composer George Gershwin, at 33, had in previous years joined forces with his lyricist brother, Ira, to provide the scores for *Lady Be Good*, *Tip Toes*, *Strike Up the Band*, *Girl Crazy*, *Funny Face* and *Treasure Girl*.

As originally planned, *Of Thee I Sing* was to have been called *Tweedle-Dee*, and was to have involved a presidential campaign, with the two major parties sponsoring rival national anthems. The Gershwins were in on the project from the beginning, and George had actually gotten so far as to plan a "contrapuntal lark" for the first-act finale, in which the opposing anthems were sung against each other. There was, however, no love interest in *Tweedle-Dee*, a large lack in any musical comedy, no matter how biting its satire. Kaufman and Ryskind finally scrapped their first idea and started all over again, with *Of Thee I Sing* (stuffed with various varieties of love, as well as with malice) the happy result.

Some of the notices:

J. Brooks Atkinson in *The New York Times*:

"This loud and blaring circus is no jerry-built musical comedy, although occasionally it subsides into the musical comedy formula. George Gershwin's most brilliant score amplifies the show. Satire in the sharp, chill, biting mood of today needs the warmth of Victor Moore's fooling and the virtuosity of Mr. Gershwin's music. Without them *Of Thee I Sing* would be the best topical travesty our musical stage has cre-

Lois Moran, William Gaxton

ated. With them it has the depth of artistry and the glow and pathos of comedy that are needed in the book."

John Anderson in the *Journal*:

"*Of Thee I Sing* exploded its way into the hearts and funnybones of its First Audience Saturday night. It is grand fun. In it the Messrs. George S. Kaufman and Morrie Ryskind have conspired to apply a burlesque slapstick to the seat of Uncle Sam's political pants. The brothers Gershwin, George and Ira, emerge with all honor and laughter, George for music that is fresh and humorously inventive, and Ira for lyrics that are wonders of rhyme and reason, the witty reason of really sparkling foolishness. The exuberant William Gaxton gives it the added impact of a performance that seems rich in vitamins."

Burns Mantle in the *Daily News*:

"It is all grand spoofing, adult, intelligent, observant and never coarse. The newest, maddest and brightest of musical satires."

Gilbert W. Gabriel in the *American*:

"We first-nighters were in at the liberation of musical comedy from twaddle and treacle and garden-party truck. We were laughing gratefully along at a new date in stage history."

Richard Lockridge in the *Evening Sun*:

"The grandest American stage satire I have any knowledge of. *Of Thee I Sing* is rushing, grotesque and merciless as it ranges through the political scene, knocking down the political scenery."

John Mason Brown in the *Evening Post*:

"A production of such a happy and exhilarating sort that it nearly makes up for all the feeble mediocrity which has cluttered our stages during the present season. Here at last is a musical show which dodges nearly all the clichés of its kind, which has wit and intelligence behind it, which brings

Victor Moore, William Gaxton

Gilbert and Sullivan to mind without being derived from them, and which makes hilarious satiric use of the American scene in general and Washington politics in particular. Alexander Throttlebottom emerges, in Victor Moore's superlatively excellent performance, as one of the most unforgettable characterizations of recent years."

George Jean Nathan in *Judge*:

"*Of Thee I Sing* is the sharpest, wittiest, and by all odds the most salubrious cathartic applied to American customs and morals that the stage, whether dramatic or musical, has offered us in an unnecessarily long time. It is a grand show."

One of the very few dissents came from Robert Benchley, of all people. Writing in *The New Yorker*, Mr. Benchley said:

"I was definitely disappointed in *Of Thee I Sing*. Compared with *Strike Up the Band*, the distinguished work of this same combination, *Of Thee I Sing* struck me (and me alone, evidently) as being dull musically, repetitious, and not particularly fresh satirically (the ancient Vice-President gag, the firebrand Congressional oratory, and the Gridiron Club of official Washington can hardly be classed as inventions), and the whole thing, during great stretches, reminiscent of an old Hasty Pudding 'spoop' in which *lèse-majesté* was considered funny enough in itself without straining for any more mature elements of comedy."

Not all of the critics accepted the *Of Thee I Sing* award happily. J. Brooks Atkinson commented in *The New York Times*:

"When the committee turns its back on the drama in a season that has yielded several excellent plays and starts equivocating about the book of a musical comedy, the Pulitzer Prize loses a great deal of its value. There is more whim than judgment in this year's award."

Mrs. Wintergreen (Lois Moran) gives birth to twins, and the Republic is saved

Burns Mantle wrote in the same vein in the *Daily News*:

"*Of Thee I Sing* is the most intelligent, the most consistent, the most timely satire of American politics the native theatre has entertained. But by no conceivable stretch can it be classed as a play in the accepted sense of that term. Strip it of its lyrics and its music and there will be little left of the prize winner but a half-hour of farcical and satirical sketches."

Among its other accomplishments, *Of Thee I Sing* blew up a minor international storm. It contained the following snatch of dialogue between the French Ambassador and the President of the United States:

AMBASSADOR: You will pardon the intrusion, Monsieur, but I have another note from my country.

PRESIDENT: That's all right. We've got a lot of notes from your country, and some of them were due ten years ago.

AMBASSADOR: But this is not a promise to pay. This is serious!

Innocuous as that exchange may now seem, it stirred Bishop William T. Manning to get the France-American Society to adopt a resolution calling for the deletion of the offending lines. Kaufman was amiability itself.

"If Bishop Manning can give me another line that gets as big a laugh," said the playwright, "it will go in."

The Bishop never did come up with a substitute snapper. The controversial dialogue stayed in.

Had *Of Thee I Sing* done nothing more than provide the American stage with Alexander Throttlebottom, that delightful achievement alone would have assured it a measure of immortality. Victor Moore crowned a lifetime of comedy acting with his bumbling, altogether enchanting portrayal of the hapless Vice-President.

John Chapman, then a columnist on the *Daily News*, later its critic, felicitously wrapped up the general feeling about Mr. Moore. Said Chapman to his redheaded wife, Georgia:

"I could not love thee dear, so much,
Loved I not Victor Moore."

ALSO-RANS: *Mourning Becomes Electra, The House of Connelly, Counsellor-at-Law, Reunion in Vienna, The Animal Kingdom*

SUMMATION

Hooray! An excellent choice that few observers would have thought the Pulitzer committee capable of making. It took a great deal of cockeyed courage to give *Of Thee I Sing* the nod over *Mourning Becomes Electra*. In a leaner year, any one of the also-rans could have won handily.

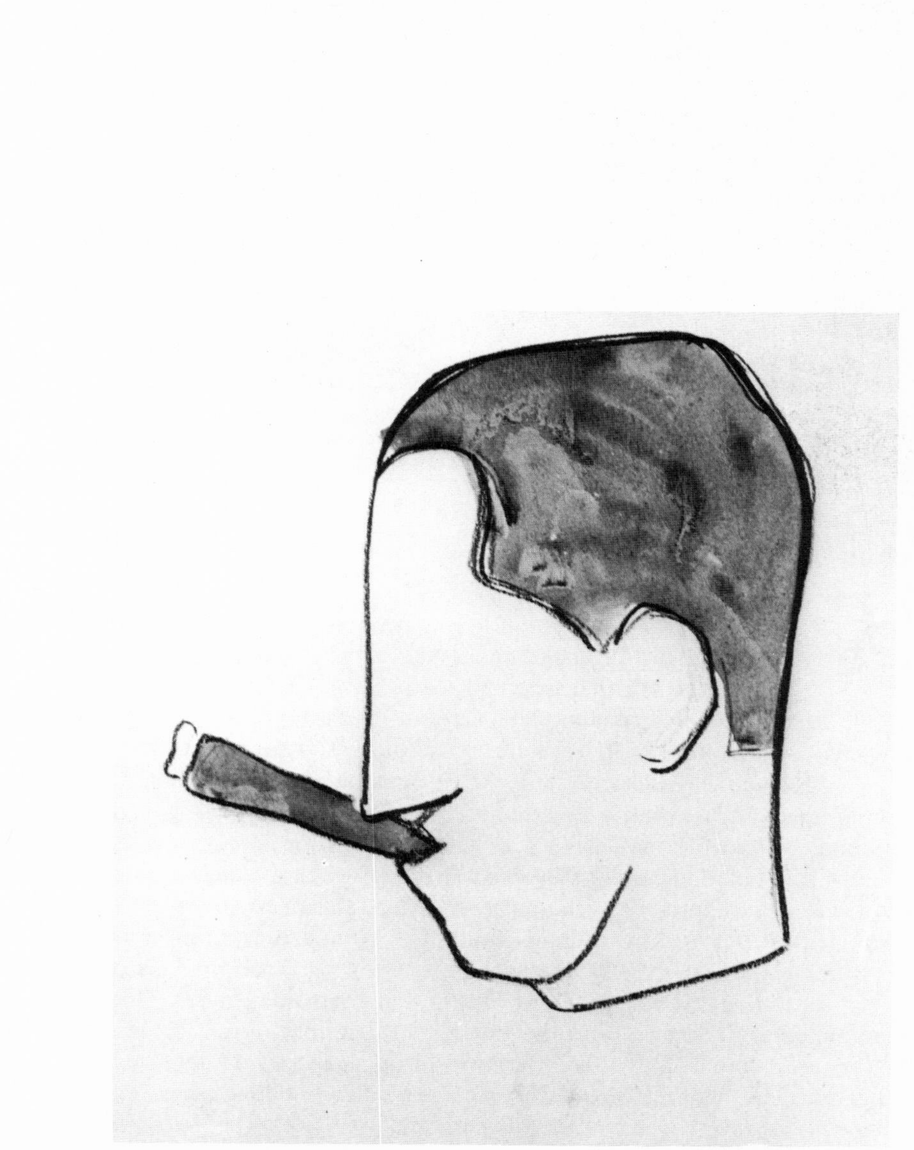

George Gershwin as seen by William Auerbach-Levy

Walter C. Kelly, Shepperd Strudwick, Mary Philips

1932-33

Young Alan McClean has just been elected to Congress for the first time, and comes to Washington full of idealistic vigor. Named to sit on the Appropriations Committee, he is shocked to find that a bill that originally stood at $40,000,000 has been inflated to more than $275,000,000 so that it can accommodate various "pork barrel" projects. The Committee is now attempting to cut it down somewhat, but only because blatant greed might evoke a presidential veto.

McClean has been elected by his Nevada constituents on a platform combining a strong reform program with a promise to attempt to get a million-dollar government appropriation for Nevada irrigation. McClean is willing to sacrifice the irrigation money if his colleagues will trim the rest of the fat out of the bill. They are all shocked at the very suggestion, especially Solomon Fitzmaurice, a Washington veteran of forty years, and Simeon Grey, Chairman of the Committee. Grey particularly needs the inflated bill, as it now contains funds for a building appropriation that will shore up a shaky bank in his home state. If the bill does not pass, Grey faces jail, but his pleas do not budge McClean.

In a maneuver designed to kill the bill by making it ridiculously top-heavy, McClean inflates it by adding every conceivable rider, but his strategy backfires—it not only passes the House, but passes by a margin comfortably over the two-thirds necessary to override a veto. McClean, saddened but enlightened by his first brush with Congressional skulduggery, vows to keep fighting the good fight. The indications are that it will be a losing one.

Aleta Freel, Shepperd Strudwick

Walter C. Kelly, J. Edward Bromberg, Russell Collins

BOTH YOUR HOUSES

THE CREDITS

A Drama in Three Acts by Maxwell Anderson.
Produced by The Theatre Guild, Inc.
Staged by Worthington Minor.
Opened at the Royale Theatre, March 6, 1933, and ran for 120 performances.

THE CAST

Marjorie Gray	Aleta Freel
Bus	Mary Philips
Eddie Wister	Robert Shayne
Solomon Fitzmaurice	Walter C. Kelly
Mark	Oscar Polk
Simeon Gray	Robert Strange
Levering	Morris Carnovsky
Merton	John Butler

Mary Philips, Shepperd Strudwick

DELL	William Foran
SNEDEN	Jerome Cowan
MISS MCMURTRY	Jane Seymour
WINGBLATT	J. Edward Bromberg
PEEBLES	Russell Collins
FARNUM	John F. Morrissey
ALAN MCCLEAN	Shepperd Strudwick
EBNER	Joseph Sweeney

The play takes place in the House Office Building, Washington, D.C.

ACT I

SCENE 1. *The Office of the Chairman of the Appropriations Committee. A Morning in Early Spring.*

SCENE 2. *The Committee Room.*

ACT II

SCENE 1. *The Office of the Chairman of the Appropriations Committee. Late Afternoon, Three Days Later.*

SCENE 2. *The Committee Room. One Hour Later.*

ACT III

SCENE 1. *The Committee Room. Evening, Three Days Later.*

SCENE 2. *The Same. Three Hours Later.*

HISTORY AND REVIEWS

"An unimportant though skillful enough play that has some interesting if disheartening things to say. . . ."

With *Both Your Houses*, the Pulitzer Prize went for the second season in a row to a production with a political background. *Of Thee I Sing* had been amusingly irreverent about incompetence and corruption in Washington, but *Both Your Houses* was fighting mad about those evils, and was as much a polemic as a play.

Maxwell Anderson, 45 when *Both Your Houses* was produced, had been both a schoolteacher and a newspaperman before *The White Desert* introduced him to Broadway in 1923. In his ten years as a playwright he had been a perennial also-ran for the Pulitzer Prize, losing with *What Price Glory?* in 1924–25, and with *Elizabeth the Queen* in 1930–31. In the season to come, 1933–34, he was to lose another close decision with *Mary of Scotland*, and none of his later plays, many of them highly regarded —*Valley Forge*, *Winterset*, *High Tor*—ever won favor with the Pulitzer judges.

Anderson, an outspoken man who once identified the Broadway critics as "the Jukes family of journalism" (after they had thoroughly trounced one of his minor efforts, *Truckline Café*) always thought that *The White Desert* was his best play, and that *Both Your Houses* was by all odds his worst one. In the spring of 1936, a few years prior to his *Truckline Café* disaster, Anderson had kinder words for the critics, and some harsh ones for the Pulitzer committee. Speaking at a Critics' Circle dinner, when he accepted an award for *Winterset*, the playwright said:

"Except for the theatre critics of New York no body of men in the country is qualified by training, education and professional experience to render judgment on a season's plays. I am, I assure you seriously, much more interested in that aspect of the ceremony than the fact that the first award goes to *Winterset*.

"Anybody with the requisite cash can offer a prize for excellence in the theatre, but in order to encourage excellence it is necessary to know it when it appears, and a knowledge of what is excellent is more difficult to obtain than cash. I have never been greatly impressed with the Pulitzer Prize for the best play of the year because the final authority for its presentation rests with a committee which is aware only dimly and at second hand of most of what occurs in the theatres of Broadway. It follows that so far as the Pulitzer Prize has had any influence on our theatre it has been a confusing and misleading influence, an encouragement to mediocrity, a gift passed out to a lucky winner by authorities who possess in this field neither standards nor information. But neither ignorance nor lack of standards can be charged against the Critics' Circle."

Both Your Houses was peculiarly a play of its time. In the early 1930's, echoes of the Teapot Dome scandal were still reverberating in Washington, and a dramatic crusade against political venality was apt enough, at least when the play was actually being written. By the time it was produced on Broadway, however, Franklin D. Roosevelt had been inaugurated only three days before; the temper of the country was tuned to the exciting change that had just taken place, and Anderson was inadvertently placed in the position of flogging a horse that had just died quite publicly.

Even so, *Both Your Houses* was considered topical enough to rate a symposium at the Royale Theatre, on a Sunday evening in April; such authorities as critic Ernest Boyd, playwright Paul Sifton, and commentator H. V. Kaltenborn gathered to discuss Mr. Anderson's new play. Boyd didn't think much of it, but his colleagues were more favorable. They all dismissed the relevancy of worrying about the effects upon *Both Your Houses* of the Roosevelt victory, but in retrospect it does seem that the play opened at the most inappropriate time possible.

Some of the notices:

Brooks Atkinson in *The New York Times*:

"Of all the theatrical attacks upon the depravity of representative government Maxwell Anderson's *Both Your Houses* is the most stirring and direct. It is not only an angry crying of names and cases but an excellent play that will interest those whom it is convincing. As a performance under the auspices of The Theatre Guild it is muscular, colorful and salty. As Solomon Fitzmaurice, Walter C. Kelly ('The

Virginia Judge') is blissfully unscrupulous. Robert Strange has a grim and forceful command of the part of the committee chairman. Shepperd Strudwick is superb as the Nevada rebel. Both as a play and a performance *Both Your Houses* is real and stimulating."

Percy Hammond in the *Herald Tribune*:

"*Both Your Houses* is an entertainment as well as an alarum, very showy at times and earnestly oracular. There may be discerned in it the same spirit of cynical compromise against which Mr. Anderson rails when he complains about the star-spangled though defective government of the U.S.A."

Gilbert W. Gabriel in the *American*:

"Maxwell Anderson is beginning to rival Elmer Rice as our Jack-of-all-plays. He is one day's poet, the next day's preacher, and still the next day's clown. In *Both Your Houses* he intends to be nothing except funny, savagely, gustily, whole-mindedly funny, and he certainly is. Seeing it, you'll be apt to think that *Both Your Houses* lacks impetus, wants a hotter pace, should command more of a roar. I know I thought that, anyhow. I was willing to have it come in like a lamb, but somewhere toward the end I had to be a shade chagrined that it would not treat us to the wrathy decibels of a lion. It is this, perhaps, which keeps it a play of contented unimportance."

Robert Garland in the *World-Telegram*:

"If it is propaganda, it is talking out of turn. And if it is a play, it is talking around in circles. Either is unfortunate. And unexpectedly dull, as entertainment goes."

Richard Lockridge in the *Evening Sun*:

"As an editorial plea it is competent enough, if familiar, but it is somewhat perfunctory drama and quite lacking in that poetic thrust which Mr. Anderson has often in the past achieved. And circumstances quite foreign to the drama have worked against the play, reducing it to a minor footnote on a page just now prodigiously crowded with more relevant excitements. But even if the surge of events did not dwarf *Both Your Houses*, it would hardly rise to prodigious heights. It is merely competent playwriting, inspired by neither deep thought nor deep feeling."

John Mason Brown in the *Evening Post*:

"*Both Your Houses* is well worth seeing. It is an unimportant though skillful enough play that has

Shepperd Strudwick, Robert Strange, Aleta Freel

some interesting if disheartening things to say. And it is at all times given the aid of an unusually helpful production."

John Anderson in the *Evening Journal*:

"*Both Your Houses* is a passionate and furious play about the ineptitude of Congressional Government. If it turns out to be more a debate than a full-bodied drama, if its talk often seems more diatribe than dialogue, admit at least that Mr. Anderson flings full strength against an interesting subject, that he has the courage to turn his platform over to an urgent public problem, and the intelligence to make it plain. He doesn't, unfortunately, make it very dramatic."

After the prize had been awarded, Richard Lockridge had this to say in the *Evening Sun*:

"The award of the Pulitzer Prize to Maxwell Anderson's *Both Your Houses* can best be applauded on the assumption that it is really an award to Mr. Anderson, who so clearly stands well forward among the country's playwrights. The cantankerous may urge that the committee has seen fit to honor Mr. Anderson's worst play."

The Pulitzer jurors divided on this award, with *Both Your Houses* squeezing out a two-to-one recommendation over *One Sunday Afternoon*.

ALSO-RANS: *One Sunday Afternoon, Dinner at Eight, We, the People, Alien Corn, Biography*

SUMMATION

A satisfactory enough decision; no injured cries arose, or at least not many, and probably none would have arisen had James Hagen's nostalgic *One Sunday Afternoon* won. *Both Your Houses* was as good a choice as any in a non-vintage year for Prize Play candidates.

Shepperd Strudwick, Mary Philips

Walter C. Kelly, Aleta Freel, Robert Strange

Playwright Sidney Kingsley

(Opposite Page) *The famous operating room scene; center, wearing glasses, J. Edward Bromberg*

1933-34

ALL OF THE ACTION takes place in New York's St. George's Hospital, where Dr. Hochberg is the attending chief of the surgical staff. Hochberg is a classically dedicated medical man, and he foresees a great future for one of his internes, Dr. George Ferguson.

Ferguson is engaged to Laura Hudson, a rich young society girl. When pressing hospital duties force him to break a date with her one evening, they quarrel bitterly, and it is obvious that the broken date has brought into focus their different attitudes toward what a doctor's life should be. In his room at the hospital that same night, Ferguson is visited by Barbara Dennin, a pretty student nurse who has come to borrow some notes. Drawn together by mutual loneliness, they make love.

Three months later, Barbara is in the hospital as a patient—she has had an abortion that has gone sour, and she now needs a hysterectomy if she is to have a chance to live. Hochberg supervises the operation, with Ferguson in attendance, and with Laura on hand as a spectator. Laura discovers the relationship between Barbara and Ferguson.

Barbara dies after the operation, and Ferguson is thereby released from his quixotic decision to marry her. As the play ends, Ferguson is determined to pursue his medical career on the highest possible level, although he realizes that the grinding work involved may destroy his chances for a normal personal life. Laura will wait for him while he spends a year studying in Vienna, and there are broad hints that she will eventually adapt herself, however reluctantly, to his proposed spartan regime.

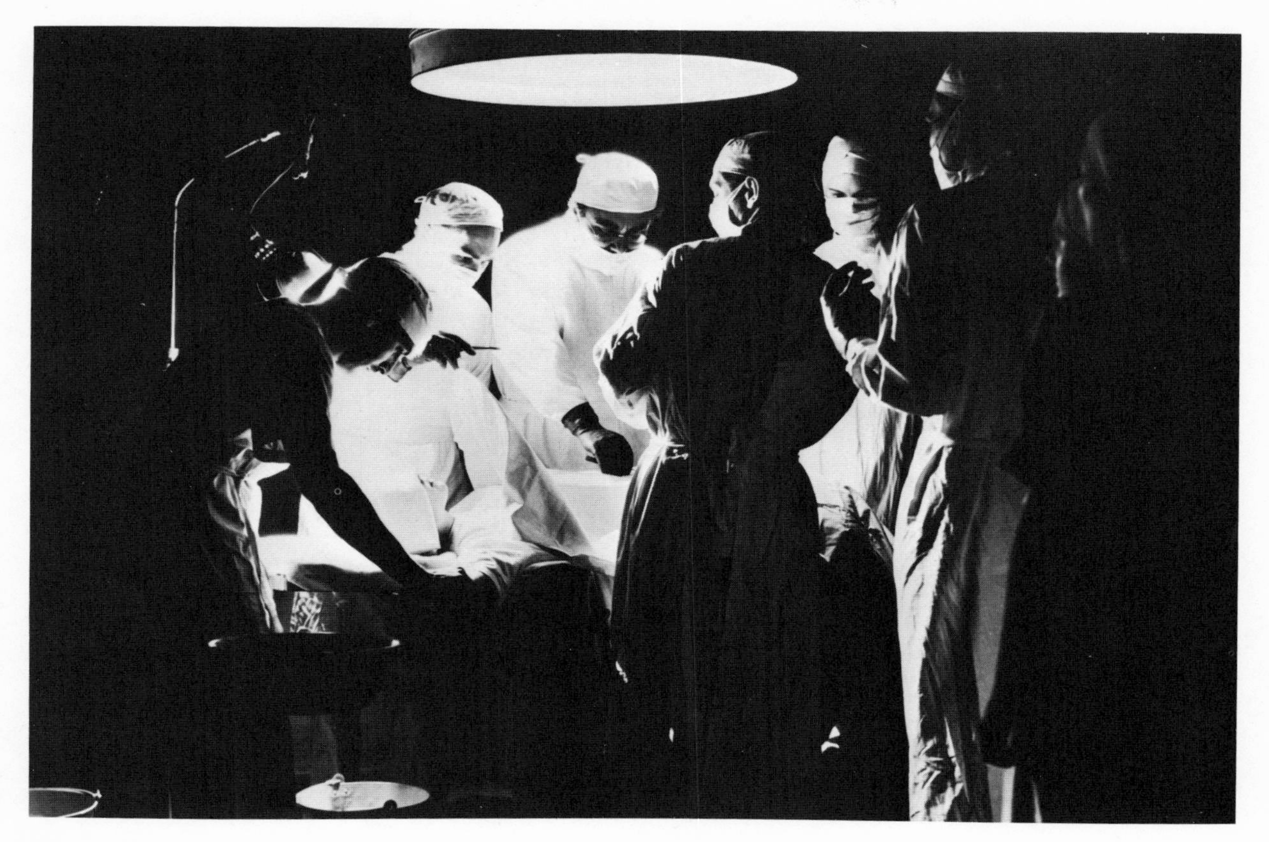

MEN IN WHITE

THE CREDITS

A DRAMA IN THREE ACTS BY SIDNEY KINGSLEY.
PRODUCED BY THE GROUP THEATRE, SIDNEY HARMON AND JAMES R. ULLMAN.
STAGED BY LEE STRASBERG.
OPENED AT THE BROADHURST THEATRE, SEPTEMBER 26, 1933, AND RAN FOR 351 PERFORMANCES.

THE CAST

DR. GORDON	Luther Adler
DR. HOCHBERG	J. Edward Bromberg
DR. MICHAELSON	William Challee
DR. VITALE	Herbert Ratner
DR. MCCABE	Grover Burgess
DR. FERGUSON	Alexander Kirkland
DR. WREN	Sanford Meisner
DR. OTIS (SHORTY)	Bob Lewis

DR. LEVINE	Morris Carnovsky
DR. BRADLEY (PETE)	Walter Coy
DR. CRAWFORD (MAC)	Alan Baxter
NURSE JAMISON	Eunice Stoddard
MR. HUDSON	Art Smith
JAMES MOONEY	Gerrit Kraber
LAURA HUDSON	Margaret Barker
MR. SMITH	Sanford Meisner
MRS. SMITH	Ruth Nelson
DOROTHY SMITH	Mab Maynard
BARBARA DENNIN	Phoebe Brand
DR. CUNNINGHAM	Russell Collins
FIRST NURSE	Paula Miller
NURSE MARY RYAN	Dorothy Patten
ORDERLY	Elia Kazan
MR. HOUGHTON	Clifford Odets
MR. SPENCER	Lewis Leverett
MRS. D'ANDREA	Mary Virginia Farmer
SECOND NURSE	Elena Karem

ACT I

SCENE 1. *Staff Library, St. George's Hospital.*
SCENE 2. *Mr. Hudson's Room.*
SCENE 3. *Children's Ward.*
SCENE 4. *George Ferguson's Room.*

ACT II

SCENE 1. *Board Room.*
SCENE 2. *Staff Library.*
SCENE 3. *Corridor.*
SCENE 4. *Operating Room.*

ACT III

George Ferguson's Room.

HISTORY AND REVIEWS

"Mary of Scotland *certainly would seem to have been a choice at once more logical and more challenging. . . .*"

Men in White, the first real success produced by the Group Theatre, was the granddaddy of the host of medical shows that twenty-five years later were to swamp television. It laid down the pattern: the idealistic-young-doctor/crusty-old-doctor relationship, the preoccupation with technical minutiae ("Scalpel!"), the soap-opera plot.

When the award to *Men in White* was announced, all three jurors resigned their positions, having unanimously recommended that the prize be given to Maxwell Anderson's *Mary of Scotland*. In a statement issued by Columbia's Frank D. Fackenthal, the jurors (Clayton Hamilton, Walter Prichard Eaton and Austin Strong) were quoted as saying they knew that they were retained in an advisory capacity only, and that they did not question the right of the Advisory Board to exercise its own judgment, but they did want the public to realize their preference for *Mary of Scotland*.

The jurors subsequently used much stronger language. Hamilton called the overruling "an outrage." Eaton said:

"The Advisory Board consists of a group of newspaper editors, mostly from out of town, who come up to Columbia once a year. I have no doubt they are excellent men, but they don't know a thing about the theatre." He added: "They don't want dramatic experts any more—they want office boys. No self-respecting, intelligent critic would serve on such a jury."

Fackenthal took the position that the jurors couldn't "resign," as technically they had been appointed for only a single year. But custom had indicated that all such appointments were almost inevitably renewed, unless Columbia itself had reason to decide otherwise.

Russell Collins, Clifford Odets, Gerrit Kraber, Sanford Meisner, Luther Adler, J. Edward Bromberg, Lewis Leverett

An ex-juror got into the act, too. Playwright A. E. Thomas wrote a scorching letter to the *Herald Tribune*:

"If the Pulitzer Prize awards are to carry any weight whatever, the public has a right to know the reasons that lie behind the awards. As it is, the Council of the Columbia School of Journalism says in effect: 'We make these awards. That is enough for you to know.' Well, it isn't enough, especially when this Council is composed of men whose incompetence to make these awards is perfectly demonstrated by the mere reading of their names. No future Pulitzer Prize award will be good for anything but a hearty laugh, until confession of error is made. Until then, to any Pulitzer Prize award the answer will be: 'What of it?' Or perhaps, 'Oh, yeah?' "

Playwright Sidney Kingsley, just short of his 27th birthday when *Men in White* opened, had completed the first draft of his play two years earlier; it had then been known as *Crisis*. After it had been optioned and then dropped by a couple of Broadway producers, the script drifted over to the scenario department at Columbia Pictures, where Sidney Harmon read it. Harmon decided to produce it with James R. Ullman as his partner; they later brought in the Group Theatre as co-producer on the theory that the Kingsley script called for ensemble playing of the highest order, a challenge the Group was particularly qualified to meet.

Kingsley had done research for the play at many New York hospitals—Montefiore, Lebanon, Beth Israel, Bellevue—and, wearing the traditional white uniform, had been introduced into various operating rooms as "a student of surgery." So well had he done his observing that the play's most famous scene, set in an operating room during an operation, was generally accepted as a model of realism. Nine-tenths of the scene was done in pantomime, and it was as rigidly choreographed as any ballet, with twelve actors going through the intricate motions of scrubbing their hands, dipping them into chemical solutions, donning rubber gloves and boiled gowns, and then weaving precisely through the patterns of the operation proper. Hourglasses hidden at various spots around the setting permitted the actors to time their scrubbing to a split-second, so that they could swing around exactly on cue to thrust their arms into the sterilized gowns. It was a most professional-looking effect.

Some of the notices:

Brooks Atkinson in *The New York Times*:

"*Men in White* is the first engrossing play of the season. Although Sidney Kingsley is not a medical man, he has written about the ideals and conflicts of loyalty of the medical profession with fervent convictions, disclosing uncommon familiarity with his subject. It is a good, brave play, despite a certain austerity in the writing and a slavish fondness for medical terms."

Percy Hammond in the *Herald Tribune*:

"A serious and gripping new drama. An honest, tricky and propaganda show, *Men in White* can be attended without a sacrifice of intelligence."

Burns Mantle in the *Daily News*:

"The Group Theatre's presentation of Sidney Kingsley's *Men in White* last night revealed as stirring

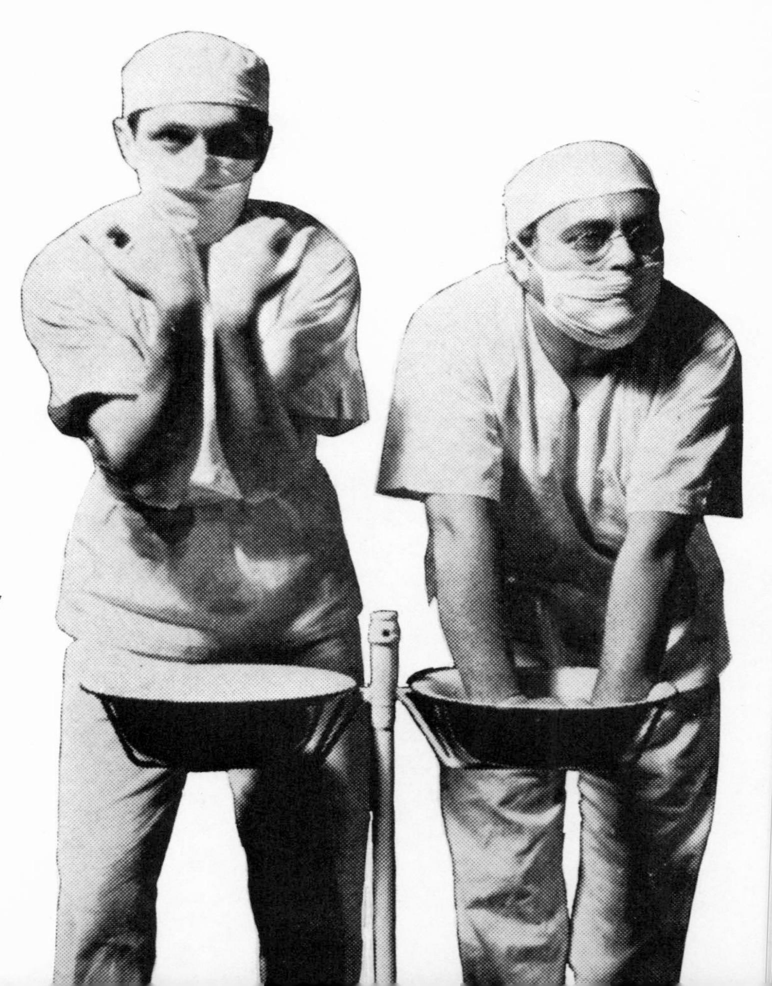

Alexander Kirkland, J. Edward Bromberg

Alexander Kirkland

Margaret Barker, Alexander Kirkland

a job of play presentation as it is given producing units to achieve. *Men in White* proved as absorbing a play, too, as you are likely to come upon the season through. It is realism in the raw, and yet it is never emotionally depressing. It manages to achieve a convincing reality without resort to obvious theatre tricks."

Gilbert W. Gabriel in the *American*:

"*Men in White* is an intensely phoney and an intensely harrowing play. Medicine is too grim a subject to allow itself to be patted on the head by a hokum-locutory drama. It bites back at the footlights. It bites back when they try to make it merely realistic. Blood is thicker than greasepaint. So much sickness before you begets sickness in the theatre itself."

John Mason Brown in the *Evening Post*:

"The truth compels me to admit that it is not much of a play. In certain vital respects it is the very same old hokum script that has been used and reused by the motion pictures whenever they have taken to anesthetics and the operating room in a big way. Some of its incidental observation is amusing. Many of its atmospheric touches are novel. And at least one of its characters—a great, all-knowing and compassionate surgeon—is compelling in a fool-proof manner. But, if it were not for what the Group has done for it to fake it into life by means of an excellent production, the play itself would be as dead as are some of the patients at the hospital where it is laid. The scene of scenes is, of course, the one in the operating room, where the only detail Mr. Strasberg has overlooked is an anesthetic for his audience. It is skillfully staged and makes suspensive use of pauses, but is no more agreeable than was your last operation. I suspect that no playhouse is a proper home for *Men in White*. It belongs in Bellevue."

After *Men in White* had its crown settled uneasily on its head, Richard Lockridge wrote in the *Evening Sun*:

"*Mary of Scotland* certainly would seem to have been a choice at once more logical and more challenging. There is beauty in the writing of Maxwell Anderson's play which we have not found elsewhere this season, and the only real objection which seems to have been entered against it is that it is not a good history.

"*Tobacco Road* would have been a more stimulating choice, and perhaps the most stimulating choice that could have been made. There is, as both defenders and assailants have almost too conclusively proved, the meat of argument in that rather appalling picture of 'poor white' life in the South. It would, at any rate, have been fun to write a long column indignantly protesting the selection of *Tobacco Road*. As for *Men in White*, it provides an interesting evening, chiefly because it is so brilliantly produced and so honestly acted."

Burns Mantle, one of the play's strongest champions, took a mild view of the controversy that the award engendered:

"By winning the Prize *Men in White* again reveals the Pulitzer Prize committee, as it represents the Columbia School of Journalism and Columbia College, as an interesting human body of men. They evidently vote their minds as playgoers and not as experts. And when their judgment is at variance with that of experts who are chosen to guide them, they speak up and say so. As a result the Pulitzer Prize play may not always represent the finest literary effort, or the most courageous theme, or the most

The founders of the Group Theatre: Cheryl Crawford, Lee Strasberg, Harold Clurman

Luther Adler, J. Edward Bromberg, Morris Carnovsky

progressive production of the year, but it is pretty sure to stand each year as the honest choice of honest playgoers who are satisfied to give the award to that drama which returns them the greatest emotional satisfaction as theatre patrons. So long as the Pulitzer Prize represents the whole theatre thus honestly it will never stray far from the intent Joseph Pulitzer had in mind when he wrote his will, however frequently he might have disagreed with the committee's choice."

The powers at Columbia were quite stirred by the fuss that arose over their rejection of *Mary of Scotland*, and finally issued this pronunciamento:

"The Advisory Board has felt embarrassment more than once in years past at being faced by the alternative of rejecting the recommendation of one of the carefully chosen juries, or of being constrained to accept that recommendation against their own judgment. The Advisory Board has, therefore, directed that hereafter the Juries of Selection and Recommendation shall be invited not to propose a definite recipient for a prize but to submit what the members of the jury regard as an eligible list of possible recipients, with a summary of their reasons for the recommendation in each case. Each jury might, if it thought best, go so far as to arrange its recommendations in order of preference. But by refraining from making a distinct recommendation, the embarrassment which the Advisory Board has sometimes felt would be avoided."

This statement provoked the *Evening Post* into an editorial which deplored the 1933–34 choice:

"The prize was withheld from an honest and important drama and given to a play generally recognized as a melodramatic rehash of a stale situation; the doctor who attends at an operation on the woman he has wronged."

As for the Advisory Board's attempt to "avoid embarrassment" in future years, the very next season was to bring down the *Old Maid/Children's Hour* thunderstorm on the Board's head—the worst and most disputed decision in the history of the Prize.

ALSO-RANS: *Mary of Scotland, Dodsworth, Wednesday's Child, Ah, Wilderness!, They Shall Not Die, Tobacco Road, Yellow Jack*

SUMMATION

This was one of the poorer decisions. Even assuming the validity of by-passing *Mary of Scotland*, either *Dodsworth, Ah, Wilderness!* or the stirring *Yellow Jack* would have been a sounder choice. Mr. Lockridge was obviously joking about *Tobacco Road*; for all its crude vigor, it could never conceivably have been chosen.

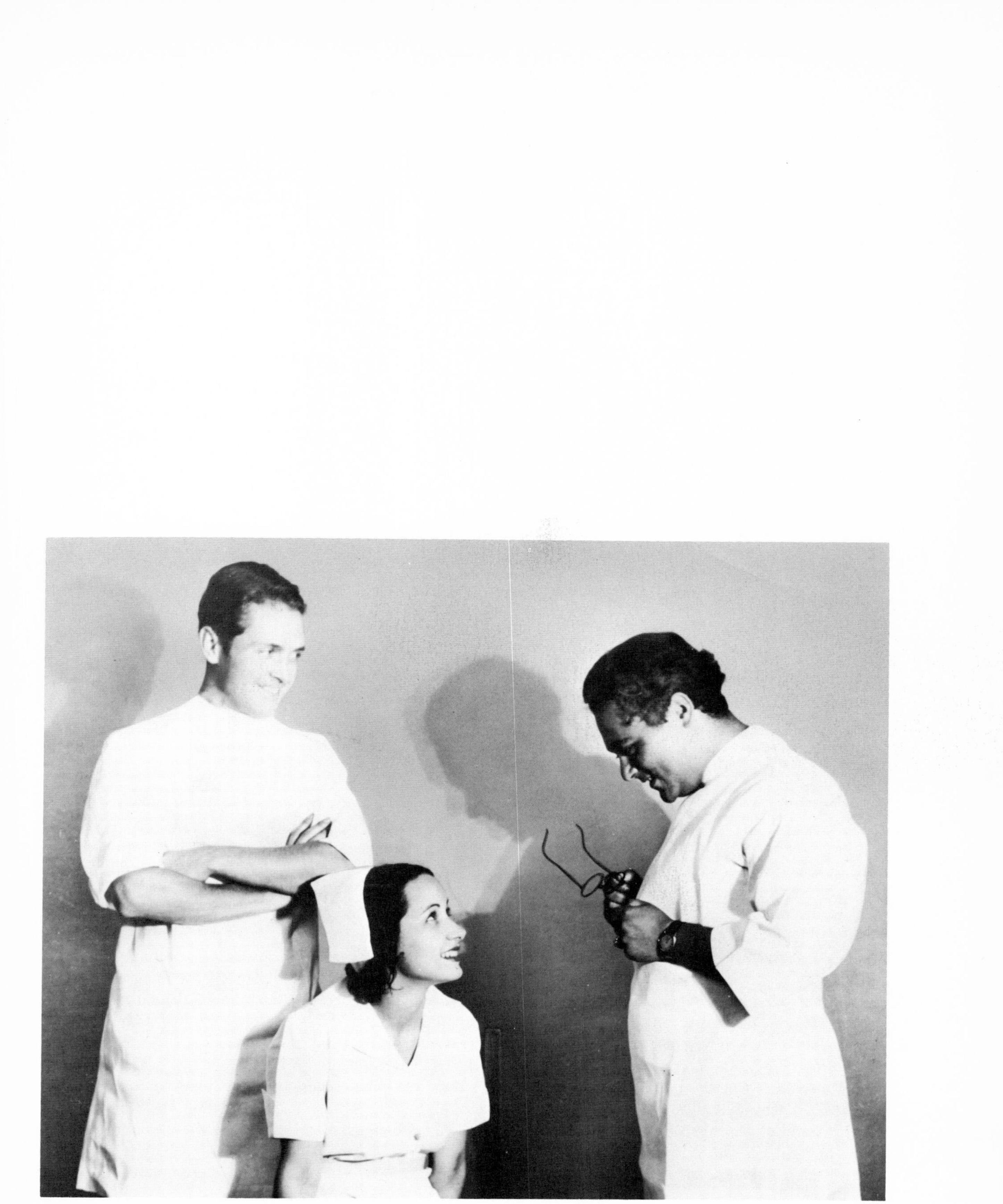

Alexander Kirkland, Phoebe Brand, J. Edward Bromberg

Judith Anderson, Helen Menken

1934-35

THE PLAY COVERS A PERIOD of more than twenty years, from 1833 to 1854. Delia and Charlotte Lovell are cousins, and when Delia marries James Ralston, Charlotte comforts Clem Spender, Delia's old flame. They have one night of brief, casual passion, and Charlotte becomes pregnant. She takes a trip down South and has her illegitimate baby in secret, and then places the little girl with the old Negress who had been her own nurse.

Charlotte organizes a day nursery so that she may have an acceptable reason for helping to take care of her daughter, Tina, who is one of the nursery's charges; in the meantime she has become engaged to James Ralston's brother, Joseph. Delia comes to the nursery, quickly discovers Charlotte's secret, and arbitrarily decides that Charlotte cannot marry Joseph under such circumstances. Delia breaks up the proposed marriage by lying to Joseph about a purported recurrence of Charlotte's old lung trouble; she then gets her husband to put up the money for a small house in which Charlotte can live with Tina. The child, however, is never told that Charlotte is her real mother.

Fourteen years later, James Ralston has died, and Charlotte and Tina are living in Delia's house. Charlotte has turned into a typical "old maid," and Tina has fallen into the habit of calling Delia "Mama." Delia actually does adopt Tina, in order to give the girl the social standing and wealth necessary to attract a proper husband. On the eve of Tina's wedding, Charlotte desperately wants to reveal the long-hidden truth to her child, but finds herself unable to. Delia, of course, will not reveal the truth either, but she does ask Tina to save her very last kiss at the wedding reception for Cousin Charlotte.

Helen Menken holds Yvonne Mann on her lap. The program does not identify the other children.

THE OLD MAID

THE CREDITS

A Drama in Three Acts by Zoe Akins.
Based on a Novel by Edith Wharton.
Produced by Harry Moses.
Staged by Guthrie McClintic.
Opened at the Empire Theatre, January 7, 1935, and ran for 305 performances.

THE CAST

Delia Lovell (later Mrs. James Ralston)	Judith Anderson
Charlotte Lovell	Helen Menken
Mrs. Jennie Meade	Mary Ricard
Bridget	Hope Landin
Clementina	Yvonne Mann
Dr. Lanskell	George Nash
Mrs. Mingott	Margaret Dale
Joseph Ralston	Robert Wallsten

Hope Landin, Judith Anderson, Yvonne Mann

JAMES RALSTON	Frederick Voight
SERVANT	Gail Reade
DEE	Florence Williams
JOHN HALSEY	Warren Trent
LANNING HALSEY	John Cromwell
TINA	Margaret Anderson

The Scene is New York

ACT I

SCENE 1. *Delia Lovell's Room, Lovell Place, 1830.*
SCENE 2. *A Day-Nursery in Mercer Street, 1836.*

ACT II

The Ralston Drawing Room, Gramercy Park, That Evening.

ACT III

SCENE 1. *The Same Room—Fourteen Years Later.*
SCENE 2. *The Same Room—Five Hours Later.*
SCENE 3. *The Same Room—The Following June.*

HISTORY AND REVIEWS

"I think it's quite the worst selection the committee could possibly have made from all the plays now current on Broadway. . . ."

The Pulitzer Prize committee's selection of *The Old Maid* over *The Children's Hour* (and, incidentally, over *Awake and Sing*, *The Petrified Forest* and *Valley Forge*—the season of 1934–35 was a remarkably good one) was the most peculiar blunder in the entire history of the Pulitzer drama awards.

There had been many other questionable decisions in the past—*Miss Lulu Bett* over *The First Year*, *Hell Bent fer Heaven* over *The Show-Off*, *They Knew What They Wanted* over *What Price Glory?*, *Alison's House* over *Elizabeth the Queen*, and, most recently, *Men in White* over *Mary of Scotland*. But this gaffe outranked them all.

Lillian Hellman's *The Children's Hour* was her first play; she was in her late twenties when she wrote it, working in her spare time while serving as a play reader for Herman Shumlin. In the middle 1930's, Lesbianism was not quite as taboo a subject as it had been ten years earlier, when *The Captive*, a high-minded and innocently dull play that dealt glancingly with Lesbians, had been closed by the police, but it still had a certain shock effect, and *The Children's Hour* was regarded as a somewhat daring trailblazer. By no wild stretch of the imagination, however, could an intelligent theatregoer have called it "dirty"; the solidity of its writing and the integrity of its author were plain for the world to see.

Miss Hellman had taken the basic plot of *The Children's Hour* from a Scottish case history set down by William Roughead in *The Great Drumsheugh Case*; she made no bones about her source material, and technically *The Children's Hour* was not an "original American play." This was at best a quibble; how original had *The Green Pastures* been, for that matter?

This was the season in which the phrase "preferably dealing with American life" was added to the Pulitzer citation; it was a comparatively meaningless addition, because of the gaping "preferably" loophole.

The Children's Hour undoubtedly lost out because of its Lesbian theme; Mr. Phelps, for instance, was reliably reported to have walked out on it, outraged that such a subject should have been thought fit for dramatization.

On April 21, 1935, Burns Mantle, in the *Daily News*, ran a list of the odds then being quoted against the various Pulitzer candidates:

The Children's Hour	9 to 5
Awake and Sing	5 to 2
The Petrified Forest	7 to 2
Valley Forge	10 to 1
Rain from Heaven	12 to 1
The Farmer Takes a Wife	15 to 1
Accent on Youth	20 to 1
Merrily We Roll Along	25 to 1
Gold Eagle Guy	30 to 1
The Old Maid	40 to 1
The First Legion	100 to 1

"Practically everybody is agreed," said Mantle, "that *The Children's Hour* is the strongest drama produced in 1934–35. But because of the disturbing nature of its motivating theme, everybody is equally convinced that the judges will not elect to hold *The Children's Hour* up for all and sundry, including Nicholas Murray Butler, to look upon and discuss as a great university's choice in drama." He added, farsightedly, "*The Old Maid* has a chance, at 40 to 1. Stark Young is on record as an admirer of Zoe Akins' drama; it is the sort of drama that belongs definitely to Professor Phelps' playgoing past, and that he instinctively endorses most heartily, and Professor Erskine could no doubt be easily won over if the vote were close."

Edith Wharton, author of *Ethan Frome* and *The Age of Innocence*, had originally written *The Old Maid* as a short novel; it was adapted for the stage by Zoe Akins, a playwright who earlier in her career had written *Papa, Déclassée, The Texas Nightingale* and *The Greeks Had a Word For It.*

Because *The Old Maid* was scheduled to open on Broadway on the same night as Robert E. Sherwood's *The Petrified Forest*, its producer, Harry Moses, invited the critics to cover it at a matinee performance in Baltimore, where it was winding up its pre-Broadway tour. Thus the reviewers saw what was essentially a "woman's play" under optimum circumstances, with an audience that was preponderantly feminine.

Some of the notices:

Brooks Atkinson in *The New York Times*:

"Once Zoe Akins was celebrated for the purple grandeur of her imagination and literary style. Now she is the author of *The Old Maid*, and now her style is plain and thorough. Out of Edith Wharton's novel about agonized motherhood, Miss Akins has fashioned a reticent and finely contemplated period drama, in which Judith Anderson gives a glowing performance. In the parallel role of the defeated spinster Helen Menken gives a haggard, gasping performance that is personally unattractive and communicates little of the character's hidden anguish. It is difficult to decide whether the uneven acting or the truncated narrative is the main source of disintegration. Whatever the source, *The Old Maid* leaves no

Robert Wallsten, Frederick Voight, Judith Anderson

single impression. With so much human emotion whipped up into passion, *The Old Maid* ought to be a masterpiece. This reviewer cannot pretend to know exactly why it is a good deal less than that."

Arthur Ruhl in the *Herald Tribune*:

"That Miss Akins' play is not all that it might have been, perhaps, were it an original play written from the outset on this particular theme, goes almost without saying. But it is an affecting work, nevertheless, beautifully played by Miss Anderson as the more tough-minded Delia and by Miss Menken as the hapless Charlotte. So plausibly is the old-New-York atmosphere, both material and mental, built up, that the spectator drops his modern impatiences to accept, for the time, the mood and customs of the day as they are presented."

Burns Mantle in the *Daily News*:

"The plot in essentials, of course, is as old as *Miss Multon* and as new as *Madame X*. It is always holding, even when played badly. When it is done as superbly as it is by these experienced technicians of the theatre, Judith Anderson and Helen Menken, it becomes a fine and moving dramatic exhibit. On Saturday afternoon in Baltimore the audience was as heavily feminine as the play, and the response was perfect. This is not to say that men will not like *The Old Maid*. To the contrary, a majority will revel in its perfectly normal emotional sweeps as completely as do women. But naturally and biologically, as you might say, it will mean less to them."

Wilella Waldorf in the *Evening Post*:

"*The Old Maid* has a certain charm about it—the charm of a series of pretty pictures of the Thirties, Forties and Fifties, but as a play it is slow moving, labored and unconvincing. Although the story in Mrs. Wharton's book has always seemed to us a very moving one, its dramatic cousin at the Empire failed to arouse us to the extent of a single sniff."

William Boehnel in the *World-Telegram*:

"Let others complain about *The Old Maid's* wordiness and thinness. I prefer to give thanks for its pitifully tragic moments, for its finely modulated performances which infuse this acutely moving tragedy with beauty, for the charm of its settings and for the exquisite staging that Guthrie McClintic has brought to it. Am I wrong when I suspect that in spite of its diffuseness this *The Old Maid* is not only a deeply touching but also a good play? Not that it is a great play or a significant one. But it has strength in spite of its weakness, and it says what it has to say with an honorable simplicity and a true emotional power."

John Anderson in the *Evening Journal*:

"As a short novel *The Old Maid* formed a part of Mrs. Wharton's four-volume study of old New York. As a play it has been adapted, not so much to the stage as to the vanishing point, so that it has become an elegant theatrical antique full of everything, I should say, except interest, drama and life. It is a miniature that has been expanded too far, and so is not much of anything."

After the prize was awarded, ex-juror Clayton Hamilton went on Station WJZ to say:

"The prize jury has labored and brought forth a mouse. Miss Zoe Akins herself very likely would be the last to claim that this is an original American play. The characters were created by Miss Wharton; the atmosphere was created by Miss Wharton, and the emotions and sentiments were worked out by Miss Wharton."

Percy Hammond took a milder view in the *Herald Tribune*, on May 12:

"The Pulitzer committee has been judicious, tolerant, intelligent and prudent in blue-ribboning a first-class second-rater. I believe *The Children's Hour* to be the best play of the year. Yet had I been an occupant of the Pulitzer bench I would have known better than to vote for it."

Maxwell Anderson, who had won the prize for *Both Your Houses* in 1932–33, but in the next two seasons had seen *Mary of Scotland* and *Valley Forge* go down in defeat, had a glum sour-grapes remark to make:

"Nobody cares any more."

Herman Shumlin, producer and director of *The Children's Hour*, was understandably apoplectic:

"I think it's quite the worst selection the committee could possibly have made from all the plays now current on Broadway."

George S. Kaufman, a winner three years earlier for *Of Thee I Sing*, and a current loser with *Merrily We Roll Along*, simply smiled and said:

"I'm in a swell spot to keep my mouth shut."

ALSO-RANS: *The Children's Hour, Awake and Sing, The Petrified Forest, Valley Forge, Rain from Heaven, The Farmer Takes a Wife, Merrily We Roll Along*

SUMMATION

The silliest and most disgraceful decision in the 50-year history of the Prize, not because *The Old Maid* itself was an atrociously bad play (it was not), but because of the unmentioned censorship that eliminated consideration of a genuine American classic, *The Children's Hour*. Miss Hellman's play should have won in a walk; failing that, Clifford Odets could well have won his first prize (it turned out he never did win one) for his tender *Awake and Sing*. The decision was Nice-Nellieism at its worst, and clouded the Pulitzer cachet for years thereafter.

Florence Williams, John Cromwell

Playwright Robert E. Sherwood

1935-36

THE HOTEL MONTE GABRIELE, in the Italian Alps, is situated dangerously close to a large Italian air base, and thus is a potential target in the World War that is on the verge of erupting. Because of the touchy international situation, all of the hotel's patrons are quarantined, and it is a motley assortment that has been bound together—a radical Frenchman who is summarily shot for making an inflammatory speech, a German doctor anxious to get back to his laboratory, a honeymooning English couple. There is vaudevillian Harry Van, an American touring Europe with an act called *Les Blondes*. And there is the mysterious Irene, mistress of munitions maker Achille Weber. Weber, it is broadly hinted, has had much to do with stirring up the present chaotic state of the world.

Harry believes that he recognizes Irene as a redhead he knew long ago, for one flaming night at the Governor Bryan Hotel in Omaha; she laughingly but unconvincingly denies the relationship. Soon, however, she turns to Harry for friendship and support, as a quarrel with her lover, Weber, over his dubious method of making a living has left her alone and unprotected at the hotel.

The Italians bomb Paris, and a reprisal on the Monte Gabriele air base is expected shortly. Harry manages to send *Les Blondes* to safety, but will not leave himself; that would mean abandoning Irene, and they are now openly in love. The play ends in a thunderous explosion of bombs. As a gallant, mocking counterpoint, Harry is at the piano, hammering out "Onward, Christian Soldiers."

Alfred Lunt at the piano

IDIOT'S DELIGHT

THE CREDITS

A Comedy in Three Acts by Robert E. Sherwood.
Produced by The Theatre Guild, Inc.
Staged by Bretaigne Windust.
Opened at the Shubert Theatre, March 24, 1936, and ran for 300 performances.

THE CAST

Dumptsy	George Meader
Signor Palota	Stephen Sandes
Donald Vavadel	Barry Thomson
Pittaluga	S. Thomas Gomez
Auguste	Edgar Barrier
Captain Locicero	Edward Raquello
Dr. Waldersee	Sydney Greenstreet

Alfred Lunt, Richard Whorf

Mr. Cherry	Bretaigne Windust
Mrs. Cherry	Jean Macintyre
Harry Van	Alfred Lunt
Shirley	Jacqueline Paige
Beulah	Connie Crowell
Edna	Frances Foley
Francine	Etna Ross
Elaine	Marjorie Baglin
Bebe	Ruth Timmons
1st Officer	Alan Hewitt
2nd Officer	Winston Ross
3rd Officer	Gilmore Bush
4th Officer	Tomasso Tittoni
Quillery	Richard Whorf
Signor Rossi	Le Roi Operti
Signora Rossi	Ernestine De Becker
Major	Murry O'Neill
Anna	Una Val
Irene	Lynn Fontanne
Achille Weber	Francis Compton
Musicians	Gerald Kunz
	Max Rich
	Joseph Knopf

ACTS I, II and III

Cocktail Lounge in Hotel Monte Gabriele in Italian Alps, Near Frontiers of Switzerland and Austria.

HISTORY AND REVIEWS

"A play of flashing moods, racing and shining like quicksilver from comedy to stinging protest. . . ."

Robert E. Sherwood stood six foot seven, and was a gregarious man who used to delight his friends by singing "When the Red Red Robin Comes Bob-Bob-Bobbin' Along" at parties. For over twenty years he was one of America's most successful playwrights, and *Idiot's Delight* gave him the first of his three Pulitzer Prizes for drama. He was to win a fourth Pulitzer Prize for a biography, *Roosevelt and Hopkins.*

In October of 1935 the Advisory Board of the Columbia School of Journalism, in a most ill-advised statement, announced that thereafter the drama Prize would be given only once to any one person. Perhaps the Board was sensitive about Eugene O'Neill's having won the Prize three times, but if so the reaction was a delayed one, for O'Neill had not won since 1927–28, with *Strange Interlude.* In any case, there it was: one Prize per playwright.

It turned out that the new rule did not govern even a single season's selections, for it was rescinded in May of 1936, before the 1935–36 award was announced. It was just as well for the Board's peace of mind that the foolish regulation was withdrawn, for otherwise there would have been another *cause célèbre*, right on the heels of the *Old Maid/Children's Hour* fiasco. Just after *Idiot's Delight* had won the Prize, Sherwood said in a transatlantic telephone interview with the Theatre Guild:

"I am extremely happy to have won the Pulitzer Prize, and, with the removal by the committee of the restrictions which would have barred former Pulitzer Prize winners from the competition, consider it a high honor, particularly in this season.

"Had not these restrictions been removed, I would have been forced to refuse the Prize and believe any self-respecting dramatist would have done the same. The elimination of consideration of the plays of Marc Connelly, Maxwell Anderson, Eugene O'Neill, Sidney Howard, George S. Kaufman, Elmer Rice and other former winners would have made the winning of the Prize a doubtful honor.

"The restoration of the former rules has corrected this. However, I hope that in the future the awarding of the Pulitzer Prize for the best play of the year will be placed in the hands of the Critics' Circle."

There was no chance, of course, that such a major procedural change would be made. The New York Drama Critics' Circle had originally been formed in the fall of 1931, but did not go officially into action until this season of 1935–36, when its first award was made to Maxwell Anderson's *Winterset.* Why were the critics suddenly stirred to activity, after four years of marking time? Writing in *Theatre Annual* in 1942, John Anderson, president of the Circle, explained:

"The answer to this question was implicit in the theatrical seasons of the eight or ten years before 1935–36, and especially in the history of the Pulitzer Prize awards. For years there had been growing disrespect, not to say ridicule, for the administration of the Pulitzer Award by Columbia University. This attitude toward the Pulitzer Prize was based not only on the plays honored, which often provided causes enough, but because it was a well-known fact that the Award Board could and did disregard the decision of the Advisory Board (usually made up of discriminating playgoers) and handed the prize to some play of its own whimsical or possibly expedient choosing."

Besides mixing up the Advisory Board and the panel of jurors, Mr. Anderson failed to mention the woman who had been a prime mover in the activation of the Critics' Circle, an energetic Broadway press agent named Helen Deutsch. Miss Deutsch, a personal friend of many of the critics, had informally suggested that they start giving their own award each season, as a professional rebuke to the inadequacy of some of the Pulitzer decisions. Miss Deutsch was not without guile in her suggestion, as one of her clients was *Winterset*, and she suspected that the critics might just happen to anoint it. It turned out that she was right.

While the critics were banding together, the Pulitzer Advisory Board contented itself with making a minor alteration in the wording of its own award, changing the phrase "which shall *best represent* the educational value and power of the stage" to "which shall represent *in marked fashion* the educational value and power of the stage." This bit of academic hairsplitting perhaps opened the door a little wider for some of the Pulitzer plays that were to come along in succeeding years, notably *Harvey* and the Tennessee Williams dramas.

Lynn Fontanne, Francis Compton

Robert E. Sherwood had a highly developed social conscience, and many of his most successful plays, *Idiot's Delight* among them, were blends of moralizing, melodrama and humor. Even in such a light sex comedy as *The Road to Rome* he had managed to have his say about the problems of power, and in *Idiot's Delight* he plunged an American hoofer and a phony Russian countess right into the middle of Armageddon, with most felicitous results.

Alfred Lunt and Lynn Fontanne had acted together once before in a Sherwood play, in the romantic *Reunion in Vienna. Idiot's Delight* cast Miss Fontanne in a familiar enough role, and she was pretty much her old soignée self; Lunt, however, had never before played a character like Harry Van, a brash American vaudevillian touring war-torn Europe with a chorus of pretty girls at his heels. The effect was as startlingly incongruous as if John Barrymore had suddenly turned up in *Abie's Irish Rose*.

Underneath its façade of comic melodrama, *Idiot's Delight* was a serious preachment. Sherwood emphasized this in his introduction to the published version:

"I believe that the world is populated largely by decent people, and decent people don't want war. Nor do they make war. They fight and die, to be sure—but that is because they have been deluded by their exploiters, who are members of the indecent minority.

"Of course, this delusion may still go on. If decent people will continue to be intoxicated by the synthetic spirit of patriotism, pumped into them by megalomaniac leaders, and will continue to have faith in the 'security' provided by those lethal weapons sold to them by the armaments industry, then war is inevitable; and the world will soon resolve itself into the semblance of an ant hill, governed by commissars who owe their power to the profundity of their contempt for the individual members of their species."

Some of the notices:

Brooks Atkinson in *The New York Times*:

"Mr. Sherwood's love of a good time and his anxiety about world affairs result in one of his most likable entertainments, *Idiot's Delight*. If this column observes that the discussion of war is inconclusive

Alfred Lunt, Lynn Fontanne

Jean Macintyre,
Lynn Fontanne, Bretaigne Windust

Alfred Lunt

and that the mood of the play is somewhat too trivial for such a macabre subject, it is probably taking *Idiot's Delight* much too seriously. For Mr. Sherwood's new play is a robust theatre charade, not quite so heroic and ebullient as *The Petrified Forest*, but well inside the same tradition. Mr. Sherwood has spoken passionately about a grave subject and settled down to writing a gusty show."

Percy Hammond in the *Herald Tribune*:

"Mr. Sherwood's excellent play has two major purposes, the comparative values of which it is difficult to estimate. One of these is seriously to discuss the inglorious triumphs and dishonest scars of battle; the other is to introduce the plastic Mr. Alfred Lunt for the initial time on any stage as a song-and-dance man, specializing in humorous anecdotes and homely philosophy. Mr. Lunt's display of finished alacrity is the most entertaining of his many superlative exhibitions. Lynn Fontanne gives one of her exquisitely lavish characterizations. My guess is that *Idiot's Delight* is the best of the entertainments of the season."

Gilbert W. Gabriel in the *American*:

"Here the Lunts, those two arch-exponents of the mischief of all heaven and earth and West 52nd Street, have—as usual—a great time. Or an even greater than usual. Then, so does their audience. Impossible not to at a party which combines the most entertaining features of a *Broadway*, a *Grand Hotel*, a *The Deluge*, a *Peace on Earth* and a *Custer's Last Stand*. Here, even more than in *The Petrified Forest*, is a demonstration of Mr. Sherwood's forte, his expertness in mixing hectic melodrama in precise

Lynn Fontanne, Alfred Lunt

proportion with fizzy and gay-hearted farce and—by way of miracle—getting thereby a tremendously powerful potion that tastes, besides, of strong social and philosophical meaning."

John Mason Brown in the *Evening Post*:

"In *Idiot's Delight* Mr. Sherwood shows once again his uncommon ability to combine entertainment of a fleet and satisfying sort with an allegory which reaches for a larger meaning. Although the allegory hovers rather hazily over the script, it does not interfere with the evening's entertainment values. The simple truth is that *Idiot's Delight* finds the Lunts at their topnotch best. Surely that is praise of the most superlative kind."

Richard Lockridge in the *Evening Sun*:

"*Idiot's Delight* is a play of flashing moods, racing and shining like quicksilver from comedy to stinging protest; it is at once brilliant entertainment and bitter questioning of the idiot stupidity which lets war happen. It is, beyond any possible doubt, Mr. Sherwood's best play."

John Anderson in the *Evening Journal*:

"*Idiot's Delight* is superb playmaking, the author's best to rank with our drama's best, full of substance and power, and full, too, of sheer, absorbing entertainment."

Commenting on the Pulitzer award, Howard Barnes said in the *Herald Tribune*:

"The award of the Pulitzer Prize to Robert E. Sherwood's *Idiot's Delight* is an accolade that is likely to cause scant dissension. Whether consciously or not, the judges have played safe in their choice this year, restoring a measure of distinction to a prize that was becoming increasingly the subject for scoffing in theatrical circles."

Alfred Lunt and Les Blondes: *Connie Crowell, Frances Foley, Jacqueline Paige, Etna Ross, Marjorie Baglin, Ruth Timmons*

ALSO-RANS: *Winterset, First Lady, Paradise Lost, Dead End, End of Summer, Porgy and Bess, Ethan Frome*

SUMMATION

A good choice; Mr. Sherwood's powerful, if sugar-coated, anti-war play was to just about everybody's taste. *Porgy and Bess* was a much more lasting contribution to the American theatre, but its derivation from a previously produced play made it ineligible.

Lynn Fontanne

Playwrights George S. Kaufman and Moss Hart

1936-37

THE NEW YORK APARTMENT OF MARTIN VANDERHOF, a salty eccentric who won't pay any income tax because he "doesn't believe in it," is crowded with his engagingly raffish family: his daughter, Penny Sycamore, who writes plays; Penny's husband, Paul, who makes fireworks in the cellar; and the two Sycamore daughters, Essie and Alice. Essie takes toedancing lessons from a Russian émigré, Boris Kolenkhov. Alice, the only member of the family with a regular job, is in love with young Tony Kirby, her boss's son, and it is on Alice's invitation that the elder Kirbys come to the Vanderhof–Sycamore household for dinner.

They arrive, unfortunately, a night too soon, and are baffled by the goings-on that constitute a "normal" evening in that somewhat different apartment. Essie is in her ballet costume; Mr. De Pinna, a permanent house guest, is in a Roman toga, modeling *The Discus Thrower* as Penny paints him; a drunken actress, Gay Wellington, is sleeping off a monumental binge on the sofa. As the climax of the evening, three Justice Department agents arrive to investigate some revolutionary literature that Ed, Essie's husband, has been grinding out on his printing press. Ed has merely been printing the inflammatory tracts for practice, but the agents don't know that, and when the fireworks in the cellar suddenly go up with a roar, everyone in the house, including the stuffy Mr. and Mrs. Kirby, is clapped into jail.

Alice is of course convinced that this means the end of her romance with Tony, but as this is a warmhearted farce, everything turns out all right in the end. The Kirbys return to the apartment, now charmed rather than bewildered, and are being served blintzes by the Grand Duchess Olga (who else would you expect to find serving blintzes at the Sycamores?) as the curtain falls on a happy communal meal.

Josephine Hull

YOU CAN'T TAKE IT WITH YOU

THE CREDITS

A Play in Three Acts by Moss Hart and George S. Kaufman.
Produced by Sam H. Harris.
Staged by George S. Kaufman.
Opened at the Booth Theatre, December 14, 1936, and ran for 837 performances.

THE CAST

Penelope Sycamore	Josephine Hull
Essie	Paula Trueman
Rheba	Ruth Attaway
Paul Sycamore	Frank Wilcox
Mr. De Pinna	Frank Conlan
Ed	George Heller
Donald	Oscar Polk
Martin Vanderhof	Henry Travers
Alice	Margot Stevenson
Henderson	Hugh Rennie
Tony Kirby	Jess Barker

Mitzi Hajos, Paula Trueman, George Tobias, George Heller, Henry Travers, Oscar Polk, Frank Conlan, Josephine Hull

BORIS KOLENKHOV	George Tobias
GAY WELLINGTON	Mitzi Hajos
MR. KIRBY	William J. Kelly
MRS. KIRBY	Virginia Hammond
THREE MEN	George Leach
	Ralph Holmes
	Franklin Heller
OLGA	Anna Lubowe

SCENE: *The Home of Martin Vanderhof, New York.*

ACT I

A Wednesday Evening.
(During this act the curtain is lowered to denote the passing of several hours.)

ACT II

A Week Later.

ACT III

The Next Day.

HISTORY AND REVIEWS

"A giddy family album viewed in a cockeyed mirror. . . ."

You Can't Take It With You, one of the most successful and best-loved comedies ever written in America, had an unostentatious beginning as Moss Hart's "other idea."

Hart and George S. Kaufman had first joined forces six years earlier, when they collaborated on *Once in a Lifetime*, a free-swinging satire on the newborn art of talking pictures; later, in the 1934–35 season, they wrote *Merrily We Roll Along*, a play whose chief claim to fame was its reverse chronology (its first scene was set in 1934, its second scene a few years earlier, its final one in 1916).

In the spring of 1936 Hart was living in Hollywood, in Frances Marion's house, and Kaufman joined him there to discuss a new project they had in mind, a dramatization of a Dalton Trumbo novel, *Washington Jitters*.

A few desultory conferences got them nowhere, and they began to search for something else to work on. Kaufman finally suggested that they talk about the "other idea" that Hart had had the year before, to build a comedy around a group of mad but lovable people who behaved exactly as they pleased, and the hell with the consequences.

In three days they had the Sycamore household down on paper: playwright Mama, who wrote plays because eight years earlier someone had left a typewriter at the house by mistake; gentle Papa, who made firecrackers in the cellar; salty old Grandpa Vanderhof, who wouldn't pay any income tax; toedancing Essie; and a group of house guests who ranged from a marvelously drunken actress to a Grand Duchess who was working as a Child's waitress.

Allotting ten days to each act (a remarkably fast working pace for Kaufman, who frequently spent as much as a year on a play), they finished the new comedy in a month. Then there was much discussion about a title. *Grandpa's Other Snake, Money in the Bank*, *Foxy Grandpa* and *The King is Naked* were all weighed and discarded before they finally decided to call it *You Can't Take It With You.*

The cozy, crackpot charm of *You Can't Take It With You* is epitomized in the Kaufman–Hart description, in the Farrar and Rinehart published version, of the living room which served as the play's single setting:

"The home of Martin Vanderhof—just around the corner from Columbia University, but don't go looking for it. The room we see is what is customarily described as a living room, but in this house the term is something of an understatement. The every-man-for-himself room would be more like it. For here meals are eaten, plays are written, snakes collected, ballet steps practiced, xylophones played, printing presses operated—if there were room enough there would probably be ice skating. In short, the brood presided over by Martin Vanderhof goes on about the business of living in the fullest sense of the word. This is a house where you do as you like, and no questions asked."

Some of the notices:

Brooks Atkinson in *The New York Times*:

"Moss Hart and George S. Kaufman have written their most thoroughly ingratiating comedy. They have been more rigidly brilliant in the past, but they have never scooped up an evening of such tickling fun. Their current lark is a much more spontaneous piece of hilarity than *Once in a Lifetime*; it is written with a dash of affection to season the humor and played with gayety and simple good spirit."

Burns Mantle in the *Daily News*:

"As fantastic as anything in the modern farce line that has been produced these many seasons. The theme is so good, the bit of philosophy with which Grandpa composes the drama in the end, and gives it just a wisp of dignity, is so sound I acknowledge a regret that the Messrs. Kaufman and Hart did not restrain their sense of the ridiculous a bit and give a little more weight to the serious thread of their comedy."

John Anderson in the *Journal*:

"Sam H. Harris opened not so much a play as a madhouse at the Booth last night, loosed a set of magnificent zanies on the town and set his audience down at 11 o'clock still laughing over the delirious doings of *You Can't Take It With You*. It is a giddy family album viewed in a cockeyed mirror, a combination of Mr. Odets' Bronx-life studies and the funnypapers. And it is all crazy enough to make a little sense. Once the farce is afloat it sails dizzily and the sky's the limit. It is great fun."

Gilbert W. Gabriel in the *American*:

"Moss Hart and George S. Kaufman have seldom been funnier, prankier, collected so many caricatures of the human race with such crazycat bodies, such thistledown souls. But that's where they fool you completely, this time. Instead of in an acid bath of scorn and fury, these collaborators put these foolish folk of theirs in a sun-pool of purest amiability, of sheer, unashamed lovableness. You come away from *You Can't Take It With You* hugging close your memory of every affectionate loon they've shown you on the stage."

Richard Watts, Jr., in the *Herald Tribune*:

"Not bothering their handsome heads over such triviality as a plot, the illustrious collaborators devote their time and attention to the amiable antics of the mad Sycamores and the crazy Vanderhofs, contemplating the merry eccentricities of the interrelated clan with admiration and approval. The result is a merry and engaging vaudeville that assuredly belongs among the first-rank hits of the season."

Richard Lockridge in the *Evening Sun*:

"Gargantuan absurdity, hilarious preposterous antics and the rumble of friendly laughter with madly comic people. It is all much funnier than the family album, and quite as unexpected."

Clockwise from Henry Travers (Center, in armchair): *Frank Wilcox, George Tobias, Jess Barker, Oscar Polk, Margot Stevenson, William J. Kelly, Paula Trueman, Frank Conlan, Ruth Attaway* (Standing), *Josephine Hull, George Heller, Anna Lubowe*

George S. Kaufman gloomily inspects his smash hit from a spot in the rear of the theatre.

The award of the Pulitzer Prize to *You Can't Take It With You* was not universally applauded, however much the play was loved. On the eve of the dinner at which the Prize was to be announced, John Anderson wrote in the *Journal*:

"When Dr. Butler rings the dinner bell at the Biltmore Monday night for the Pulitzer Prize Picnic the town will hold its breath (if not its sides). If the Pulitzer judges are wise they will give the prize to *Johnny Johnson*; if they are bold they will give it to *High Tor*; and if they are cowards they will give it to *You Can't Take It With You*."

A few days later, after the award had been made, John Mason Brown did some good-natured grumbling in the *Evening Post*:

"Mr. Hart's and Mr. Kaufman's play is a comedy which is unusually entertaining and immensely lovable. Yet vastly as I enjoyed it, I still think that the judges showed a disregard of standard. I may be wrong, but my own belief is that a prize play should stand for more than a box-office success. To my way of thinking *You Can't Take It With You* is a box-office play, pure and simple minded, and admirable as such. But to crown it as the season's most distinguished drama is quite another matter, and does not seem to me to make much sense."

A small civil war broke out at the *Daily News*. The *News* commented editorially:

"*You Can't Take It With You* is a perfectly swell hit show, humorous, human, beautifully acted. We fear the reason why the professional critics snoot this play is that from long theatre-going they have become somewhat sombre minded; contract the feeling that if a play is not built upon a heavy theme, it does not deserve a dignified prize award. We can't concur. We like the prize award to *You Can't Take It With You* 100 percent."

Burns Mantle, the *News'* drama critic, answered his editors:

"If a prize for the best play of this or any season is to be given with the understanding that 'best play' means the most entertaining play, the happiest play, the maddest play, the surest laughter play, or the best box-office play, that is one thing. But if the Kaufman–Hart comedy in any way suggests such a prize play as Joseph Pulitzer himself would endorse, then my editor is right and I'm a Chinaman, or something.

"The trouble with prize play awards is, ever has been and always will be, that it is quite impossible to define actually just what specific virtues in a play are to be considered. The theatre fulfills its truest function only so long as the actions it inspires are 90 per cent emotional reactions, and emotional reactions are as varied as the humans who experience them. Hence every award is a compromise of sorts. Which starts arguments like this."

You Can't Take It With You did not travel well; in 1938 it was a one-week failure in London. Charles Morgan wrote back to *The New York Times*:

"These people seem to have no link connecting them with that life of which farce is, or should be, a recognizable distortion and fantastication. *You Can't Take It With You* might have been written about the inhabitants of Mars."

A predominantly English cast may have suffocated the comedy's Yankee charm. Anyway, Grandpa Vanderhof was so purely and cantankerously American that it is small wonder our English cousins found him difficult to understand or accept. The silly old man wouldn't even pay his rates.

ALSO-RANS: *High Tor* (Critics' Circle Award), *Johnny Johnson, Excursion, The Women, Having Wonderful Time*

SUMMATION

A peculiar if delightful choice. Maxwell Anderson's *High Tor* was the logical selection, but the Sycamores and Grandpa were accustomed to riding roughshod over logic.

The entire company, staff and backstage crew. Playwrights Hart and Kaufman are standing in the center, rear, while producer Sam H. Harris sits at the center of the table, flanked by Henry Travers and Mitzi Hajos.

Playwright Thornton Wilder

1937-38

OUR TOWN is performed without scenery, and with a minimum of properties. Its leading character is a folksy Stage Manager who throughout the play comments upon the universal commonplaces of life in Grover's Corners, New Hampshire, in the early days of the twentieth century. Artfully artless, with a surface naïveté but with complex roots that go very deep indeed, *Our Town* is a bold attempt to come to grips with reality on an informal, cracker-barrel level.

In Act One, set in 1901, the residents of the town are introduced, particular emphasis being placed on two families, the Gibbses and the Webbs. The town's background is sketched in some detail by the Stage Manager: a newsboy on his rounds, a choir rehearsal, all of the sweet, shirtsleeve simplicities of everyday life. Young George Gibbs and young Emily Webb, next-door neighbors, are obviously beginning to fall in love.

In Act Two the year is 1904, and it is George and Emily's wedding day. In a tender flashback, the Stage Manager recreates the moment when the two young people first saw each other plain, over sodas

Helen Carew,
Doro Merande, Evelyn Varden

OUR TOWN

Martha Scott,
John Craven

at a drug store. In the moments just before the wedding, both of them are frightened and insecure, but their doubts dissolve at the service, performed by the Stage Manager. They run joyously offstage as the act ends.

Nine years have passed by the time Act Three opens; it is the summer of 1913, the scene is the town's graveyard, with the dead sitting quietly upon rows of chairs. A funeral procession brings a shy newcomer to join them—it is Emily. Nervous, unsettled by the placid resignation of her graveyard companions, Emily quickly seizes an opportunity to relive one day of her life, her twelfth birthday. The journey back to childhood is a heartbreaking one, and gives Emily a poignant realization of the transitory quality of all human actions and hopes. As the play ends she is back in the cemetery, sadly watching her young husband as he throws himself weeping on her grave, unable to tell him the melancholy lesson she has learned, that the living do not understand very much about life.

THE CREDITS

A Drama in Three Acts by Thornton Wilder.
Produced and Staged by Jed Harris.
Opened at Henry Miller's Theatre, February 4, 1938, and ran for 336 performances.

THE CAST

Stage Manager	Frank Craven
Dr. Gibbs	Jay Fassett
Joe Crowell	Raymond Roe
Howie Newsome	Tom Fadden
Mrs. Gibbs	Evelyn Varden
Mrs. Webb	Helen Carew
George Gibbs	John Craven
Rebecca Gibbs	Marilyn Erskine
Wally Webb	Charles Wiley, Jr.
Emily Webb	Martha Scott
Professor Pepper	Arthur Allen
Mr. Webb	Thomas W. Ross
Woman in the Balcony	Carrie Weller
Man in the Auditorium	Walter O. Hill
Lady in the Box	Aline McDermott

The wedding of Emily and George (Martha Scott and John Craven, with Frank Craven in background)

SIMON STIMSON	Philip Coolidge
MRS. SOAMES	Doro Merande
CONSTABLE WARREN	E. Irving Locke
SI CROWELL	Billy Redfield
BASEBALL PLAYERS	Alfred Ryder
	William Roehrick
	Thomas Coley
SAM CRAIG	Francis G. Cleveland
JOE STODDARD	William Wadsworth

PEOPLE OF THE TOWN: Carrie Weller, Alice Donaldson, Walter O. Hill, Arthur Allen, Charles Mellody, Katharine Raht, Mary Elizabeth Forbes, Dorothy Nolan, Jean Platt, Barbara Brown, Alda Stanley, Barbara Burton, Lyn Swann, Dorothy Ryan, Shirley Osborn, Emily Boileau, Ann Weston, Leon Rose, John Irving Finn, Van Shem, Charles Walters, William Short, Frank Howell, Max Beck, James Malaidy.

ACTS I, II and III

Grover's Corners, New Hampshire, 1901 to 1913.

HISTORY AND REVIEWS

"Mr. Wilder has transmuted the simple events of human life into universal reverie. . . ."

Alexander Woollcott, no longer a mere drama critic but an established international celebrity, was spotted at a performance of *Our Town* by the play's press agent, who asked him to volunteer a quotable opinion.

"Certainly not!" said Woollcott indignantly. "I'd as soon think of endorsing the Twenty-Third Psalm!"

Some time later, Woollcott spoiled a good story by successfully conquering his indignation and saying, for publication: "In all my days as a theatregoer, no play ever moved me so deeply."

He was not alone in that judgment; many others felt equal admiration for this sceneryless, plotless play that dealt in deliberately simple terms with life and love and death. There were equally strong negative reactions to the play, with some critics feeling that Wilder had fobbed off on the public an over-simplified, shallow trick. However, thirty years after its opening *Our Town* seems fixed in a quite exalted place at the top of any list of American dramas, jostling three or four other candidates for the mythical laurel of The Great American Play.

Our Town's genesis can be traced directly to a one-act play that Wilder had written some years earlier, *Pullman Car Hiawatha*, which used the same system of inspecting a microcosm to discover a series of large truths.

Thornton Wilder, 42 years old when *Our Town* was produced, had become world-famous in 1927 with the publication of *The Bridge of San Luis Rey*, a novel which won him the first of his three Pulitzer Prizes (the third came in 1942–43, for *The Skin of Our Teeth*). Wilder also wrote such other novels as *The Cabala*, *The Ides of March* and *Heaven's My Destination*, and such excellent one-act plays as *The Happy Journey from Trenton to Camden* and *The Long Christmas Dinner*. In 1939 he wrote *The Merchant of Yonkers*, an adaptation of an old German play; it was a failure, but in 1955, zipped up by the vigorous direction of Tyrone Guthrie, it was very successful under its new title of *The Matchmaker*. Still later, *The Matchmaker* was trimmed with songs and became *Hello, Dolly!*

Frank Craven

Writing in *The New York Times* a week or two after the *Our Town* opening, Wilder had this to say about his new play:

"I wished to record a village's life on the stage, with realism and with generality. The theatre longs to represent the symbols of things, not the things themselves. All the lies it tells—the lie that that young lady is Caesar's wife; the lie that people can go through life talking in blank verse; the lie that that man just killed that man—all those lies enhance the one truth that is there— the truth that dictated the story, the myth. The theatre asks for as many conventions as possible. A convention is an agreed-upon falsehood, an accepted untruth. When the theatre pretends to give the real thing in canvas and wood and metal it loses something of the realer thing which is its true business. Ibsen and Chekhov carried realism as far as it could go and it took all their genius to do it. Now the camera is carrying it on and is in great 'theoretical peril' of falling short of literature. But the writing of the play was not accompanied by any such conscious argumentation as this. It sprang from a deep admiration for those little, white towns in the hills and from a deep devotion to the theatre. These are but the belated gropings to reconstruct what may have taken place when the play first presented itself—the life of a village against the life of the stars."

Some of the notices:

Brooks Atkinson in *The New York Times*:

"Thornton Wilder's *Our Town* is a beautifully evocative play. Taking as his material three periods in the history of a placid New Hampshire town, Mr. Wilder has transmuted the simple events of human life into universal reverie. He has given familiar facts a deeply moving, philosophical perspective. Staged without scenery and with the curtain always up, *Our Town* has escaped from the formal barrier of the modern theatre into the quintessence of acting, thought and speculation. In the staging, Jed Harris has appreciated the rare quality of Mr. Wilder's handiwork and illuminated it with a shining performance. *Our Town* is one of the finest achievements of the current stage. It is a microcosm. It is also a hauntingly beautiful play. As chorus, preacher, drugstore proprietor and finally as shepherd of the flock, Frank Craven plays with great sincerity and understanding, keeping the sublime well within his homespun style. As the boy and girl, John Craven and Martha Scott turn youth into tremulous idealization; some of their scenes are lovely past all enduring. Under the leisurely monotone of the production there is a fragment of the immortal truth."

Richard Watts, Jr., in the *Herald Tribune*:

"Another interesting and provocative, if occasionally maddening, evening in the theatre is provided by Thornton Wilder's *Our Town*. Combining some of the distinguishing traits of the Greek, the Chinese and the Mercury Theatres, the new work is done without scenery. As long as the gentle love story of the young people is being told, the simple annals of a rural community are being tenderly set down and the homely philosophy of the commentator is being shrewdly expressed by Frank Craven, *Our Town* is both beautiful and touching. I suspect it of being merely pretentious in its occasional outbursts of cosmic brooding."

Richard Lockridge in the *Evening Sun*:

"Experimental in form, the play yet achieves moments of rare simplicity and truth; at its best it

Jay Fassett,
Evelyn Varden

reaches into the past of America and evokes movingly a way of life which is lost in our present turmoil, but is good to remember. In the third act 'our town' becomes, symbolically, our earth and our life on it and the author begins to suspect that he is touching the garments of eternal truth. This I doubt very much, suspecting rather that he is groping in the equally eternal mist. *Our Town* seems to me both more moving and more significant, before its author reaches his hands towards significance. But it is, in any case, an original and extremely interesting play and a stimulating employment of experimental stagecraft."

John Anderson in the *Journal-American*:

"What Mr. Wilder has written is not a play, in the accepted sense, but a sort of retrospective edition of the Living Newspaper. I must confess that Mr. Wilder's play, in spite of its admirable writing, left me completely cold. In his production, Jed Harris would have his cake and eat it, too. He would avoid the common illusion of the theatre, by eliminating scenery and properties, but he would grab for it in every gesture and inflection of his players, and in a whole catalogue of off-stage noises. Thus he has stripped the production of the customary theatrical claptrap, but has substituted for it another brand of hokum that is obligingly abetted by the audience. There is no doubt that the First Audience was completely engrossed. I wasn't."

John Chapman in the *Daily News*:

"*Our Town* is a poet's conception; but in the eyes of this regretful reporter it is not quite a poet's achievement. Sometimes, as it skips through the lives in a small New Hampshire town, it soars; but again it is earthbound by its folksy attention to humdrum detail. However it may add up, it is an intelligent and rewarding theatrical experiment."

(Right) *Martha Scott as a bewildered newcomer to* Our Town*'s graveyard*

The universal appeal of *Our Town* made it popular in productions around the world, under such titles as *Var Lilla Stad*, *Ma Petite Ville*, *Nuestra Ciudad* and *Unsere Kleine Stadt*. Here in the United States it has long been a staple for amateur companies and schools, and Mr. Wilder himself loves to appear in it—he has played the Stage Manager on eight separate occasions, including a two-week engagement on Broadway.

ALSO-RANS: *Of Mice and Men* (Critics' Circle Award), *Golden Boy, Susan and God, On Borrowed Time, Prologue to Glory*

SUMMATION

An excellent choice. *Our Town* would have won against almost any competition, and was pressed seriously only by *Of Mice and Men*. *Of Mice and Men* was a brilliantly staged, superbly earthy play; unfortunately, its earthiness was forced to compete with a combination of spirituality, nostalgia and novelty.

The original members of The Playwright's Company: S. N. Behrman, Maxwell Anderson, Robert E. Sherwood, Elmer Rice

1938-39

THE PLAY'S SPAN OF YEARS—1830 to 1861—presents Abe Lincoln as a gangling youth who gradually changes into a gentle, bearded man on his way to Washington to assume the duties of the presidency.

Lincoln's brief, sad romance with Ann Rutledge is lightly sketched in, and his embittered agony at her early death makes him equivocate for years before he can bring himself to marry the drivingly ambitious Mary Todd. In the meantime his political career has begun, with his election to the Illinois Assembly.

By 1858, Lincoln has come far enough along as a politician to be running for United States Senator from Illinois. His opponent is Judge Stephen A. Douglas, and the first long scene of Act III recreates one of their famous debates. Douglas speaks first, giving an eloquent pro-slavery speech; Lincoln's rebuttal is even more eloquent, and ends with the famous phrase: "This government cannot endure permanently, half slave and half free."

In 1860, Lincoln is nominated to run for the presidency. On election night he and Mary have a dreadful quarrel, in which her hysteria foreshadows her eventual madness. Wearily Lincoln listens to the returns, and when he carries New York, he realizes that he has been elected.

As the play ends, the Lincolns are on the back platform of a railroad train at Springfield, ready to leave for Washington. The five terrible years of the Civil War lie just ahead. A band is playing "Glory, Glory Hallelujah" as the train pulls out.

Raymond Massey, Muriel Kirkland

ABE LINCOLN IN ILLINOIS

THE CREDITS

A Drama in Three Acts by Robert E. Sherwood.
Produced by The Playwrights' Company.
Staged by Elmer Rice.
Opened at the Plymouth Theatre, October 15, 1938, and ran for 472 performances.

THE CAST

Mentor Graham	Frank Andrews
Abe Lincoln	Raymond Massey
Ann Rutledge	Adele Longmire
Judith	Iris Whitney
Ben Mattling	George Christie
Judge Bowling Green	Arthur Griffin
Ninian Edwards	Lewis Martin
Joshua Speed	Calvin Thomas
Trum Cogdal	Harry Levian

Howard da Silva, Raymond Massey, Marion Rooney, Howard Sherman, Hubert Brown

Jack Armstrong	Howard da Silva
Bab	Everett Charlton
Feargus	David Clarke
Jasp	Kevin McCarthy
Seth Gale	Herbert Rudley
Nancy Green	Lillian Foster
William Herndon	Wendell K. Phillips
Elizabeth Edwards	May Collins
Mary Todd	Muriel Kirkland
The Edwards' Maid	Dorothy Allan
Jimmy Gale	Howard Sherman
Aggie Gale	Marion Rooney
Gobey	Hubert Brown
Stephen A. Douglas	Albert Phillips
Willie Lincoln	Lex Parrish
Tad Lincoln	Lloyd Barry
Robert Lincoln	John Payne
The Lincolns' Maid	Iris Whitney
Crimmin	Frank Tweddell
Barrick	John Gerard
Sturveson	Thomas F. Tracey
Jed	Harry Levian
Phil	Kevin McCarthy
Kavanagh	Glenn Coulter
Ogleby	John Triggs
Donner	David Clarke
Cavalry Captain	Everett Charlton

Raymond Massey and Howard da Silva (Center, in undershirt) *decide to shake hands rather than fight.*

SOLDIERS, RAILROAD MEN, TOWNSPEOPLE: Stuart McClure, Allen Shaw, Phillip Caplan, David Hewes, Dearon Darnay, Harrison Woodhull, Robert Fitzsimmons, Joseph Wiseman, Walter Kapp, George Malcolm, Bert Schorr, Augusta Dabney, Bette Benfield, Ann Stevenson.

ACT I

SCENE 1. *Mentor Graham's Cabin near New Salem, Ill. About 1830.*
SCENE 2. *The Rutledge Tavern.*
SCENE 3. *Bowling Green's House.*

ACT II

SCENE 1. *Law Office of Stuart and Lincoln on Second Floor of Court House, Springfield. About 1840.*
SCENE 2. *Parlor of the Edwards House.*
SCENE 3. *The Law Office.*
SCENE 4. *On the Prairie, About 1847.*
SCENE 5. *The Parlor.*

ACT III

SCENE 1. *A Speaker's Platform in an Illinois Town. 1858.*
SCENE 2. *Parlor of the Edwards Home, Now Used by the Lincolns.*
SCENE 3. *Lincoln Campaign Headquarters, Illinois State House. November 6, 1860.*
SCENE 4. *Yards of Railroad Station, Springfield, February 11, 1861.*

"A profoundly moving portrait of our human lore and our spiritual heritage. . . ."

Three years after he had won his first Pulitzer Prize for *Idiot's Delight*, Robert E. Sherwood came up with another winner, *Abe Lincoln in Illinois*, an episodic account of the thirty years that preceded Lincoln's tenure as President of the United States.

Unlike John Drinkwater (whose *Abraham Lincoln* the judges had so reluctantly disqualified back in 1919–20), Sherwood chose not to go into the Washington period of Lincoln's life at all. In his introduction to the published script of the play (Scribner's) the playwright said that he had been much impressed by Carl Sandburg's interpretation of Lincoln's life, and had also made use of William H. Herndon's writings and the Lincoln biographies by Nathaniel Wright Stephenson and Albert J. Beveridge. Sherwood had read Lord Charnwood's biography (upon which the Drinkwater play had been based), but felt that the other men probed deeper.

In his Scribner's introduction, Sherwood said:

"Lincoln's life, as he lived it, was a work of art, forming a veritable allegory of the growth of the democratic spirit, with its humble origins, its inward struggles, its seemingly timid policy of 'live and let live' and 'mind your own business,' its slow awakening to the dreadful problems of reality, its battles with and conquests of these problems, its death at the hands of a crazed assassin, and its perpetual renewal caused by the perpetual human need for it. Furthermore, just as Lincoln's life needs no adornments of symbolism to make it pertinent, his character needs no romanticizing, no sentimentalizing, no dramatizing.

Raymond Massey, Adele Longmire

Raymond Massey

"Lincoln's great achievement, most of which was accomplished by the echoes of his words, long after his death, was the solidification of the American ideal. But this is not a play about his achievement; it is, rather, a play about the solidification of Lincoln himself—a long, uncertain process, effected by influences, some of which came from within his own reasoning mind, some from sources which we cannot comprehend. As many as possible of these influences are indicated in this play; the rest are left to the imagination of the audience, because they are beyond mine."

Abe Lincoln in Illinois was the first production of the newly organized Playwright's Company, which Sherwood, Elmer Rice, Sidney Howard, Maxwell Anderson and S. N. Behrman had formed to produce their own plays. Scoffers thought the mixture of temperaments too potentially explosive, but The Playwrights managed to stay together for many years, with comparatively little friction. *Abe Lincoln* got them off and running with a big commercial success. For the most part it received superlative notices that verged on the reverent, but there was a surprisingly strong undercurrent of dissent from some reviewers who felt that Mr. Sherwood had leaned far too heavily on the crutch of the Lincoln legend, and had been guilty of using that legend to shore up the weaker early portions of his play.

Some of the notices:

Brooks Atkinson in *The New York Times*:

"Mr. Sherwood has written his finest play. *Abe Lincoln in Illinois* is part of the living truth of America. In the breadth and depth of its understanding it is far above the general level of commercial theatre. Mr. Sherwood has looked down with compassion into the lonely blackness of Lincoln's heart and seen some of the fateful things that lived there. *Abe Lincoln in Illinois* is a profoundly moving portrait of our human lore and our spiritual heritage. Mr. Massey has an exhaustingly long part to play. He is the center of every scene; he has a great many lines and several long speeches to deliver. An actor might be forgiven for not mastering all the details. But Mr. Massey, too, has drawn inspiration from the theme he is conveying, and he plays it with an artless honesty that is completely overwhelming at the end. Fortunately, he looks the part. But he goes deeper than surface resemblances. He has the artistic stature to measure the great things that lie beneath. From the careless, good-natured boy to the towering man of melancholy who goes on leaden feet to face his destiny, is a long road for any actor to travel in one night. But Mr. Massey tells the whole story in terms of humanity with the diffident eloquence of a man who knows what it means."

Burns Mantle in the *Daily News*:

"*Abe Lincoln in Illinois* is a biographical drama with a soul. Probably no finer, no more human, more understanding, more intelligently analyzed study of Lincoln has been written into the record of American letters. But as a drama of cumulative emotional interest it is, to me, weakened by the fact that the dramatist has tried to wedge too much into the pattern."

Richard Lockridge in the *Evening Sun*:

"Writing and acting are combined to make a satisfying and deeply impressive play, catching in reflection the greatness of its central character and the mystery of his mind."

Richard Watts, Jr., in the *Herald Tribune*:

"One of the most stirring of American plays. A beautiful and moving portrait of the greatest and most lovable of our national heroes, the new drama is not only the finest of modern stage biographies but a lovely, eloquent and endearing tribute to all that is best in the spirit of democracy. *Abe Lincoln in Illinois* is one of the great achievements of the American theatre and the American spirit."

Here, however, is John Mason Brown, dissenting in the *Evening Post*:

"The program at the Plymouth names Mr. Sherwood as the author of *Abe Lincoln in Illinois*. And so he is. But he does not work without collaborators whose aid at times proves far more potent than any contribution he has to make. One of these collaborators is our own foreknowledge as members of

Albert Phillips, Lewis Martin, Raymond Massey

the audience of Lincoln, the man and the martyr. Mr. Sherwood's other collaborator is Mr. Lincoln himself. Had there been calls of 'Author! Author!' at the Plymouth Saturday night, Mr. Sherwood would have had to appear behind the footlights hand-in-hand with Honest Abe. Failing him, he would have been compelled to walk on with a copy of the Lincoln–Douglas debates in his hand. Except for its enlivening moments here and there during the earlier scenes, and the three touching episodes of its last act, this first production of The Playwrights' Company comes as a disappointment for which ironically a well-intentioned dramatist must be blamed."

Muriel Kirkland, Frank Tweddell, Calvin Thomas,
Lewis Martin, Raymond Massey, Wendell K. Phillips

Making much the same point, John Gassner had this to say in *One Act Play Magazine*:

"It is a mistake to let our zeal for Abe Lincoln blind us to the fact that *Abe Lincoln in Illinois* is a rather indifferent piece of playmaking. The third act is, on the whole, superlative; it contains the best serious writing of Mr. Sherwood's career. But the first acts consist of loosely connected, lagging and fumbling episodes. There is little excitement in watching Abe Lincoln moving about in a fog, not knowing what to do, and just 'hanging around' scene after scene. If the character had been John Doe the experience would have been devastatingly dull. Only our prior knowledge that Lincoln turned out to be a great leader pulls the play out of the morass."

The enthusiasts far outweighed the grumblers, however, and Heywood Broun spoke for most of his fellow newspapermen when he wrote in the *World-Telegram*, after the Pulitzer Prize had been awarded:

"The Pulitzer Prize committee has double-crossed me; I'm sore this year because I have nothing about which I can holler. Not only is *Abe Lincoln in Illinois* a magnificent play but it represents the peak of a fine artist who has constantly grown in stature through several seasons."

There was no Critics' Circle Award this season, as under the Circle rules (subsequently amended) a play had to receive twelve votes out of a possible fifteen in order to win. On the final ballot, Lillian Hellman's *The Little Foxes* led, with six votes to *Abe Lincoln's* five. William Saroyan's *My Heart's in the Highlands* was third, with two votes, and there were two abstentions.

ALSO-RANS: *The Little Foxes, My Heart's in the Highlands, Rocket to the Moon, The Philadelphia Story, The American Way, No Time for Comedy*

SUMMATION

An excellent choice, even if an almost preordained one; how could the committee have turned down a play about America's greatest folk hero, written by one of the country's top playwrights? Tough timing for Miss Hellman, as in another season *The Little Foxes* would almost surely have won her some belated balm for the *Children's Hour* slight.

Mr. and Mrs. Lincoln on their departure from Springfield for Washington (Muriel Kirkland, Raymond Massey)

Will Lee

1939-40

NICK'S PACIFIC STREET SALOON, on the Embarcadero in San Francisco, is William Saroyan's neon-lit version of the cosmos. As originally planned, the play's theme was to have been stated over a loudspeaker at the beginning of the first act. The speech was subsequently eliminated, but nevertheless it embodies Saroyan's theme:

"In the time of your life, live—so that in that good time there shall be no ugliness or death for yourself or for any life your life touches. Seek goodness everywhere, and when it is found, bring it out of its hiding place and let it be free and unashamed. Place in matter and in flesh the least of the values, for these are the things that hold death and must pass away. In the time of your life, live—so that in that wondrous time you shall not add to the misery and sorrow of the world, but shall smile to the infinite delight and mystery of it."

The play defies conventional synopsis, for it is deliberately random and fragmentary. Its principal

Julie Haydon, Edward Andrews, Eddie Dowling

Eddie Dowling, Julie Haydon, Edward Andrews

THE TIME OF YOUR LIFE

character is Joe, a gentle dreamer who has made Nick's saloon his headquarters. Joe's best friend is Tom, a simple, good-hearted young man who falls in love with Kitty Duval, a pathetic waterfront prostitute. Their idyll—and, indeed, the whole boozily warm camaraderie of the saloon—is menaced by Blick, a detective who is a sadistic bully. At the end of the play, Blick is killed offstage by Kit Carson, an aged eccentric given to telling tall tales about his gaudy past, such as the time he fell in love with a 39-pound midget. With Blick's death, the cancer that has begun to threaten the saloon is removed, and life can once more be lived in all of its eccentric glory.

The spice and delight of *The Time of Your Life* lie not in its ragtag plot but in its assortment of picturesque grotesques—Kit Carson, Willie the slot-machine addict, piano-playing Wesley, and the gloomy Arab whose sole comment on civilization is his often-repeated "no foundation, all the way down the line."

THE CREDITS

A PLAY IN THREE ACTS BY WILLIAM SAROYAN.
PRODUCED BY THE THEATRE GUILD, IN ASSOCIATION WITH EDDIE DOWLING.
STAGED BY EDDIE DOWLING AND WILLIAM SAROYAN, UNDER THE SUPERVISION OF THERESA HELBURN AND LAWRENCE LANGNER.
OPENED AT THE BOOTH THEATRE, OCTOBER 25, 1939, AND RAN FOR 185 PERFORMANCES.

THE CAST

NEWSBOY	Ross Bagdasarian
DRUNK	John Farrell
WILLIE	Will Lee
JOE	Eddie Dowling
NICK	Charles De Sheim
TOM	Edward Andrews
KITTY DUVAL	Julie Haydon
DUDLEY	Curt Conway
HARRY	Gene Kelly
WESLEY	Reginald Beane
LORENE	Nene Vibber
BLICK	Grover Burgess
ARAB	Houseley Stevens, Sr.
MARY L.	Celeste Holme
KRUPP	William Bendix
MCCARTHY	Tom Tully
KIT CARSON	Len Doyle
NICK'S MA	Michelette Burani
SAILOR	Randolph Wade
ELSIE	Cathie Bailey
A KILLER	Evelyn Geller
HER SIDE KICK	Mary Cheffey
A SOCIETY LADY	Eva Leonard Boyne
A SOCIETY GENTLEMAN	Ainsworth Arnold
FIRST COP	Randolph Wade
SECOND COP	John Farrell

TIME: *Afternoon and Night of a Day in October, 1939.*

ACT I

Nick's Pacific Street Saloon, Restaurant and Entertainment Palace at the Foot of the Embarcadero, San Francisco.

ACT II

Scenes 1 and 3, Same as Act I. Scene 2, Room in the New York Hotel, San Francisco.

ACT III

Same as Act I.

Len Doyle, Eddie Dowling

William Bendix, Tom Tully

Edward Andrews, Julie Haydon

"A prose poem in ragtime with a humorous and lovable point of view. . . ."

William Saroyan has been carrying on a pair of public love affairs, with Life and with William Saroyan, ever since the Thirties, when the publication of *The Daring Young Man on the Flying Trapeze* served notice that a strange new talent had shouldered its way onto the literary scene—a talent undisciplined, boozy, egotistical, and utterly individual.

In his early writing days Saroyan lived in San Francisco with his mother and sister, writing a story a day in an unheated room, bundled up in a heavy wool sweater, with the radio blaring and the floor around him littered with torn manuscripts. Although he wrote his stories in English, he painstakingly translated them all into Armenian, for his mother's benefit.

His first Broadway play was *My Heart's in the Highlands*, produced by The Theatre Guild in the

In this Don Freeman drawing, author and co-director William Saroyan perches on the orchestra rail at rehearsal, script in hand, cigarette in mouth, Armenian gleam in eye.

spring of 1939. Those few theatregoers who saw it during its six-week run were either enchanted or enraged. Eddie Dowling (enchanted) met Saroyan at the Critics' Circle dinner that year, and told him he'd buy his next play sight unseen. Six days later, Saroyan gave him the script of *The Time of Your Life*, then entitled *Sunset Sonata.*

"That really means six days—and thirty years," Saroyan later said in a *Boston Herald* interview. "After all, the stuff in the play has been gathering ever since I was old enough to see and feel life. This isn't a 'play' in the accepted sense of the word. I think there isn't enough 'play' in plays. Something ought to be done about it, and that's what I'm trying to do. You might just as well call plays 'mechanics,' because that's what most of them have become."

No one could conceivably have called *The Time of Your Life* a "mechanic"; it was one of the least mechanical plays ever produced commercially, a splendidly sprawling hodgepodge with the self-assurance of a drunken peacock.

The Time of Your Life had one of the oddest pre-Broadway tours on record. George Jean Nathan, the critic for *Newsweek*, had developed a paternalistic interest in Saroyan: he read the playwright's new scripts, and even gave him advice on casting problems. Nathan, who had admired *The Time of Your Life* in manuscript, made an unorthodox trip to New Haven to see how things were going with his protégé's latest effort. He found they weren't going well at all, and said so in a *Newsweek* column, printed before the play's Broadway opening:

"I have in my thirty-odd years of theatrical reconnaissance seen some voluptuous botches, but I have seldom seen one that surpassed the Guild's preparation of this particular exhibit."

Meanwhile, up in Boston, the "voluptuous botch" was being ripped apart and completely rebuilt. In New Haven the play had had highly stylized costumes and settings, which must have looked great on paper, but which looked ludicrous on stage. These came out. Director Robert Lewis was replaced by the new directorial team of Dowling and Saroyan. All of Lehman Engel's incidental music was jettisoned. Almost half the cast was replaced. During that two-week Boston engagement Saroyan, Dowling, and two Theatre Guild directors, Lawrence Langner and Theresa Helburn, worked frantically around the clock, with old patent attorney Langner even designing a new pinball machine that erupted gloriously with flags and music when a player finally hit the jackpot.

Everybody knows you *can't* rewrite and restage a full-length play in two weeks, but apparently nobody had told this to the dedicated workers up in Boston. The all-new *Time of Your Life* hit Broadway like a fist. On opening night, playwright George S. Kaufman was in the audience. At the first intermission an excited girl came up to him in the lobby.

"Are you Mr. Saroyan?" she asked.

"I wish I were," said Kaufman.

Eddie Dowling, Edward Andrews

Some of the notices:

Richard Watts, Jr., in the *Herald Tribune*:

"Mr. Saroyan's new play is a delight and a joy. A sort of cosmic vaudeville show, formless, plotless and shamelessly rambling, it is a helter-skelter mixture of humor, sentimentalism, philosophy and melodrama, and one of the most enchanting theatrical works imaginable. Often enormously funny, often tremendously touching but always heartily and richly alive, the new Saroyan work is a dramatic composition of beauty and originality that has the great virtue of possessing a heart. Beautifully played by Mr. Dowling and an excellent cast, it is an honor to American dramatic writing."

Brooks Atkinson in *The New York Times*:

"William Saroyan's *The Time of Your Life* is only a reverie in a bar room, without much story and none of the nervous excitement of the theatre. Nothing holds this sprawling drama together except Mr. Saroyan's affection for the tatterdemalions who are in it. But his affection is no casual sentiment. It has the force of a genuine conviction about people. It is innocent at heart and creative in art. Beautifully acted by Eddie Dowling in a bar-fly role, *The Time of Your Life* is something worth cherishing—a prose poem in ragtime with a humorous and lovable point of view."

Richard Lockridge in the *Evening Sun*:

"*The Time of Your Life* is ambling and almost plotless; fantasy and gags and nitwit stories bound together very lightly with melodrama. It is two-thirds sheer delight; a third mere fumbling. And it is not for worlds to be missed. It doesn't matter a hoot what *The Time of Your Life* is all about. Just about people being alive, maybe."

John Mason Brown in the *Evening Post*:

"William Saroyan's new play offers an uncommon and delightful experience in theatregoing. It is at once gleeful and heartbreaking, tender and hilarious, probing and elusive. Formless or not, Mr. Saroyan's script has enormous vigor. It has beauty, too. And its compassion is as irresistible as its humor is gay or its insight is exceptional. To respond to *The Time of Your Life* one does not have to know precisely what it is about. One only has to be willing to feel. Its people are not greasepaint creations. They have blood in their veins, real air in their lungs, and joy in their hearts."

John Chapman in the *Daily News*:

"Did you ever go out on a party and get very tight and have all sorts of amusing things happen—and never, from the next day on, quite remember what made it so much fun? So it is with Mr. Saroyan's *The Time of Your Life*. It is screwy, it is chopped-up, one or two of its scenes are pretty bad letdowns and only the most serious of the playgoers will try to read a weighty message into it. But on the whole I think it is exciting theatre."

John Anderson in the *Evening Journal*:

"Altogether, the play makes up an amusing and provocative evening, rich in color and texture, and full of a fresh, undisciplined talent, that makes Saroyan his own best friend and the theatre's newest hope."

Wolcott Gibbs in *The New Yorker*:

"The trouble with Mr. Saroyan, generally speaking, is his impression that the entire content of any man's mind automatically becomes a great play when produced on the stage; his virtue is that for rather more than half the evening you are apt to believe the same thing yourself."

Saroyan rejected the Pulitzer Prize and returned the $1,000 check, the only playwright ever to do so. It was not that he didn't agree with the judges (he thought he had written "a good, perhaps great theatrical work"), but he did not like being patronized by wealth.

"I would be no more guilty of bad taste," he said, "if I made an annual William Saroyan award to one or another of the great magnificently organized industries for most effectively profiting more than any other similar industry during the year. I do not know why, but I am sure such an industry would not be proud of my recognition of its great skill in accumulating profits."

The Pulitzer Prize committee shrugged off the rejection, and the award stood. *The Time of Your Life* also won the Critics' Circle Award. This was the first year (there were subsequently to be many more) in which the critics agreed with the Pulitzer committee.

ALSO-RANS: *Life With Father, The Male Animal, The Man Who Came To Dinner, Morning's At Seven*

SUMMATION

In this decision, sentiment seems to have carried the day. Granting *The Time of Your Life*'s ragamuffin appeal, worthier plays were brushed aside: *Life With Father* was an endearing and sturdy piece of Americana, and *The Male Animal* wrapped a trenchant plea for academic freedom in a delightful web of Thurber-Nugent dialogue. A debatable choice.

Charles De Sheim, Eddie Dowling, Gene Kelly

(Center) *Alfred Lunt*

1940-41

THE PLAY'S FIRST ACT IS SET IN 1938, in the Helsinki home of Dr. Kaarlo Valkonen, a world-famous neurologist who has won the Nobel Prize. He has an American-born wife, Miranda, and one son, Erik. Much of the act is taken up by a radio talk that Dr. Valkonen broadcasts to America, condemning Hitler. Finland is still at peace.

A year later, Erik is planning to marry his fiancée, Kaatri, even though Soviet invasion seems imminent. Erik will fight if war comes. So will his father, for that matter; although Dr. Valkonen is convinced that fighting means a renouncement of all his scientific training, he grimly points out that "even a scientist must try to put out a fire that threatens his laboratory." Kaatri reveals that she is pregnant, and is reluctant to bring the baby into the war-torn world of 1939, but the Valkonens insist that she go through with the pregnancy.

Some months later, the Russo-Finnish war is on. Erik has been killed, and Kaatri is sent to America with her child. While Dr. Valkonen is at an outpost near Viipuri, close to the advancing Soviet lines, he hears of his son's death. The doctor then straps on a revolver and goes out to meet his own death.

Back at the Valkonen home in Helsinki, a shaken Miranda sits with Kaarlo's Uncle Waldemar. Her son is dead, and her husband too, but Miranda has no intention of leaving Helsinki. When the Russians come she will burn the beautiful house, and then she and Uncle Waldemar will take rifles and go out into the garden for a last stand.

Shown at rehearsal: Playwright Robert E. Sherwood, Richard Whorf, Lynn Fontanne, Alfred Lunt, Sydney Greenstreet

THERE SHALL BE NO NIGHT

THE CREDITS

A DRAMA IN THREE ACTS BY ROBERT E. SHERWOOD.
PRODUCED BY THE PLAYWRIGHTS' COMPANY, IN ASSOCIATION WITH THE THEATRE GUILD, INC.
STAGED BY ALFRED LUNT.
OPENED AT THE ALVIN THEATRE, APRIL 29, 1940, AND RAN FOR 115 PERFORMANCES.

THE CAST

DR. KAARLO VALKONEN	Alfred Lunt
MIRANDA VALKONEN	Lynn Fontanne
DAVE CORWEEN	Richard Whorf
UNCLE WALDEMAR	Sydney Greenstreet
GUS SHUMAN	Brooks West
ERIK VALKONEN	Montgomery Clift
KAATRI ALQUIST	Elisabeth Fraser
DR. ZIEMSSEN	Maurice Colbourne

(Far Left) *Sydney Greenstreet.* (Far Right) *Lynn Fontanne, Alfred Lunt*

MAJOR RUTKOWSKI	Edward Raquello
JOE BURNETT	Charles Ansley
BEN GICHNER	Thomas Gomez
FRANK OLMSTEAD	William Le Massena
SERGEANT GOSDEN	Claude Horton
LEMPI	Phyllis Thaxter
ILMA	Charva Chester
PHOTOGRAPHERS	Ralph Nelson
	Robert Downing

ACTS I and II

Living Room of the Valkonens' House in Helsinki. October, 1938, to January, 1940.

ACT III

SCENE 1. *Dave Corween's Rooms, Hotel Kamp, Helsinki. February, 1940.*

SCENE 2. *Classroom in School House Near Viipuri Bay.*

SCENE 3. *The Valkonens' Living Room.*

HISTORY AND REVIEWS

"A moving play, thoughtfully written and beautifully played, but marred, and gravely marred, by inconclusiveness. . . ."

On Christmas Day of 1939, playwright Robert E. Sherwood was at home in his Sutton Place apartment, listening to the radio, when he heard a broadcast by William L. White from the Finnish front-line defenses on the Karelian Isthmus. The program's title was "Christmas on the Mannerheim Line," and it described the embattled Finns celebrating the holiday as best they could, with a Christmas tree strung from a tent pole, festooned with a few cheap celluloid ornaments which danced in the concussion of the Russian artillery.

Strongly moved, Sherwood began thinking about a play which would have the Finns as its heroes. At the time he was working on a revision of his own *Acropolis*, a 1935 failure in London. He put it aside (forever, it turned out), but told no one about the new idea. He began writing on January 15, and had his first draft finished by February 10; the play simply poured out of him, in an angry torrent. He originally intended to call it *Revelation*, and did take his final title from the Bible's Book of Revelations:

"And they shall see His face; and His name shall be in their foreheads. And there shall be no night there; and they need no candle, neither light of the sun; for the Lord God giveth them light: and they shall reign forever and ever."

At the time, Alfred Lunt and Lynn Fontanne, Sherwood's old cronies from *Reunion in Vienna* and *Idiot's Delight*, were finishing up an engagement in *The Taming of the Shrew*, having tacked on an extra week during which they were devoting their receipts, appropriately enough, to Finnish War Relief. Lunt's stepfather, Dr. Karl Sederholme, was a Finn, and Lunt had been in the habit of visiting Finland since his boyhood.

Sherwood took the play backstage to the Lunts on Saturday night and left it with them, saying only: "Here's a new play. I've got to catch a train." The Lunts also had a train to catch that night, as they were going out to their country home in Genosee Depot, Wisconsin, for a brief vacation. Once they had settled into their compartment, Miss Fontanne (ladies first) got first crack at the manuscript. At Harrisburg she wired Sherwood:

"This half of the combination returns in two weeks for rehearsals."

It was then Lunt's turn to read it. He did, staying up all night, and in the morning at Chicago he sent his own wire:

"So does this half."

The venture had a number of "labor of love" aspects. Lunt staged the play, but would take no directorial fee. The Theatre Guild contributed several thousand dollars' worth of electrical equipment, for which the production was never charged; and for the first four weeks of the run, Sherwood split his considerable royalties between the Red Cross and Finnish Relief.

There Shall Be No Night was the first Pulitzer Prize play which did not have Americans as protagonists—Richard Whorf did play an American correspondent, but the role was a comparatively minor one. This did not actually contradict the Pulitzer terms, which called for a play "preferably" dealing with American life, and fifteen years later, in the season of 1955–56, *The Diary of Anne Frank* was to slip smoothly through the same loophole.

The play gave Sherwood his third Pulitzer Prize, following as it did such previous winners as *Idiot's Delight* and *Abe Lincoln in Illinois*. It was the last drama award he was to win, and gave him a record second only to Eugene O'Neill's four prizes.

Some of the notices:

Brooks Atkinson in *The New York Times*:

"As a play *There Shall Be No Night* is no masterpiece; it has a shiftless second act and less continuity of story than one likes to see. It does not hang together particularly well. But as acted by Mr. Lunt and Miss Fontanne with thoroughly awakened sincerity it is on the whole enormously impressive.

Alfred Lunt, Richard Whorf, Lynn Fontanne, Elisabeth Fraser, Sydney Greenstreet, Montgomery Clift

Alfred Lunt, Elisabeth Fraser, Lynn Fontanne

Lynn Fontanne, Elisabeth Fraser, Maurice Colbourne

Lynn Fontanne,
Alfred Lunt

Out of the bottom of his heart Robert E. Sherwood has faced the philosophy of the war today with the best council of which a man of principle is capable. Although *There Shall Be No Night* is uneven drama, it honors the theatre and the best parts of it speak for the truth with enkindling faith and passionate conviction."

Richard Lockridge in the *Evening Sun*:

"*There Shall Be No Night* is a moving play, thoughtfully written and beautifully played by Alfred Lunt, Lynn Fontanne and the others in the cast. But it is marred, and I think gravely marred, by inconclusiveness. Its human story is moving and real; its speculations interesting but rather confused and perhaps not very profound. Mr. Sherwood has written beautifully and with intensity. I wish he had thought longer, and more slowly."

Richard Watts, Jr., in the *Herald Tribune*:

"*There Shall Be No Night* is not a tidy nor a consistent play. Yet it is a play of stature, dignity and high emotion, thoughtful, eloquent and heartfelt, and it is brilliantly acted by the Lunts and an admirable cast. It has something of great contemporary import to say to what we call our civilization, and it speaks from both the mind and the heart."

Burns Mantle in the *Daily News*:

"*There Shall Be No Night* is a drama of our time, of the day before yesterday, into which has been poured not only the burning convictions of the author, but the impassioned and truly begotten personal sympathies of its leading players. It seems to me, therefore, that it is an outstanding contribution, not only to this particular theatre season, but to this particular time in the history of a fumbling world. *There Shall Be No Night*, accepted as preachment or stage play, is a masterly work stirringly projected."

John Anderson in the *Journal-American*:

"It is an absorbing play, written with passionate indignation, and though it loiters now and then in its dialogue and turns its plot a little neatly, it holds power and emotion and a sense of outrage that seems even more unbelievable because we know it is true. The fact that this is all recent history has several curious effects on the play. The end, of course, is a foregone conclusion. Several scenes are heightened by the immediacy of the drama in the off-stage world, and others falter slightly because we are asked to accept in the theatre material we can't comprehend outside it. As reportorial drama *There Shall Be No Night* is selective, vivid and stirring."

George Jean Nathan in *Newsweek*:

"It is honest, sincere, heartfelt, generally dignified, of passionate resolve, brave in intent, and thor-

Montgomery Clift, Elisabeth Fraser, Lynn Fontanne, Alfred Lunt

Lynn Fontanne, Montgomery Clift, Alfred Lunt

oughly high-minded, but somehow, at least to one observer, as drama defective, inconclusive, and inert."

John Chapman, in his column in the *Daily News*:

"This journalist found *There Shall Be No Night* quite on the pretentious side—as though Zoe Akins had written *Journey's End*."

Many people read into *There Shall Be No Night* an indirect plea for American intervention in World War II, although Sherwood denied that that had been his intention. Even if the play had been meant as such a plea, the message was stated vaguely enough to provoke the critics into remarks about "inconclusiveness," as noted above.

There Shall Be No Night made two tours after its brief Broadway run. The first tour, beginning in the fall of 1940, was uneventful, but the second one, which opened on October 15, 1941, had its problems. Four months earlier Hitler had invaded Russia, and Finland was now fighting at the German dictator's side. *There Shall Be No Night* closed abruptly in mid-week in Rochester, Minnesota, shortly after Pearl Harbor was attacked on December 7, 1941. The Playwrights' Company made this announcement:

"In view of the current world situation that finds Finland enrolled, reluctantly enrolled in all likelihood, but nevertheless enlisted as an ally of the Axis Powers, the best interests of this country would be served through the termination of the tour."

There Shall Be No Night did turn up in London a couple of years later, but by then its leading characters had had their names changed. The new version dealt with the Italian invasion of Greece, a much less controversial subject under the circumstances.

ALSO-RANS: *Watch on the Rhine* (see Summation below), *Native Son, Lady in the Dark, Claudia*

SUMMATION

An obviously emotional decision, and a poor one; the wartime climate swept *There Shall Be No Night* into a prize that it did not deserve. A much finer play, Lillian Hellman's *Watch on the Rhine*, opened on April 1, 1941, and may thus have technically missed the 1940–41 Pulitzer deadline by one day; the critics, however, considered the Hellman play as part of the 1940–41 season, and gave it their own award. Orson Welles' muscular *Native Son* was the most spectacular theatrical firework of the season, but was too melodramatic to be Prize material.

Peter Fernandez, Eric Roberts, Paul Lukas, and Anny Blyth in Watch on the Rhine

1941-42

NO AWARD

Lillian Hellman's *Watch on the Rhine*, a powerful and touching anti-Fascist play that managed to make its point without preaching, should by all rights have won hands down this year. It had opened on April 1, 1941, and by general theatre standards belonged to the 1940–41 season (it won the New York Drama Critics' Circle Award for that period), but by the Pulitzer yardstick it was a 1941–42 play, and as such well deserved the Prize.

Among the other plays, *In Time to Come* was a moderately successful study of Woodrow Wilson's heartbreaking involvement with the League of Nations, and John Steinbeck's *The Moon Is Down* set up a curiously bloodless conflict between the gentle mayor of a European village and a Nazi "villain" only a little less correct than Lord Chesterfield. *Junior Miss* was the season's comedy hit, but was not Pulitzer material. Neither was Maxwell Anderson's *Candle in the Wind*, nor the Kaufman-Ferber *The Land Is Bright*.

Fredric March

1942-43

Florence Reed

IN OUR TOWN Thornton Wilder compressed the world into a New England village; in *The Skin of Our Teeth* he chose a broader canvas, nothing less than the entire sweep of human history.

All of the classical unities are scrambled in this play; anachronisms abound, time and space are bent to the author's will, and a deadly serious story is told in terms of hoked-up farce.

The leading characters are Mr. and Mrs. George Antrobus; their children, Henry and Gladys; and their maid-of-all-work, Lily Sabina, who serves the play as Mistress of Ceremonies, filling much the same function as the Stage Manager in *Our Town*.

In Act One the Antrobuses successfully fight their way through the Ice Ace; as the glaciers crunch along toward Excelsior, New Jersey, Mr. Antrobus triumphantly invents the wheel and the alphabet, and discovers the number "one hundred." At the end of the act Sabina is pleading with the members of the audience to pass their chairs up to the stage, to replenish the fire that is holding back the ice.

Director Elia Kazan, producer Michael Myerberg

Tallulah Bankhead

THE SKIN OF OUR TEETH

Act Two is set on the boardwalk at Atlantic City. Young Henry (rather obviously representing Cain) is on the run from the police, having hit a man with a stone. Mr. Antrobus, now President of the Order of Mammals, Subdivision Humans, dallies for a while with Sabina, who has turned up as a beauty contest winner. This escapade is interrupted by the Flood, which has been predicted by a raffish old Fortune Teller. The ominous red balls of a hurricane signal are raised; in thunder and lightning, Mr. Antrobus sets off in a boat with his family and two animals of each kind.

In Act Three the War is over, any war. The setting is the battered Antrobus home. Father and son, bitter enemies now, grudgingly let themselves be reconciled by Sabina, who has become a uniformed camp-follower. Sitting in the ruins of his world, Mr. Antrobus finds the strength to start building again; he and the human race have escaped catastrophe after catastrophe by the skin of their teeth, and there is nothing to do but simply to hope and to go on. Sabina finally tells the audience to go home—after all, as she says, the play goes on for ages.

Florence Eldridge, Frances Heflin, Fredric March, Tallulah Bankhead

THE CREDITS

A Fantastic Comedy in Three Acts by Thornton Wilder.
Produced by Michael Myerberg.
Staged by Elia Kazan.
Opened at the Plymouth Theatre, November 18, 1942, and ran for 359 performances.

THE CAST

Sabina	Tallulah Bankhead
Mr. Fitzpatrick	E. G. Marshall
Mrs. Antrobus	Florence Eldridge
Dinosaur	Remo Buffano
Mammoth	Andrew Ratousheff
Telegraph Boy	Dickie Van Patten
Gladys	Frances Heflin
Henry	Montgomery Clift
Mr. Antrobus	Fredric March

DOCTOR	Arthur Griffin
PROFESSOR	Ralph Kellard
JUDGE	Joseph Smiley
HOMER	Ralph Cullinan
MISS E. MUSE	Edith Faversham
MISS T. MUSE	Emily Lorraine
MISS M. MUSE	Eva Mudge Nelson
USHERS	Stanley Prager
	Harry Clark
GIRLS	Elizabeth Scott
	Patricia Riordan
FORTUNE TELLER	Florence Reed
CHAIR PUSHERS	Earl Sydnor
	Carroll Clark
CONVENEERS	Stanley Weede
	Seumas Flynn
	Aubrey Fassett
	Stanley Prager
	Harry Clark
	Stephan Cole
BROADCAST OFFICIAL	Morton Dacosta
DEFEATED CANDIDATE	Joseph Smiley
MR. TREMAYNE	Ralph Kellard
HESTER	Eula Belle Moore
IVY	Viola Dean
FRED BAILEY	Stanley Prager

ACT I

Home, Excelsior, New Jersey.

ACT II

Atlantic City Boardwalk.

ACT III

Home, Excelsior, New Jersey.

HISTORY AND REVIEWS

"A play which is part circus and part comically mad allegory,
a play which jumbles all times and all places together. . . ."

When Thornton Wilder first began to write *The Skin of Our Teeth*, a play whose theme was to be the indestructibility of man, he decided that it would be insufferably pompous to treat such a serious subject with the gravity it seemed to call for. Farce was the proper approach, he felt. In his first draft the two leading characters were identified as Pa and Ma. Pa spent the whole last act in a hammock, and when he was finally ready to die, a roller-skating maid brought him a little tin bucket, which he promptly and vigorously kicked. Ed Wynn was to play Pa, with Fannie Brice as Ma.

To its everlasting regret, Broadway was denied that particular treat, but in the version of *The Skin of Our Teeth* that was ultimately produced Wilder did manage to come up with a dazzling show that played hob with every available unity of time or space.

Anachronism was piled upon anachronism. A messenger entered with a singing telegram while the Ice Age descended upon a modern New Jersey home, and Tallulah Bankhead implored the paying customers in the audience to burn their seats, to keep the cold away. Fredric March, as Mr. Antrobus, the play's battered but dauntless hero, mastered both the Wheel and the Alphabet during one busy day at the office. The Flood trapped the entire cast on the Atlantic City boardwalk, where a Bingo game was in progress.

What's that cute little animal? A dinosaur. And who's that nice-looking old gentleman standing over there in the corner? Plato, that's who. That's the kind of play *The Skin of Our Teeth* was—outrageous, unpredictable, making its own rules and then promptly breaking them, careening along through the millennia as man survived fire and flood and war "by the skin of his teeth." Flawed here and there by a kind of folksy pedantry (with Mr. Wilder being too much the deliberately unbuttoned don, having his joke), *The Skin of Our Teeth* was nevertheless blithe and bracing. Many theatregoers were baffled by it; some hated it; more, many more, simply relaxed and enjoyed it.

Some of the notices:

John Anderson in the *Journal-American*:

"By setting down the story of the human race in the terms of a sort of cosmic vaudeville, Thornton Wilder has turned out an odd, often provocative, and sometimes richly amusing play. The plight of the

Montgomery Clift

Frances Heflin, Fredric March, Montgomery Clift

human race if taken comically ought to produce laughter beyond tears, ought to spring from a valiant humor that rises above tragedy. Yet it seems to me that the fun is too often superficial, that it touches no serious depths of emotion, so that the play fails to reach the wrenching intensity for which its laughter should be a profound release. It has a funnypaper inventiveness which finally gets in the way of what Mr. Wilder is trying to say. Eliza Kazan has directed the players with great energy and perception. Fredric March plays Mr. Antrobus with deep sincerity and simplicity. Florence Eldridge is better at the fatuous humors of the eternal housewife than with the rest of it, and Florence Reed provides a vivid and fascinating sketch of a boardwalk fortune teller. Tallulah Bankhead is irresistibly comic and entertaining, but when she is out of sight the play sags badly, and loses its fragile atmosphere of sophisticated innocence."

Richard Lockridge in the *Evening Sun*:

"Thornton Wilder turns handsprings through history in *The Skin of Our Teeth.* He celebrates the persistence of man against all odds in a play which is part circus and part comically mad allegory, a play which jumbles all times and all places together, introduces a New Jersey couple who have been married 5,000 years and throws off sparks like a pinwheel. *The Skin of Our Teeth* is funny and tonic; it is one of the theatre's lively jokes. And don't let the term 'allegory' frighten. *The Skin of Our Teeth* is as easy to enjoy as a circus. No homework is required. It is not profound, nor does it pretend to be. It is comedy, outrageous and unexpected and full of tricks. Rather often the gay mood is not fully sustained;

Florence Eldridge

once or twice the author can be detected giving nonsense a worried shove. But by and large *The Skin of Our Teeth* seems to me a fresh and delightful jest."

Burns Mantle in the *Daily News*:

"I couldn't promise that you will enjoy *The Skin of Our Teeth*, knowing nothing of your reactions to fantastic comedy, but I can say, with conviction, that I think you will be sorry if you do not see it. It is quite sure to prove the supreme novelty of this theatre season. Last night's audience laughed a lot and cheered a little."

Lewis Nichols in *The New York Times*:

"Thornton Wilder has wrtiten a comedy about man which is the best play the Forties have seen in many months, the best pure theatre. Tallulah Bankhead is magnificent—breezy, hard, practical by turns. As of last evening the theatre was looking up. Definitely."

Howard Barnes in the *Herald Tribune*:

"Theatregoing became a rare and electrifying experience last night. Viewed merely as a prank, *The Skin of Our Teeth* is frequently amusing, but often wearisome. Contemplated as a sometimes stuttering but splendidly sincere attempt to make some sense out of this poor old world, it is a challenging and unforgettable communication between a group of artists and spectators. *The Skin of Our Teeth* is a bit crazy, but it is a vital and wonderful piece of theatre."

Wilella Waldorf in the *Evening Post*:

"*The Skin of Our Teeth* actually is neither a profound nor particularly impressive drama. It is merely a stunt show with everything tossed into it that the author could dream up. Like all wacky extravaganzas it doesn't always come off, and it is occasionally rather dull, but the evening is saved by some good performances in the leading roles."

Remo Buffano, Tallulah Bankhead, Andrew Ratousheff

A fine brouhaha erupted after *The Skin of Our Teeth* won the Pulitzer Prize. Henry Morton Robinson, a senior editor of the *Readers' Digest*, and Professor Joseph Campbell, of Sarah Lawrence College, lodged a formal protest with the Pulitzer Prize committee, describing the award as "a committee whitewashing of Wilder's literary grave-robbing," and complaining that the play was "a bold and unacknowledged appropriation of the late James Joyce's *Finnegans Wake*."

In two separate articles in the *Saturday Review of Literature* (December 19, 1942 and February 13, 1943) the Messrs. Robinson and Campbell, co-authors of a book called *A Skeleton Key to Finnegans Wake*, had cited more than fifty "deadly parallels" between the Wilder play and the Joyce book. Wilder, one of the world's most renowned authorities on Joyce, chose to make no public comment. Said Robinson: "He probably has a reason for not answering, and if so I am interested to know what it is."

Actually, Wilder did take note of the Robinson–Campbell charges, affably making an attempt to refute them in a few informal remarks he made to the cast of *The Skin of Our Teeth* at a backstage party. He said, in substance, that his play contained ideas that were sprinkled all through literature. Certainly Joyce had also used a great many of them—most of them were essential if you were writing any sort of Everyman story. He implied that if he cared to, he could take most of the alleged parallels cited by Robinson and Campbell and trace them to even more obscure sources. Wilder even pointed out a couple of things that his critics had overlooked. Longfellow had never written a poem called *The Star*, quoted in the play; *The Star* had simply sounded to Wilder like a good Longfellow title. And a passage credited in the play to Plato had really been written by Wilder himself; he had combed Plato's works, hadn't been able to find as apt a quotation as he wanted, and so had written a brief paragraph in Plato's style.

The *Finnegans Wake* controversy cost Wilder the Critics' Circle Award. When those gentlemen met in solemn session, they were prepared to give their own prize to *The Skin of Our Teeth* when one of them uneasily brought up the Joyce matter. It turned out that nobody could speak knowledgeably about *Finnegans Wake*, for not one of them had read more than brief portions of it. The critics decided not to take any chances; they played safe and gave their prize to Sidney Kingsley's *The Patriots*, which was about as far away from Joyce as a play can get.

ALSO-RANS: *The Patriots, The Eve of St. Mark, Tomorrow the World*

SUMMATION

A good choice, and not a particularly unorthodox one, despite *The Skin of Our Teeth*'s clown face. Wilder was an established author who had already won one Pulitzer Prize for drama, which tended to make his present foolery "respectable"; also, the opposition was scarcely formidable.

As the Slate Brothers (Left) *and Red Buttons* (Right) *do an imitation of the Andrews Sisters, playwright-director Moss Hart gets into the act, in this shot taken at a* Winged Victory *rehearsal.*

1943-44

NO AWARD

This wartime year was one of the poorest seasons on record and produced nothing worthy of the Prize. Moss Hart's *Winged Victory*, a huge popular success, was simply a lavish primer on Air Force training. The only other possible candidate, Lillian Hellman's *The Searching Wind*, condemned the appeasers and politicians who had been responsible for two world wars, but lacked the forcefulness of her near-miss of two years before, *Watch on the Rhine*.

Rodgers and Hammerstein's *Oklahoma!* (which had opened on March 31, 1943, late enough for the Pulitzer judges to consider it as part of the following season) was given a "special citation of excellence," but was not eligible for the Prize, having been based on an earlier play, Lynn Riggs's *Green Grow the Lilacs*.

Josephine Hull

1944-45

ELWOOD P. DOWD is a gentle, boozy man of forty-seven who lives with his widowed sister, Veta, and her daughter, Myrtle May, in a fine old-fashioned mansion. The mansion's other boarder is Harvey, a giant rabbit who is Elwood's best friend and constant companion. Harvey is usually invisible to everyone except Elwood, although Veta has managed to catch a couple of glimpses of him.

Elwood's preoccupation with Harvey makes living in the Dowd home difficult for Veta and her daughter, and Veta would like to have Elwood committed to Chumley's Rest, a sanitarium. Elwood willingly goes out there with her to look the place over, but through a misunderstanding it is Veta, not Elwood, who gets plunged into hydrotherapy.

Elwood spends an evening on the town with Dr. Chumley and Harvey, and Chumley, after seeing the rabbit himself, becomes much friendlier with Elwood. However, Veta still wants Elwood to be given a shock treatment that will banish Harvey once and for all, and she finds a strong ally in Dr. Sanderson, Chumley's assistant.

Elwood, always a man to be obliging, is willing to take the shock treatment and abandon Harvey, if this will make Veta happy. Just as Elwood is about to be treated, though, Veta has a sudden change of heart. If Harvey means so much to her brother, she reasons, why should they be forced to give each other up? At the final curtain Elwood and Harvey stroll off arm in arm, inseparable as ever.

HARVEY

Frank Fay

THE CREDITS

A Comedy in Three Acts by Mary Coyle Chase.
Produced by Brock Pemberton.
Staged by Antoinette Perry.
Opened at the 48th Street Theatre, November 1, 1944, and ran for 1,775 performances.

THE CAST

Myrtle Mae Simmons	Jane Van Duser
Veta Louise Simmons	Josephine Hull
Elwood P. Dowd	Frank Fay
Miss Johnson	Eloise Sheldon
Mrs. Ethel Chauvenet	Frederica Going
Ruth Kelly, R.N.	Janet Tyler
Marvin Wilson	Jesse White

LYMAN SANDERSON, M.D.	Tom Seidel
WILLIAM R. CHUMLEY, M.D.	Fred Irving Lewis
BETTY CHUMLEY	Dora Clement
MR. PEEPLES	Lawrence Hayes
JUDGE OMAR GAFFNEY	John Kirk
E. J. LOFGREN	Robert Gist

ACTS I and II

SCENE 1. *The Library of the Old Dowd Family Mansion in a City in the Far West.*

SCENE 2. *Reception Room of Chumley's Rest.*

ACT III

Chumley's Rest.

HISTORY AND REVIEWS

"The greatest intemperance document that the American stage has ever offered. . . ."

With the possible exception of Hamlet's father and Peter Pan's Tinker Bell, Harvey must have been the most famous invisible character ever to "appear" on a stage. He was also, without a doubt, the only rabbit who ever had a play named after him. A sturdy 6 feet 1½ inches tall, affectionate and amiably philosophical, Harvey was the confidant and drinking companion of one Elwood P. Dowd, a gentleman in more or less constant need of a drinking companion.

This peculiar but altogether engaging animal sprang from the vivid imagination of 37-year-old Mary Coyle Chase, a Denver newspaperwoman who early in her career had been the most accomplished picture stealer on the *Rocky Mountain News*. Picture stealers insinuate themselves into households that have somehow become involved in messy news stories, and walk out with photographs of either the criminal or the victim. It is an occupation requiring equal parts of guile, charm and nerve. Miss Chase, Irish and comely, was well equipped with all three.

It took her two years to write *Harvey*, working at her dining room table in Denver with a miniature stage propped up in front of her, and manipulating empty spools to simulate the movements of her various characters. When she had been a pigtailed little girl her three Irish uncles, Pete, Tim and Jamie, had spun her tales about "pookas," who appeared in Celtic mythology as the spirits of large animals. A pooka had a way of scraping up an acquaintance with any friendly person who happened to catch his fancy, and this struck Miss Chase as a dandy springboard for a play. *Harvey*, in fact, was originally titled *The Pooka*, and was first copyrighted as *The White Rabbit*.

Over those two years, Miss Chase wrote three separate versions of *Harvey*. In the first one, the pooka was a man-sized canary; in the second, the canary had become a rabbit, but the central character of the play was a woman. It was not until the third version that Elwood P. Dowd finally emerged in all his tipsy masculine splendor.

Harvey was produced by Brock Pemberton, who seven years earlier had sponsored a Chase flop called *Now You've Done It*. Pemberton soon found that he was dealing with an authoress who knew just what she wanted. In a letter to him some six months before the Broadway opening, Miss Chase said:

"The thing that concerns me most is the overall impression of the play. It must be bold humor, with a folk-lore quality to it. It must be the kind of production about which the audience would say later, 'It's a play about a man who goes around with a 6-foot white rabbit,' rather than 'It's a play about a woman who tries to get her brother in a sanitarium.' That is my main concern—that it does not pull any punches, that it does not sacrifice its integrity, and that the laughs are deep and rooted in truth—that it has genuine humor instead of gags, and that it gives the audience genuine satisfaction."

Pemberton first offered the play to Harold Lloyd, but Lloyd had never had any stage experience, and bowed out rather than face the rigors of Broadway so late in his career. The role of Elwood went to an ex-vaudevillian, Frank Fay, a famous M.C. of the Twenties who for the past few years had been a virtual hermit on his $250,000 California estate. Rarely have role and actor blended more happily.

When *Harvey* had its pre-Broadway tryout in Boston, Pemberton insisted that the imaginary rabbit become visible in at least one scene. Miss Chase was appalled, but Pemberton persuaded her that his idea should be tried once, at a special preview that was being given for soldiers. He bought a $650 rabbit suit, and an actor was duly stuffed into it and sent trotting across the stage for five seconds at the end of the second act. It ruined the play. The suit was retired after its lone taste of glory, having cost Pemberton a cool $130 per second. Harvey never again appeared in the flesh.

Some of the notices:

John Chapman in the *Daily News*:

"*Harvey* is the most delightful, droll, endearing, funny and touching piece of stage whimsey I ever saw, and in it Frank Fay gives a performance so perfect that forever hence he will be identified with the

Frank Fay, playwright Mary Coyle Chase, producer Brock Pemberton

character he plays, as was Joseph Jefferson with Rip van Winkle and Frank Bacon with Lightnin' Bill Jones."

Howard Barnes in the *Herald Tribune*:

"Fantasy has charm and infinite delight in *Harvey*. The new play is as wise as it is witty; as occult as it is obvious. It is full of laughter and delicate meaning. It is stage sorcery at its whimsical best. A lively and utterly charming show. Frank Fay's performance of the bum is memorable; Josephine Hull's daffy dowager is a performance not to be missed."

Lewis Nichols in *The New York Times*:

"A very delightful evening—one of the treats of the fall theatre. Frank Fay and Josephine Hull are providing the last word in acting."

Burton Rascoe in the *World-Telegram*:

"I can't recall that I ever laughed so hard and so continuously at any show as I did last night at the opening of *Harvey*. The whole fantasy is delicious, subtle, clever and very funny."

Louis Kronenberger in *PM*:

"*Harvey*, for all its shortcomings, gave me the pleasantest theatrical lift I have had in a long time. The play itself is often wonderfully funny, and occasionally touched with something that goes deeper than fun. Frank Fay is superb. To say that nobody else could have done it better is to say nothing; so far as I can see, nobody else could have done it at all. *Harvey* has a first act that keeps going way too long, and a last act that, in a sense, can't keep going at all. But on a Broadway so given to staleness, it is a refreshing play."

Time Magazine:

"The funniest and most likable fantasy that Broadway has seen in years."

The New Yorker:

"A work of pure enchantment—touching, eloquent, and lit with a fresh, surprising humor that has nothing to do with standard comedy formulas. The funniest play in town."

A dissent from Wilella Waldorf in the *Post*:

"Elwood is a delightful fellow and Harvey is an entrancing, though invisible rabbit. But the vehicle their creator has knocked together for them to wander around in is a slipshod farce in which all of the other characters are stock figures hacked rather crudely out of a very low grade of theatrical cardboard."

George Jean Nathan had a few amusing comments to make in the *Journal-American* after the Pulitzer Prize had been awarded.

"The present terms of the Pulitzer Award," said Nathan, "are for 'an original American play, performed in New York, which shall represent in marked fashion the educational value and power of the stage, preferably dealing with American life.' " Nathan was willing to admit that *Harvey* was original, that it dealt with American life, that it had been performed in New York, and that it represented the power of the stage. "But," he went on, "that it represents in marked fashion the educational value of the stage, at least in the accepted Pulitzer intent and meaning, is enough to make the Bartender's Union laugh its combined head off. The educational value of *Harvey*, which is a delightful fantastic farce-comedy, consists simply and solely, as everybody but the Pulitzer judges by this time knows, in the instruction that it is far more contributive to human happiness to be good and drunk, and to stay good and drunk, than it is to be dismaliy sober. The play is the greatest intemperance document that the American stage has ever offered."

During its four-year run, *Harvey* pretty much took over Fay's whole life, both inside the theatre and out. His dressing room was awash with all sorts of rabbits, both live and stuffed; his telephone answering service was forever coping with messages that Harvey had called; and whenever he made a reservation at a restaurant, he was bound to find that the waiter had set an extra place, usually a small plate containing some lettuce and a carrot, for the ubiquitous rabbit. Fay got monumentally bored with the offstage whimsey after a while, but gamely put up with it to the end. After all, not many actors ever get a chance to be bored for *four* long years.

The success of the play naturally enriched Miss Chase beyond her rosiest dreams. She and her husband had been on such a thin financial edge that they had borrowed $300 from a Denver bank in order to get to New York for the opening. She never had to do *that* again.

ALSO-RANS: *The Glass Menagerie, A Bell for Adano, The Late George Apley, Anna Lucasta, I Remember Mama, Soldier's Wife*

SUMMATION

An unorthodox selection (who would ever have thought that the Pulitzer Prize would be awarded to a paean to drunkenness?), and a poor one. Despite *Harvey*'s undeniable charm, the Prize should have gone to Tennessee Williams' *The Glass Menagerie*, the warmest and most poetic play that this talented author has yet written.

Playwrights Howard Lindsay and Russel Crouse

1945-46

Grant Matthews, a successful airplane manufacturer with a rugged, forceful personality, is regarded by political boss Jim Conover as a possible Republican candidate for President. Before committing himself to supporting this candidacy, however, Conover would first have Matthews make a series of informal speeches across the country. It will soon become apparent, Conover feels, how the public takes to this strangely compelling political greenhorn.

For a year Matthews has been carrying on a casual affair with Kay Thorndyke, publisher of a string of newspapers. When this comes to Conover's attention he is quick to insist that Mary, Matthews' estranged wife, accompany him on the proposed tour, to quash any rumors about his private life.

Mary is shrewd enough to realize that she is being used, but tours with her husband anyway. Her salty observations do much to deflate his regrettable tendency toward pomposity, and when Matthews is briefly induced to temporize in some of his speeches, so that various powerful factions shall not be antagonized, it is Mary who finally convinces him that he must determine to be his own man, whatever the consequences.

As the play ends it is obvious that Mary has won her husband back from Kay, and while his nomination is still questionable, it is strongly implied that the party's politicians may be forced to take Matthews on his own terms.

Ralph Bellamy, Myron McCormick, George Spelvin, Ruth Hussey, George Bradley, Lew Thomas, Minor Watson

STATE OF THE UNION

THE CREDITS

A Comedy in Three Acts by Howard Lindsay and Russel Crouse.
Produced by Leland Hayward.
Staged by Bretaigne Windust.
Opened at the Hudson Theatre, November 14, 1945, and ran for 765 performances.

THE CAST

James Conover	Minor Watson
Spike McManus	Myron McCormick
Kay Thorndyke	Kay Johnson
Grant Matthews	Ralph Bellamy
Norah	Helen Ray
Mary Matthews	Ruth Hussey
Stevens	John Rowe

Ralph Bellamy, Ruth Hussey

BELLBOY	Howard Graham
WAITER	Robert Toms
SAM PARRISH	Herbert Heyes
SWENSON	Fred Ayres Cotton
JUDGE JEFFERSON DAVIS ALEXANDER	G. Albert Smith
MRS. ALEXANDER	Maidel Turner
JENNIE	Madeline King
MRS. DRAPER	Aline McDermott
WILLIAM HARDY	Victor Sutherland
SENATOR LAUTERBACK	George Lessey

ACT I

SCENE 1. *Study in James Conover's Home in Washington, D.C.*
SCENE 2. *Bedroom in Conover's Home.*

ACT II

Living Room of a Suite in Book-Cadillac Hotel in Detroit.

ACT III

Living Room of the Matthews' Apartment in New York City.

HISTORY AND REVIEWS

"An adult, witty play about politics, spiced with verbal jabs and wisecracks. . . ."

Howard Lindsay and Russel Crouse were for years one of Broadway's most successful teams, a superbly matched pair of theatrical carpenters, with Lindsay as the constructor, nailing up the planks, and Crouse as the ebullient funny man, painting the trim. *State of the Union* brought them their first Pulitzer Prize, an honor many observers thought they should have won some years before, with their 1939–40 *Life With Father.*

Lindsay, 57 when *State of the Union* opened, had originally been an actor, and made his New York stage debut in *A Young Man's Fancy*, starring Jeanne Eagels. He soon turned director, with such plays and musicals as *Dulcy*, *To the Ladies*, *The Poor Nut*, *Anything Goes*, *The Gay Divorce*, *Red, Hot and Blue,* and *Hooray for What.* As a playwright, he collaborated with Bertrand Robinson on *Tommy*, *Your Uncle Dudley* and *Oh, Promise Me*, then did a solo adaptation of *She Loves Me Not.* He returned to acting with *Life With Father*, when producer Oscar Serlin failed in his attempts to get Walter Huston for the leading role. Lindsay, drafted as a last resort into his own comedy, played Father Day for many years at New York's Empire Theatre, with Mrs. Lindsay, Dorothy Stickney, opposite him as Mother.

Crouse, an Ohio boy, was 52 in 1945. He started off as a reporter for the Cincinnati *Commercial Tribune* and the Kansas City *Star*, wrote a column called "Left at the Post" for the New York *Post*, and served a five-year term as press agent for The Theatre Guild. Crouse's only acting assignment was the role of Bellflower in *Gentlemen of the Press*, although in later years he long nursed a secret ambition to walk on as Dr. Findlay in *Life With Father*, and actually did so at one performance, sporting a fine set of prop whiskers. His explanation: "I wanted to see if there was a doctor in the Crouse."

Lindsay and Crouse owed their first association to a shipwreck. Back in the fall of 1934, *Anything Goes*, with William Gaxton, Victor Moore and Ethel Merman, was about to go into rehearsal under Lindsay's direction when the *Morro Castle* tragically burned and sank off Asbury Park. Unfortunately, the original plot of *Anything Goes* dealt with the jolly complications of a fire at sea. A new book was called for, but the show's authors, Guy Bolton and P. G. Wodehouse, were unavailable. Lindsay agreed to help rewrite the book himself, if a suitable collaborator could be found; Crouse was tapped for the job, and the partnership was born. It was to endure for over thirty years, with the men remaining the closest of personal friends, and ended with Crouse's death in 1966; it provided Broadway with a long string of successes either written or produced by the partners.

Among other shows, Lindsay and Crouse produced *Arsenic and Old Lace* (Crouse once remarked to Boris Karloff, when Karloff burped during a lunch they were sharing: "Someone you ate, no doubt"), *Detective Story* and *The Hasty Heart.* Their *Life With Father* ran longer than any other production in Broadway history (3,133 performances, from 1939 to 1946), and their sentimental book for *The Sound of Music* helped make that somewhat saccharine show one of the biggest musical hits ever.

Lindsay was forced to return briefly to acting during *State of the Union's* pre-Broadway tour; in Detroit, Minor Watson came down with laryngitis, and Lindsay stepped into the 50-side role of James Conover, the longest one in the play, for two performances.

The original title of *State of the Union* was *I'd Rather Be Left*, a switch on the title of the Kaufman–Hart musical satire of five years earlier, *I'd Rather Be Right.* Lindsay and Crouse always had a fondness for punning titles, viz., *Strip for Action* and *Remains to be Seen*, one a story about a burlesque troupe, the other a comedy-melodrama.

In awarding the Prize to *State of the Union*, the Pulitzer committee once more demonstrated its fondness for shows with political backgrounds. This was the third one to be anointed; the first of the three had been *Of Thee I Sing*, followed the next season by *Both Your Houses.* A few years later, with remarkable consistency, they were to give the award to *Fiorello!*

Some of the notices:

Lewis Nichols in *The New York Times*:

"With wonderfully funny lines and situations, this new comedy about politics also has enough sentiment to keep it from being farce, enough idea to show that its heart is in the right place. Probably *State of the Union* will not do away with the party system in America, but it has at least driven away the dark clouds hovering over the theatre. Since a couple of states are usually out of step at election time, set down part of the second act as being too peaceful for comfort. But *State of the Union* wins by a landslide nevertheless."

Howard Barnes in the *Herald Tribune*:

"A literate and amusing comedy has come to the Hudson to renew one's wavering faith in the theatre. *State of the Union* is that happy combination of wit and sense which makes playgoing the delight it should be. Howard Lindsay and Russel Crouse have written it wisely and well, fashioning a political satire which is as good-humored as it is pertinent. They have threaded it with engaging, and sometimes touching human relationships. Ralph Bellamy, Minor Watson and Myron McCormick are all three perfect for their parts. Ruth Hussey is wonderfully good, and Kay Johnson brings a brittle brilliance to her role. *State of the Union* speaks out loud about things that need stating. It does so with gayety and conviction."

Wilella Waldorf in the *Evening Post*:

"Reports from the tryout tour must have led you to believe that *State of the Union* was the sensation of the decade. It isn't. It's just a good show. We advise you to see it, but we also think it would be a good idea not to rush to the Hudson under the impression that a great, stupendous drama has come to town. *State of the Union* starts a bit slowly but once it gets under way it gains momentum fast. The third act is particularly diverting and also pretty exciting stuff."

Minor Watson, Myron McCormick, Ralph Bellamy, Kay Johnson

Myron McCormick,
Ralph Bellamy, Ruth Hussey

Ralph Bellamy,
Myron McCormick, Ruth Hussey

Myron McCormick, Ralph Bellamy, Minor Watson, Kay Johnson

Burton Rascoe in the *World-Telegram*:

"It is entertaining; it is nice on the eyes and ears; it is instructive, witty, wise and bright. A very enjoyable and instructive evening in the theatre. This is a play worth your attention."

John Chapman in the *Daily News*:

"An adult, witty play about politics. At its best, *State of the Union* examines the American political system with high-humored cynicism, and the play is spiced with verbal jabs and wisecracks. At its worst it is a shade too long and its pace falters, particularly in the third act. But considering the overall excellence of *State of the Union*, this trouble is minor."

Ward Morehouse in the *Evening Sun*:

"A brisk, entertaining and discerning play. Howard Lindsay and Russel Crouse have deftly woven politics, a domestic story and observations on the state of the union into a timely, topical and engaging piece of theatre."

State of the Union made such a point of being topical that one of its speeches was actually changed nightly. In a scene in the second act, Ralph Bellamy was called upon to read a newspaper headline to Ruth Hussey. The headline was always chosen from that particular day's evening paper.

ALSO-RANS: *Home of the Brave, The Magnificent Yankee, Deep are the Roots, Born Yesterday, Dream Girl*

SUMMATION

A satisfactory enough decision, although two or three other plays could with as much justice have been chosen. *Born Yesterday* was a marvelously funny indictment of corruption, and *Home of the Brave* was an effective war play which said some telling things about prejudice. *The Magnificent Yankee* took a loving look at a great American character, Oliver Wendell Holmes. *State of the Union* by an eyelash; no landslide. The Critics Circle gave no Best Play award this season. They did establish a separate new category, Best Musical, and chose *Carousel.*

Victor Sutherland, Kay Johnson, Aline McDermott, Ralph Bellamy, Minor Watson, Herbert Heyes, George Lessey, Maidel Turner, G. Albert Smith, Ruth Hussey

Carl Benton Reid, James Barton, Dudley Digges and Nicholas Joy in The Iceman Cometh

1946-47

NO AWARD

It is difficult to understand why no production was considered worthy of the Prize in 1946–47, for there were many outstanding candidates, and at least one of them could have held its own in any company. This was Eugene O'Neill's *The Iceman Cometh*, his first Broadway offering in years and a strikingly powerful, if discursive, study of man's desperate need for illusions. Ten years later *The Iceman Cometh* was revived with great success by the Circle in the Square, and was then finally accepted as a major work in the O'Neill canon. It seems unfortunate and unfair that it was not given its due when it first appeared.

Arthur Miller's *All My Sons* would have made an almost equally satisfactory winner, and did win the New York Drama Critics' Circle Award that season. Lillian Hellman's *Another Part of the Forest* took the rapacious Hubbards of *The Little Foxes* back a few years in time, and quite felicitously, but with no more Pulitzer luck than its famous predecessor had had. On the musical side, *Finian's Rainbow* was a marvelous blend of fantasy and social comment. The Critics' Circle chose the delightful *Brigadoon* as Best Musical.

Kim Hunter (Rear), *Jessica Tandy*

Producer Irene M. Selznick, playwright Tennessee Williams

1947-48

STANLEY KOWALSKI, an earthy young brute, lives with his wife, Stella, in a seedy section of New Orleans. An unexpected house guest arrives; she is Blanche Du Bois, Stella's older sister, a faded Southern belle with pathetic delusions of grandeur. Stanley and Blanche hate each other on sight.

The Kowalski household soon explodes. Stanley breaks open Blanche's trunk and strews her tattered finery around the room, and accuses her of financial trickery in her disposal of the old family plantation, Belle Reve.

Mitch, a poker-playing crony of Stanley's, is attracted to Blanche, and she dares to dream of marrying him. She tells him about the horror of her first marriage, at sixteen, to a homosexual who shot himself after Blanche found him with an older man. Mitch is sympathetic, but all of his sympathy vanishes after Stanley tells him a few sordid truths about Blanche's recent past—before coming to New Orleans, she

The final scene, as Blanche (Background) *is being led off to the asylum.*

A STREETCAR NAMED DESIRE

had been living in frantic promiscuity at the notorious Flamingo Hotel, after losing both her plantation and her teaching job.

Mitch cruelly rejects Blanche, in a scene in which he thrusts her aging face under the glare of a naked light bulb. Deranged, Blanche dresses up in an old white satin gown and a rhinestone tiara, and finds herself alone in the house with Stanley; Stella is in the hospital, having a baby. Blanche talks wildly of a Caribbean cruise that she plans to go on with an old admirer. Stanley mocks her, then brutally rapes her.

In the play's final scene, Stella is home from the hospital with her baby, not daring to believe Blanche's story of the rape, but desperate to get her sister out of the house as quickly as possible. A doctor and a matron appear to take Blanche away to an asylum, and Blanche goes with them quietly, almost timidly, remarking as she leaves that she "has always been dependent on the kindness of strangers." Stanley is comforting Stella as the curtain falls.

THE CREDITS

A PLAY IN THREE ACTS BY TENNESSEE WILLIAMS.
PRODUCED BY IRENE M. SELZNICK.
STAGED BY ELIA KAZAN.
OPENED AT THE ETHEL BARRYMORE THEATRE, DECEMBER 3, 1947, AND RAN FOR 855 PERFORMANCES.

THE CAST

NEGRO WOMAN	Gee Gee James
EUNICE HUBBEL	Peg Hillias
STANLEY KOWALSKI	Marlon Brando
STELLA KOWALSKI	Kim Hunter
STEVE HUBBEL	Rudy Bond
HAROLD MITCHELL (MITCH)	Karl Malden
MEXICAN WOMAN	Edna Thomas
BLANCHE DU BOIS	Jessica Tandy
PABLO GONZALES	Nick Dennis
A YOUNG COLLECTOR	Vito Christi
A STRANGE WOMAN	Ann Dere
A STRANGE MAN	Richard Garrick

The Action of the Play Takes Place in the Kowalski Apartment in the French Quarter in New Orleans.

ACT I

SCENE 1. *Early Evening.*
SCENE 2. *Six O'Clock the Following Evening.*
SCENE 3. *Later That Evening.*
SCENE 4. *Early the Following Morning.*

ACT II

SCENE 1. *Some Weeks Later.*
SCENE 2. *Later—About 2 a.m.*

ACT III

SCENE 1. *Some Weeks Later.*
SCENE 2. *Three-quarters of an Hour Later.*
SCENE 3. *A While Later That Evening.*
SCENE 4. *A Few Hours Later That Night.*
SCENE 5. *Some Days Later.*

HISTORY AND REVIEWS

"A genuinely poetic playwright whose knowledge of people is honest and whose sympathy is profoundly human. . . ."

Tennessee Williams was born Thomas Lanier Williams in Columbus, Mississippi, on March 26, 1911.

"I changed my name to Tennessee Williams," he once said, "because the Williamses had fought the Indians for Tennessee, and I had discovered that the life of a young writer was going to be similar to the defense of a stockade against a band of savages."

Williams sold his first short story when he was sixteen years old, receiving $35.00 for it from *Weird Tales*. It was borrowed from a passage in Herodotus, and was called *The Vengeance of Nitocris*. Nitocris was an Egyptian queen who prepared a banquet in a stone cellar for a number of her enemies, then opened a hidden sluice gate and let the Nile in to drown them all.

As he grew up Williams was by turn a bellhop, a movie usher, and a waiter in a Greenwich Village night club. In his spare time he wrote short stories and plays, and by 1939 he was serious enough about his playwriting to be studying at the New School Playwriting Seminar, under the supervision of Theresa Helburn and John Gassner. For the seminar he wrote a play called *Battle of Angels*, which The Theatre Guild decided was worth producing. It was not the happiest of decisions.

The Boston opening of *Battle of Angels*, in December of 1940, was a first-class fiasco, and at the very end of the play clouds of smoke from a simulated onstage fire billowed out into the auditorium, driving the choking and coughing audience into the street. The Boston critics were unkind, the City Councilor of Boston indignantly denounced the play as "putrid," and it was withdrawn two weeks later. The planned Broadway opening was abandoned. (Rewritten, and retitled *Orpheus Descending*, *Battle of Angels* finally did get to Broadway a number of years later. It would have been better for all concerned had it rested peacefully in Boston.)

Williams struggled along for the next few years, then scored his first major success with *The Glass Menagerie*. With Laurette Taylor giving one of the great performances of the American stage as a tattered Southern gentlewoman ("She floated through the play like a cork," said the *Chicago Tribune's* Claudia Cassidy), *The Glass Menagerie* established Williams immediately as one of America's leading playwrights. The production of *A Streetcar Named Desire* in late 1947 solidified that position.

A much more harsh and violent play than *The Glass Menagerie*, *A Streetcar Named Desire* was conceived while Williams was resting in a hospital during the *Menagerie* run, convalescing from a cataract operation. He had first thought of calling the new play *The Poker Night*, but soon switched to the other title. In the hospital he began reminiscing about his days in New Orleans as a waiter in the French Quarter. Two streetcar lines had run past his door, in opposite directions. The destination of the first line was DESIRE; of the second, CEMETERY. This ironic counterpoint pleased and attracted him, and the play began to take shape.

Some time later, Williams said:

"The dominant theme in most of my writings is that the most magnificent things in human nature are valor and endurance." The valor of *Streetcar's* faded heroine, Blanche Du Bois, was the component of

Marlon Brando, Jessica Tandy, Kim Hunter

Marlon Brando,
Kim Hunter, Jessica Tandy

the play that moved audiences most deeply, far more than the vivid theatrical brutishness of Stanley Kowalski, Blanche's tormentor and eventual nemesis.

Some of the notices:

Brooks Atkinson in *The New York Times*:

"Tennessee Williams has brought us a superb drama. And Jessica Tandy gives a superb performance as the rueful heroine whose misery Mr. Williams is tenderly recording. This must be one of the most perfect marriages of acting and playwriting. Like *The Glass Menagerie*, the new play is a quietly woven study of intangibles. But to this observer it shows deeper insight and represents a great step forward toward clarity. And it reveals Mr. Williams as a genuinely poetic playwright whose knowledge of people is honest and whose sympathy is profoundly human. Elia Kazan's direction is sensitive but concrete. Mr. Williams has not forgotten that human beings are the basic subject of art. Out of poetic imagination and ordinary compassion he has spun a poignant and luminous story."

Howard Barnes in the *Herald Tribune*:

"Tennessee Williams has written a savagely arresting tragedy. His dramatization of a woman's crack-up is a work of rare discernment and craftsmanship. Although it is almost explosively theatrical at times, it is crowded with the understanding, tenderness and humor of an artist achieving maturity. As is fitting, the play is afforded a superlative production. As a whole *A Streetcar Named Desire* has tremendous dramatic excitement, honesty and impetus, leaving a spectator properly limp at the ending. A memorable show."

Richard Watts, Jr., in the *Evening Post*:

"Tennessee Williams' new play is a feverish, squalid, tumultuous, painful, steadily arresting and oddly touching study of feminine decay along the lower Mississippi. Marlon Brando's portrayal of the heroine's sullen, violent nemesis is an excellent piece of work. Even finer, though, is Karl Malden, one of the ablest young actors extant, as the girl's sentimental and disillusioned admirer. Mr. Williams is an oncoming playwright of power, imagination, and almost desperately morbid turn of mind and emotion."

Marlon Brando, Nick Dennis, Rudy Bond, Karl Malden

Jessica Tandy, Marlon Brando

Jessica Tandy, Karl Malden

John Chapman in the *Daily News*:

"Tennessee Williams, a young playwright who is not ashamed of being a poet, has given us a superb drama. *The Glass Menagerie* was a fragment, a cameo. The new play is full-scale—throbbingly alive, compassionate, heart-wrenchingly human. It has the tragic overtones of grand opera. Blanche is a pitiful figure, and she is acted gloriously by Jessica Tandy."

Louis Kronenberger in *PM*:

"*A Streetcar Named Desire* is by all odds the most creative new play of the season—the one that reveals the most talent, the one that attempts the most truth. It carries us into the only part of the theatre that really counts—not the most obviously successful part, but the part where, though people frequently blunder they seldom compromise; where imagination is seated higher than photography; and where the playwright seems to have a certain genuine interest in pleasing himself. *A Streetcar Named Desire* is by no means always a good play. It falls down in places; it goes wrong in places. But what is right about it is, in today's theatre, rare. There is a willingness to be adventurous in the pursuit of truth."

Williams has always been happy, even eager, to write or talk at length about his plays and his creative philosophy. Here he is quoted in an interview that appeared in London in 1958:

"There is a crying, almost screaming need of a great world-wide human effort to know ourselves and each other a great deal better, well enough to concede that no man has a monopoly on right or virtue any more than any man has a corner on duplicity and evil and so forth. If people, and races and nations, would start with that self-manifest truth, then I think that the world could side-step the sort of corruption which I have involuntarily chosen as the basic, allegorical theme of my plays as a whole."

In 1960, he wrote in *The New York Times Magazine*:

"There are two kinds of creative work: organic and non-organic. It is possible to reform, to change the nature of a non-organic (synthetic) work in the arts, meaning that work which is produced through something other than a necessity as built in to the worker as his heartbeat and respiration. But you could flay the skin off a writer whose work is organic and you still would not get out of him a sincere or workable recantation of his faith in what he is doing, however abominable that work may be, or strike you as being."

(Opposite Page) *Marlon Brando, Jessica Tandy*

Years after its opening, *A Streetcar Named Desire* was still Williams' favorite among his plays. In the *Evening Post* of May 2, 1958, Robert Rice quoted the playwright as saying: "*Streetcar* said everything I had to say. It has an epic quality that the others don't have."

ALSO-RANS: *Mister Roberts, Command Decision, The Heiress, Allegro*

SUMMATION

An excellent choice. *Mister Roberts*, while one of the funniest plays of the past couple of decades, was simply not in the same league with *Streetcar* as far as genuineness of emotion was concerned. *Command Decision* was a good, solid job, but no match for the haunting Williams play.

Arthur Miller

1948-49

At sixty-three Willy Loman is a failure. Once a successful traveling salesman, he is now reduced to borrowing fifty dollars a week from a friendly neighbor and pretending to his wife, Linda, that it is his salary; he cannot find the courage to tell her that he has been fired. His two sons, Biff and Happy, are shallow and worthless.

For years Willy has hidden his inadequacies under a quick smile and a glib line of chatter, but with age these defenses have crumbled, and his mind begins to disintegrate. The play moves restlessly from the seamy present into Willy's pathetic memories, and then back into the present again, with fact and fantasy and recollections all woven into one tragic pattern.

Willy's relationship with his sons is thoroughly explored; in various scenes he roughhouses with them as children, encourages them to steal sand from a building project they have been working on, listens aghast as Biff confesses to stealing a pen from a prospective employer. In a dreadful scene in a Boston

Alan Hewitt, Lee J. Cobb

Arthur Kennedy, Lee J. Cobb, Cameron Mitchell

DEATH OF A SALESMAN

hotel, Biff happens to enter a room that his father is sharing with a stray pick-up, and any relationship that father and son may have had is instantly shattered.

Rich, tough, successful Uncle Ben tempts Willy to go make his fortune in Alaska, but Willy is too frightened to try anything new. One by one all of Willy's small dreams and pretenses are shattered, while Linda fights a brave but losing battle to keep her home together, and to keep her husband from slipping over the edge into final insanity.

At the end of the play's second act Willy is out in his back yard planting seeds, muttering about his twenty thousand dollar insurance policy, which may give Biff the fresh start that the boy needs. Willy then gets into his run-down Chevrolet and drives off to his death. In the Requiem which closes the play, Linda cannot cry at first, as she cannot get over the feeling that her husband is simply "off on a trip"; at last she sobs at the thought that their house is now paid for, after so many years, and that Willy will never come home to it.

Mildred Dunnock, Lee J. Cobb, Arthur Kennedy, Cameron Mitchell

THE CREDITS

A Play in Two Acts by Arthur Miller.
Produced by Kermit Bloomgarden and Walter Fried.
Staged by Elia Kazan.
Opened at the Morosco Theatre, February 10, 1949, and ran for 742 performances.

THE CAST

Willy Loman	Lee J. Cobb
Linda	Mildred Dunnock
Biff	Arthur Kennedy
Happy	Cameron Mitchell
Bernard	Don Keefer
The Woman	Winnifred Cushing
Charley	Howard Smith
Uncle Ben	Thomas Chalmers
Howard Wagner	Alan Hewitt
Jenny	Ann Driscoll
Stanley	Tom Pedi
Miss Forsythe	Constance Ford
Letta	Hope Cameron

The Action Takes Place in Willy Loman's House and Yard and in Various Places He Visits in the New York and Boston of Today.

HISTORY AND REVIEWS

"The play sweeps along like a powerful tragic symphony. . . ."

Both of its producers, Kermit Bloomgarden and Walter Fried, hated the title of *Death of a Salesman*. Too somber, they thought; and besides, wasn't it too plain a tip-off of the ending? Playwright Arthur Miller held firm. While the argument raged, a play called *The Smile of the World* opened on Broadway, to poor notices. Miller bundled up the reviews, took them to Bloomgarden's office, and tossed them on his desk.

"So much for happy titles," he said.

Gloomy title and all, *Death of a Salesman* went to Philadelphia to begin its pre-Broadway trials, and the play's very first performance in that city was a unique theatrical event. At the end of the performance, the audience refused to go home; half an hour after the final curtain people were still standing near their seats or milling around in the lobby, sledge-hammered by the impact of one of the most poignant tragedies of the modern theatre.

More than any other contemporary American play, *Death of a Salesman* captured the heartbreak and futility of a character destroyed by forces, both internal and external, that were too overwhelming for him to cope with. It was the threadbareness of Willy Loman's ambitions, as much as his failure to achieve them, that stabbed theatregoers with a horrid sense of self-awareness. Some observers felt that Willy was a pathetic rather than a tragic figure, that he tumbled from a sadly small height in a fall that was too prosaic for the deep sense of loss that tragedy should ideally engender. But any semantic hair-

Arthur Kennedy, Lee J. Cobb

Howard Smith, Lee J. Cobb

splitting between tragedy and pathos could not have mattered less to the play's enthralled audiences; they were moved by Willy as they had rarely been moved before.

Arthur Miller, 32 when he wrote *Death of a Salesman*, had already had two other plays on Broadway, a failure called *The Man Who Had All the Luck*, and the successful *All My Sons*, which had won the Critics' Circle Award back in 1946–47.

All My Sons was a tidily carpentered drama in the Ibsen tradition, built tightly inside a formal framework; *Death of a Salesman* could not have been more different. *Salesman* was as loose and fluid and shifting as a dream. Its quicksilver darting through time and space could have made for insane confusion; instead, the play emerged as a model of lucidity, the line of its narrative always clear. Elia Kazan's staging, and Jo Mielziner's eerily effective settings and lighting, combined with an original cast that could hardly have been improved upon, made *Death of a Salesman* a polished, professional triumph.

It had taken Miller only six weeks of intense work to write the play, and for all the gloom of the

subject matter, that work had actually been fun. Writing in *The New York Times* on the first anniversary of the Broadway opening, Miller said:

"I confess that I laughed more during the writing of this play than I have ever done, when alone, in my life. I laughed because moment after moment came when I felt I had rapped it right on the head—the non sequitur, the aberrant but meaningful idea racing through Willy's head, the turns of story that kept surprising me every morning. And most of all the form, for which I have been searching since the beginning of my writing life. Writing in that form was like moving through a corridor in a dream, knowing instinctively that one would find every wriggle of it and, best of all, where the exit lay.

"To me the tragedy of Willy Loman is that he gave his life, or sold it, in order to justify the waste of it. It is a tragedy of a man who did believe that he alone was not meeting the qualifications laid down for mankind by those clean-shaven frontiersmen who inhabit the peaks of broadcasting and advertising offices."

In this Don Freeman drawing, Arthur Kennedy sits at the table, while Mildred Dunnock restrains Lee J. Cobb

Thomas Chalmers, Lee J. Cobb, Howard Smith

Some of the notices:

Brooks Atkinson in *The New York Times*:

"Arthur Miller has written a superb drama. From every point of view *Death of a Salesman* is rich and memorable drama. It is so simple in style and so inevitable in theme that it scarcely seems like a thing that has been written and acted. For Mr. Miller has looked with compassion into the hearts of some ordinary Americans and quietly transferred their hope and anguish to the theatre. Under Elia Kazan's masterly direction, Lee J. Cobb gives a heroic performance, and every member of the cast plays like a person inspired. Mildred Dunnock gives the performance of her career as the wife and mother—plain of speech but indomitable in spirit. Mr. Miller's elegy in a Brooklyn sidestreet is superb."

Howard Barnes in the *Herald Tribune*:

"A great play of our day has opened. *Death of a Salesman* has majesty, sweep and shattering dramatic impact. As it has been staged by Elia Kazan and consummately performed by Lee J. Cobb, Mildred Dunnock, Arthur Kennedy and all their associates, it is a soaring tragedy. A terrible documentation has been leavened with bursts of wild humor and more than one moment of touching grandeur, while the fluent scenes build inexorably to the climax. With Jo Mielziner's inspired setting and lighting, the offering is theatre of the first order. Cobb contributes a mammoth and magnificent portrayal of the central character. *Death of a Salesman* is a play to make history."

Cameron Mitchell, Lee J. Cobb, Thomas Chalmers, Arthur Kennedy

John Chapman in the *Daily News*:

"*Death of a Salesman* is a very fine work in the American theatre. I cannot urge it upon you too strongly. To see it is to have one of those unforgettable times in which all is right and nothing is wrong."

William Hawkins in the *World-Telegram*:

"*Death of a Salesman* is a play written along the lines of the finest classical tragedy. Often plays have been written that crossed beyond physical actuality into the realm of memory and imagination, but it is doubtful if any has so skillfully transcended the real limits of time and space. The play sweeps along like a powerful tragic symphony. The actors are attuned to the text as if they were distinct instruments. Themes rise and fade, are varied and repeated. Again as in music, an idea may be introduced as a faint echo, and afterwards developed to its fullest part in the big scheme. It is hard to imagine anyone more splendid than Lee J. Cobb is as Willy Loman."

Richard Watts, Jr., in the *Evening Post*:

"Arthur Miller, who was revealed as a 'promising' playwright in his successful *All My Sons* a couple of seasons ago, reaches fulfillment as a dramatist of individuality and power in *Death of a Salesman*. Gone is Mr. Miller's rather labored obeisance to Ibsen, and in its place is a definite quality of his own, a kind of cold intellectual clarity mixed with simple and unashamed emotional force. Under Elia Kazan's vigorous and perceptive direction, *Death of a Salesman* emerges as easily the best and most important

Mildred Dunnock, Lee J. Cobb, Arthur Kennedy, Cameron Mitchell

new American play of the year. Set down with frank emotion, the new play is, I suspect, something to make strong men weep and think. It is a play not easily to be forgotten."

Perhaps by pure coincidence, but quite possibly because of the emotional depth of the role itself, both the London and New York Willy Lomans eventually withdrew from their respective companies, each pleading exhaustion. Lee J. Cobb on Broadway, and Paul Muni (making one of his rare stage appearances) in London, found that coping with Willy's problems night in and night out was just too much to take.

That first transfixed Philadelphia audience was later to find counterparts all over the world. After the Vienna opening, for instance, a critic wrote:

"As the lights came on after the final curtain, the people in the theatre sat in complete silence for a long moment and looked, with terror, into themselves. It has been a long time since we had that kind of experience in the theatre."

ALSO-RANS: *Anne of the Thousand Days, Detective Story, Life With Mother, The Silver Whistle*

SUMMATION

No contest. *Death of a Salesman* would have been a sure-fire winner in any season, so the fact that it happened to triumph over only moderate opposition didn't really matter. The play also won the Critics' Circle Award. *South Pacific* won the Critics' Best Musical award.

Lee J. Cobb, Mildred Dunnock

Arthur Kennedy, Winnifred Cushing, Lee J. Cobb

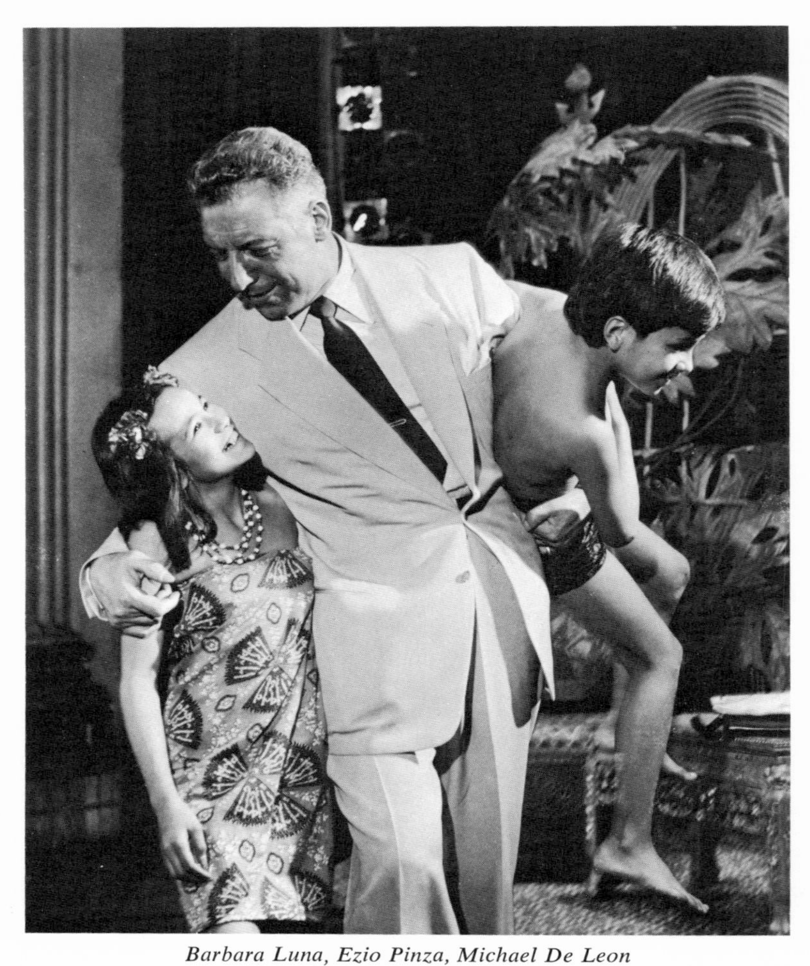

Barbara Luna, Ezio Pinza, Michael De Leon

(Opposite Page) *Director Joshua Logan, composer Richard Rodgers, librettist Oscar Hammerstein 2nd, Mary Martin, author James A. Michener*

1949-50

ALL OF THE ACTION takes place on two islands in the South Pacific, during World War II. One island is an outpost of the United States Navy, and also contains the plantation of Emile de Becque, a wealthy, middle-aged Frenchman. The other island, Bali H'ai, is peopled exclusively by natives.

De Becque and Ensign Nellie Forbush, a Navy nurse from Arkansas, fall in love, but Nellie breaks with him when she discovers that he already has two children by a Polynesian wife, who is now dead. De Becque volunteers for a dangerous mission on a neighboring island, and goes there with Lieutenant Joe Cable, a young Marine officer who has been carrying on a bittersweet, fruitless love affair with Liat, the lovely seventeen-year-old daughter of the formidable Bloody Mary.

Cable is killed on the mission, but de Becque successfully carries out his orders and then returns safely to his plantation, where a repentent Nellie is waiting for him.

South Pacific contains few choral numbers, and the other songs all flow directly out of the action. The major songs include "Some Enchanted Evening," "Bali H'ai," "There Is Nothin' Like a Dame," "Happy Talk," "Younger than Springtime," "I'm Gonna Wash that Man Right Outa My Hair," "I'm in Love with a Wonderful Guy," "You've Got to be Taught," "Honey Bun" and "This Nearly Was Mine."

SOUTH PACIFIC

THE CREDITS

A Musical Play in Two Acts by Oscar Hammerstein 2nd and Joshua Logan.
Based on James A. Michener's *Tales of the South Pacific.*
Music by Richard Rodgers. Lyrics by Oscar Hammerstein 2nd.
Produced by Richard Rodgers and Oscar Hammerstein 2nd,
in association with Leland Hayward and Joshua Logan.
Staged by Joshua Logan.
Opened at the Majestic Theatre, April 7, 1949, and ran for 1,925 performances.

THE CAST

Ngana	Barbara Luna
Jerome	Michael De Leon *or* Noel De Leon

Betta St. John, William Tabbert

HENRY	Richard Silvera
ENSIGN NELLIE FORBUSH	Mary Martin
EMILE DE BECQUE	Ezio Pinza
BLOODY MARY	Juanita Hall
BLOODY MARY'S ASSISTANT	Musa Williams
ABNER	Archie Savage
STEWPOT	Henry Slate
LUTHER BILLIS	Myron McCormick
PROFESSOR	Fred Sadoff
LT. JOSEPH CABLE, U.S.M.C.	William Tabbert
CAPT. GEORGE BRACKETT, U.S.N.	Martin Wolfson
CMDR. WILLIAM HARBISON, U.S.N.	Harvey Stephens
YEOMAN HERBERT QUALE	Alan Gilbert
SGT. KENNETH JOHNSON	Thomas Gleason
SEABEE RICHARD WEST	Dickinson Eastham
SEABEE MORTON WISE	Henry Michel
SEAMAN TOM O'BRIEN	Bill Dwyer
RADIO OPERATOR BOB MCCAFFREY	Biff McGuire
MARINE CPL. HAMILTON STEEVES	Jim Hawthorne
STAFF SGT. THOMAS HASSINGER	Jack Fontan
SEAMAN JAMES HAYES	Beau Tilden
LT. GENEVIEVE MARSHALL	Jacqueline Fisher
ENSIGN DINAH MURPHY	Roslyn Lowe
ENSIGN JANET MACGREGOR	Sandra Deel
ENSIGN CORA MACRAE	Bernice Saunders
ENSIGN SUE YAEGER	Pat Northrop
ENSIGN LISA MINELLI	Gloria Meli
ENSIGN CONNIE WALEWSKA	Mardi Bayne
ENSIGN PAMELA WHITMORE	Evelyn Colby
ENSIGN BESSIE NOONAN	Helena Schurgot
LIAT	Betta St. John
MARCEL, HENRY'S ASSISTANT	Richard Loo
LT. BUZZ ADAMS	Don Fellows

ISLANDERS, SAILORS, MARINES, OFFICERS: Mary Ann Reeve, Chin Yu, Alex Nicol, Eugene Smith, Richard Loo, William Ferguson.

The Action of the Play Takes Place on Two Islands in the South Pacific During the Recent War. There is a Week's Lapse of Time Between the Two Acts.

HISTORY AND REVIEWS

"I do not think it is first-night excess which causes me to hail it as one of the finest musical plays in the history of the American theatre. . . ."

Rodgers and Hammerstein's *South Pacific*, an unorthodox musical comedy (or "musical play," as it was identified in the program) that didn't even bother with a chorus line, was one of the biggest critical and financial successes in theatrical history, topping its authors' previous smashes, *Oklahoma!* and *Carousel.*

South Pacific was the first Pulitzer Prize play to be based upon a novel that had itself won the Pulitzer Prize, James A. Michener's *Tales of the South Pacific*. Ten years later, *All the Way Home* (derived from James Agee's *A Death in the Family*) was to hit the same double jackpot.

Producer Leland Hayward and director Joshua Logan were the first men to see the dramatic possibilities in the Michener book; they took it to Richard Rodgers, suggesting that he read it. He did so, and then passed it on to Oscar Hammerstein 2nd. With the two famous musicals cited above to their credit, they were already one of the most successful theatrical teams of the century. *South Pacific* was to sweep them to even greater heights.

In the *Saturday Review* of March 26, 1949, Rodgers was quoted by Irving Kolodin on the production's beginnings:

"Oscar and I were sitting around a swimming pool at Bel Air one morning. Up till that time we had been pondering the original story I read as the basis for the script. That's the one about Lieutenant Cable from Princeton and the Tonkinese girl Liat. 'Fo' Dolla' we were agreed is a good story; but could it carry a whole play without being *Madame Butterfly* all over again? An idea then came to treat this theme as subordinate, putting the heavier accent on the story ('Our Heroine') about the French planter and the nurse from Arkansas. Here was a mature man, away from Europe almost twenty years because he killed a man in a street fight, brought into contact with a typical American girl. How would they react? What would be their effect on each other? That was something to build on. That's where we started."

Mary Martin singing "Honey Bun"

Actually, *South Pacific* was based on three of the Michener stories that had been braided loosely together into *Tales of the South Pacific*: "Fo' Dolla," "Our Heroine" and "The Remittance Man."

For the French planter, Emile de Becque, they signed Ezio Pinza, a massive ex-bicycle rider who was the Metropolitan Opera's greatest basso, and who had never done a Broadway show before. For Nellie Forbush, the little Arkansas nurse, they decided on Mary Martin, who had made a blazing Broadway debut ten years earlier in *Leave It To Me*, when she sang "My Heart Belongs to Daddy." Miss Martin was reached by telephone in California, where she was winding up a year's tour as Annie Oakley in *Annie Get Your Gun*, an assignment that had lowered her voice half an octave below its usual range.

"Listen," said Miss Martin, when Rodgers told her that Pinza was to be her co-star, "what do you need two basses for?"

The famous *South Pacific* score was written much as Rodgers and Hammerstein had always written their songs, with Hammerstein struggling for days or even weeks over a single lyric, and with Rodgers then composing a tune for it in an incredibly short space of time; the melody for "Honey Bun" was written in twenty minutes, and that for "Bali H'ai" in only fifteen. Rodgers feels that this facility is not really very remarkable, and that it's unfair to say that he "works only a few minutes on a song"—the melody may have been simmering in the back of his mind for weeks, simply waiting for a chance to come to a boil.

Myron McCormick (Center) *leads a chorus of "There Is Nothing Like a Dame."*

South Pacific's only pre-Broadway problem consisted of an embarrassment of riches; when the show opened in New Haven it was fifteen minutes too long, but so tightly constructed that its authors couldn't figure out how to cut it. Emlyn Williams happened to be in town, as a guest of Joshua Logan. In the course of a single evening Williams sat down with a script and a copy pencil and whittled out ten minutes, a line here, a paragraph there, keeping the framework intact. Some weeks later the authors presented him with a pair of gold scissors and a gold-plated blue pencil, gratefully inscribed: "To Emlyn the Ripper."

Mary Martin

Ezio Pinza, Mary Martin

Some of the notices:

Brooks Atkinson in *The New York Times*:

"A magnificent musical drama. Essentially this is a tenderly beautiful idyll of genuine people inexplicably tossed together in a strange corner of the world; and the music, the lyrics, the singing and the acting contribute to this mood. Since we have all been more or less in love with Mary Martin for several years, it is no surprise to find her full of quicksilver, pertness and delight as the Navy nurse. Ezio Pinza's bass voice is the most beautiful that has been heard on a Broadway stage in an eon or two; he is also a fine actor. Fortunately, Mr. Rodgers and Mr. Hammerstein are the most gifted men in the business. And *South Pacific* is as lively, warm, fresh and beautiful as we had all hoped that it would be."

Howard Barnes in the *Herald Tribune*:

"A show of rare enchantment. It is novel in text and treatment, rich in dramatic substance, and eloquent in song. It is a long and prodigal entertainment, but it seems all too short. *South Pacific* is a musical play to be cherished."

Richard Watts, Jr., in the *Evening Post*:

"An utterly captivating work of art. I do not think it is first-night excess which causes me to hail it as one of the finest musical plays in the history of the American theatre. For a long time everyone has known that Mary Martin was exceedingly expert and charming in the ways of musical comedy. But nothing I have ever seen her do had prepared me for the loveliness, humor, gift for joyous characterization and sheer lovableness of her portrayal of Nellie Forbush. Hers is a completely irresistible performance. As for Ezio Pinza, the eminent refugee from opera, he, of course, sings delightfully. But he is far more than a fine singer. As the planter De Becque he emerges as an expert and charming actor, possessing rare romantic style."

Hobe Morrison in *Variety*:

"Rodgers and Hammerstein have not only done it again—they've topped themselves. *South Pacific* is one of the most enjoyable and satisfying musicals in theatre history. It's a tumultuous smash. Its score is one of Richard Rodgers' finest—possibly *the* finest. Oscar Hammerstein's lyrics are among his most graceful and moving. Joshua Logan's direction is superbly imaginative, flexible and paced."

Juanita Hall encourages Betta St. John and William Tabbert in "Happy Talk."

Ezio Pinza, Barbara Luna, Michael De Leon, Mary Martin

William Hawkins in the *World-Telegram*:

"This is the ultimate modern blending of music and popular theatre to date, with the finest kind of balance between story and song, and hilarity and heartbreak."

John Chapman in the *Daily News*:

"*South Pacific* makes a full, satisfying evening in the theatre. It is done with good taste by expert and ambitious showmen who are not afraid to dispense with old formulas and adopt a new one. It has a style of its own and this style gives it distinction. But it does not always fully realize its intentions. The libretto strikes me as being unwieldy in spite of Mr. Logan's clever staging. Mr. Michener's stories and characters have not been completely assimilated. Mr. Rodgers has provided some nice melodies, but this is by no means his most remarkable score. *South Pacific* is a very good musical which would be a success in any season. But it cannot measure up to *Carousel* as a work of art."

Time Magazine:

"Hammerstein and Logan have contrived a shrewd mixture of tear-jerking and rib-tickling, of sugar and spice and everything twice. Their musical play is far superior to the usual libretto nonsense; it is quite the equal, in fact, of the usual movie yarn. It is not the integrated work that Rodgers and Hammerstein's *Carousel* was. In *South Pacific* Rodgers' music provides only a score, not a scaffolding. His fine talent seemed far more individual when his musical shows had crunchy centers rather than gooey ones."

For the first couple of years of its run *South Pacific* was the "hottest" ticket that Broadway had ever known, and seats sold on the black market for fantastic premiums. Seven weeks after its opening, a general ticket scandal broke on Broadway, and it was revealed that single seats for the musical had been hawked for as high as $60.00. John M. Murtagh, City Commissioner of Investigation, began rumbling about the possibility of revoking the Majestic Theatre's license, but nobody took him very seriously. By then *South Pacific* was already a New York landmark; Murtagh might as well have been threatening to saw up the Statue of Liberty. The license was never revoked.

The *South Pacific* award was a popular one, as exemplified by this editorial in the *Herald Tribune*:

"Over 33 years a pattern has necessarily been set for the prizes, as in so many like and lesser contests. That a year can come when a play like *South Pacific* can stand above this pattern—a part of a great war framed in melody and tenderness and with more everlasting dramatic truth than often arrives behind Manhattan footlights—is to the credit of the American stage, the American heart and the board of Pulitzer awards."

ALSO-RANS: *The Member of the Wedding, Come Back, Little Sheba*

SUMMATION

An excellent choice; *South Pacific* was superlative theatre, and earned its honors. *The Member of the Wedding* was flawed by a weak third act, and *Come Back, Little Sheba*, William Inge's first Broadway play, was as drab as it was honest. Although *South Pacific* had actually opened in the previous season, its April 7 premiere came late enough to qualify it for the 1949–50 award. The Critics' Circle, having chosen *South Pacific* the previous season, cited *The Consul* as Best Musical and *The Member of the Wedding* as Best Play.

Mary Martin, Ezio Pinza

In Guys and Dolls, *Vivian Blaine and the Hot Box Girls get set to sing "A Bushel and a Peck"*

1950-51

NO AWARD

There were a number of productions that could have won the Prize this season with no questions asked. Chief of these was *Guys and Dolls*, a tart and tangy exploration of the never-never land of Damon Runyon's Broadway, crisp, professional, and blessed with a just-right book and a truly magnificent score.

Clifford Odets' *The Country Girl* dealt compassionately with the relationship between an alcoholic actor and his sturdy, no-nonsense wife; an award would have somewhat compensated Odets for the by-passing of *Awake and Sing* a dozen years earlier. Lillian Hellman was represented by *The Autumn Garden*, a thoughtful, literate play. Sidney Kingsley made an excellent dramatization of Arthur Koestler's *Darkness at Noon*. Tennessee Williams contributed *The Rose Tattoo*, a warmer play than his previous winner, *A Streetcar Named Desire*, but lacking *Streetcar*'s brutal theatrical intensity.

Any of the above could have won. The Drama Critics chose *Darkness at Noon* as Best Play and *Guys and Dolls* as Best Musical.

Playwright Joseph Kramm

1951-52

JIM DOWNS, a one-time successful theatrical director who has been reduced to earning money as an English tutor, is brought into City Hospital after a suicide attempt. Poverty, despair and a hopelessly unhappy marriage have driven him to take an overdose of barbiturates.

His estranged wife, Ann, comes to visit him in the ward, and it soon becomes apparent that she will go to any lengths to win him back and to reestablish his dependency upon her. It is at Ann's request that Jim is kept in the hospital for observation, making it impossible for him to keep an appointment for a promising new job.

Although Jim is obviously sane enough to be released, the obtuse hospital psychiatrists, influenced by Ann, refuse to recognize this. Ann, it turns out, has the power to request his discharge in her custody at any time, but he can only be discharged upon such a specific request. Ann is thus armed with an enormous weapon in her fight to make Jim pick up the threads of their loveless marriage.

After three weeks in the hospital, Jim realizes that he is trapped—for life. He sadly agrees to give up his old girl, Charlotte, forever; if Ann will sign the papers he will go back to live with her, on her terms. Helpless, broken, he is weeping as the final curtain falls.

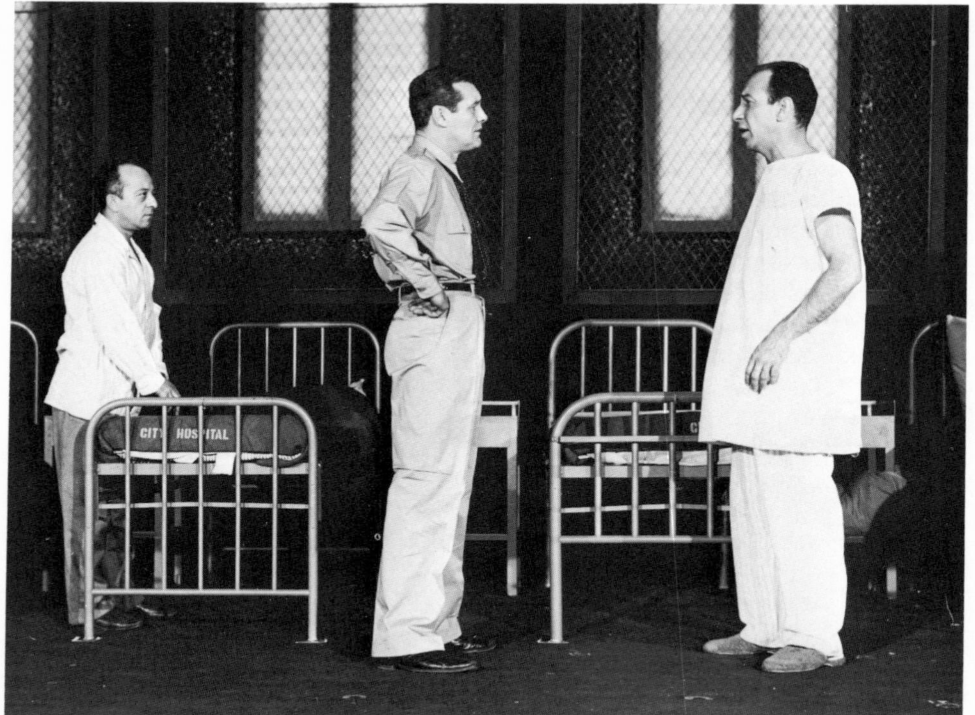

Will Lee, Philip Huston, and José Ferrer

THE SHRIKE

THE CREDITS

A PLAY IN TWO ACTS BY JOSEPH KRAMM.
PRODUCED BY JOSÉ FERRER, IN ASSOCIATION WITH MILTON BARON.
STAGED BY JOSÉ FERRER.
OPENED AT THE CORT THEATRE, JANUARY 15, 1952, AND RAN FOR 161 PERFORMANCES.

THE CAST

MISS CARDELL	Phyllis Hill
FLEMING	Tom Reynolds
MISS HANSEN	Jeannette Dowling
DR. KRAMER	Stephen Elliott
PERKINS	James Hawthorne Bey
GROSSBERG	William Bush

DR. BARROW	Isabel Bonner
PATIENT	Vincent Donahue
ANN DOWNS	Judith Evelyn
JIM DOWNS	José Ferrer
DR. SCHLESINGER	Somer Alberg
SAM TAGER	Will Lee
GEORGE O'BRIEN	Martin Newman
JOE MAJOR	Joe Comadore
DON GREGORY	Philip Huston
JOHN ANKORITIS	Will Kuluva
FRANK CARLISLE	Leigh Whipper
WILLIAM SCHLOSS	Billy M. Greene
DR. BELLMAN	Kendall Clark
MISS WINGATE	Mary Bell
HARRY DOWNS	Edward Platt
TOM BLAIR	Arthur Jarrett

All of the Action Takes Place in City Hospital.

José Ferrer, Judith Evelyn

ACT I

SCENE 1. *11:30 in the Morning—Tuesday.*
SCENE 2. *2:00 a.m., the Next Morning—Wednesday.*
SCENE 3. *Noon, Two Days Later—Friday.*
SCENE 4. *11:00 a.m., Three Days Later—Monday.*
SCENE 5. *Afternoon—Immediately Following.*

ACT II

SCENE 1. *Just Before Lunch—the Next Day—Tuesday.*
SCENE 2. *2:00 p.m., the Next Day—Wednesday.*
SCENE 3. *Close to 9:00 p.m.—the Same Day.*
SCENE 4. *2:00 p.m., the Next Day—Thursday.*
SCENE 5. *3:00 p.m., Five Days Later—Tuesday.*

ACT III

SCENE 1. *1:30 p.m., Two Days Later—Thursday.*
SCENE 2. *Afternoon, Four Days Later—Monday.*
SCENE 3. *2:00 p.m., Three Days Later—Thursday.*
SCENE 4. *10:00 a.m., the Next Day—Friday.*

HISTORY AND REVIEWS

"A cold and merciless examination of the processes by which an intelligent and normally sensitive human being can be utterly destroyed. . . ."

The Shrike was Joseph Kramm's first play, produced when its author was 44. A Philadelphian, he had turned to playwriting after a modest career as an actor, in such plays as *Bury the Dead*, *Processional*, *Golden Boy*, *Liliom* (the Ingrid Bergman–Burgess Meredith revival) and *Uncle Harry*.

Perhaps the most purely harrowing play ever to win the Pulitzer Prize, *The Shrike* was set in a city hospital, and detailed a man's systematic destruction by his wife, abetted by various psychiatrists. Most critics did not question its melodramatic power and theatrical effectiveness, but in at least one quarter (see Dr. Lawrence Kubie's letter, below) Mr. Kramm was called sharply to task for unfairly stacking the cards against his helpless protagonist.

The Shrike was in a sense a one-man triumph for José Ferrer, who produced and staged the play, and acted the leading role with enormous skill and vigor. Mr. Ferrer was all over Broadway in those days. Here is a brief summary of his activities in the thirteen months directly preceding the opening of *The Shrike*:

Produced, directed and acted one of leading roles in *Twentieth Century*.
Produced and directed *Stalag 17*.
Directed *The Fourposter*.
Acted in film, *Anything Can Happen*.
Did 11-week one-man Shakespeare show over radio station WNEW.
Recorded *Cyrano de Bergerac*, playing title role.
Worked on script of motion picture, *Moulin Rouge*.

Worked on Broadway script of *The Musical Comedy Man* (never produced).
Produced, directed and acted leading role in *The Shrike.*
Whew!

Some of the notices:

Walter Kerr in the *Herald Tribune*:

"*The Shrike* is a cold and merciless examination of the processes by which an intelligent and normally sensitive human being can be utterly destroyed. It is a relentless, bitter and clinical piece of stage work, and the way José Ferrer is playing it, Joseph Kramm's study in cannibalism packs the wallop of a pile-driver. Mr. Ferrer is downright magnificent; without him, *The Shrike* might well be in trouble. Judith Evelyn performs a small miracle as the blood-sucking wife, in intimating the savagery and the single-mindedness of this woman at the same time that she creates, inexplicably, some sympathy for herself. *The Shrike* is a cold-blooded piece of theatrical manufacture, but there is tremendous fire in its performances."

Brooks Atkinson in *The New York Times*:

"*The Shrike* is a plausible melodrama that is likely to scare the living daylights out of you. According to the program, the shrike is a 'predatory bird.' Since there is no malice in the shrike, only a fondness for slaughter, Mr. Kramm's title is not really apposite. But that is the only reservation this column has about Mr. Kramm's economically written melodrama. Mr. Ferrer has staged it with relish, and he plays it with power and dexterity."

John McClain in the *Journal-American*:

"This will probably be a highly controversial offering. I would score it a clean hit, however, since I will defy anybody to come away from the Cort without a strenuous opinion on the merits of the play—and the pleasant realization that it was, after all, just a nasty nightmare."

John Chapman in the *Daily News*:

"*The Shrike* is an odd play, a good play, and a fascinating play. Its first performance at the Cort Theatre last evening has left me emotionally frazzled. It is not a pastime, but an experience—a grim experience. I repeat, *The Shrike* is no pastime—but if you see it you will not soon forget it."

Richard Watts, Jr., in the *Evening Post*:

"Out of what is clearly a deep and impassioned conviction, Joseph Kramm has written a grim and harrowing play about a man tormented in a psychiatric ward, which he calls *The Shrike*, and which the amazingly talented José Ferrer produced, staged and acted in superlatively at the Cort Theatre last night. You will certainly not have a pleasant evening at *The Shrike*, but you are likely to have an enthralling one."

George Jean Nathan in the *Journal-American*:

"Mr. Kramm's main story often gets lost and has a time of it getting back on its feet again. The writing, moreover, though here and there not without some melodramatic power, is elementary. But almost everything else about the exhibit is so excellent that the play takes on a superficial aspect of being very much better than it is. José Ferrer's performance is top-notch acting; Judith Evelyn's evil wife is managed with uncommon intelligence; the many other characters are every one of them close to perfect. Everything, in a word, represents the theatre at its most proficient—everything, that is, but the play upon which such affectionate effort has been expended. It is all much like an elaborately wrapped and beribboned large package delivered by a flashing coach and four, which when opened and peered into discloses under the wealth of fancy paper only a small firecracker."

In a remarkable letter to *The New York Times* on March 16, 1952, two months after the play's opening, Dr. Lawrence S. Kubie, Clinical Professor of Psychiatry at the Yale University School of Medicine, wrote as follows:

"Every attempted suicide confronts the psychiatrist with questions which occur to him automatically and at once. Was the suicide due to a transient panic or to one which will recur? Was it due to a passing moment of depression or to one which carries a lasting threat of repeated similar attempts? Did the sui-

José Ferrer, Kendall Clark, Isabel Bonner

cidal effort grow out of some more malignant type of mental illness? Was it a purely commercial venture as the patient in *The Shrike* claims? Or if the would-be suicide gives this explanation of his action, is this merely a conscious or unconscious cover-up for illness?

"Whether the answer is as transparent as measles, as can happen, or whether the answer requires weeks of careful study, these are not abstruse and esoteric issues whose importance is known only to the elite of the profession. They are kindergarten questions of which even psychiatric stumblebums are aware. Yet in order to have any play at all the author had to write as though his psychiatric stooges were ignorant of such obvious and basic matters, just as he had to drag in the devouring wife for the same purpose. Without them he would have just a straight psychiatric documentary.

"This is the first of a series of distortions of reality in the play. The second arises from the failure to evaluate the patient's story and the wife's. When confronted by such a problem, hospital psychiatrists routinely make use of every possible source of information. The wife's story would have been listened to respectfully and attentively, but also as skeptically as was that of the patient. Psychiatric social service workers would have been sent out to check on their versions. Representatives of both families would have been questioned discreetly. Instead of excluding the patient's girl friend, she, too, would have been interrogated in the effort to evaluate his illness; not to mention the family doctor and the friend who was also a psychiatrist.

"Thus, it is childish nonsense for the author to portray the hospital staff as rejecting these invaluable sources of information and as warning outside doctors not to 'interfere' when they had relevant information to give. Moreover, psychological tests would have been administered, but quietly and reassuringly, not as shown in the play. In giving the tests the physicians would not have behaved like district attorneys, waiting to pounce on the patient as though he was a criminal whose guilt they were out to prove. Here again the play departs from any resemblance to reality.

"It is not necessary to catalogue every distortion which occurs in the play; but several others deserve special mention. Anyone who has ever worked around a mental hospital knows how desperately the hospital doctors and the social service workers labor to find jobs for patients. This makes quite incredible the playwright's picture of a staff that deliberately blocks a patient's rehabilitation by not allowing him to investigate a job which has actually been offered to him.

"Perhaps the ultimate piece of folly in the play is the moment when the attendant explains to the patient that the reason why the doctors will not let him out is that every suicide is a potential homicide. Here is a perfect example of the danger of meager knowledge. Of course, it is true that unconscious destructive impulses may be hidden under suicidal efforts: but they are equally hidden in every neurotic symptom, and indeed in almost every human activity. There is no evidence, statistical or clinical, that among unsuccessful suicides unconscious, latent homicidal fantasies have any special tendency to break loose. Nor does any reputable or disreputable psychiatrist make any such claim. Thus the statement that a man who has made a suicidal attempt must be a potential killer is a 'literary' fiction, introduced only to serve the author's need to contrive a plot.

"To portray all psychiatrists as ignorant or destructive is hardly calculated to dispel fear among people, so many of whom may some day have to face or deal with mental illness. Is it really too much to ask that when the stage attempts to deal seriously with matters which are essential to human progress, the playwright and the director should understand deeply and fully the subject which they are portraying?"

ALSO-RANS: *I Am a Camera, Mrs. McThing, Point of No Return, Jane*

SUMMATION

A debatable decision, justifiable only because *The Shrike* could perhaps have been considered the best of a so-so lot. *I Am a Camera* (Critics' Circle Award) owed much of its appeal to Julie Harris' superb performance. *Point of No Return* was fairly standard stuff. The Critics' Circle Best Musical award went to a revival of Rodgers and Hart's *Pal Joey*.

Judith Evelyn is very much on the distressed José Ferrer's mind in this montage by photographer Alfredo Valente

William Inge

Eileen Heckart, Arthur O'Connell

1952-53

WHEN HAL CARTER, a shallow, handsome vagabond, drifts into a little Kansas town on Labor Day, the maleness that he exudes sets all the local feminine hearts a-thumping.

Hal is looked upon with awe by tomboy Millie Owens, with love by her beautiful older sister, Madge, and with deep suspicion by their mother, Flo. Madge is Alan Seymour's girl, and Alan turns out to have been Hal's old college roommate, but that friendly relationship does not prevent Hal from seducing the virginal Madge, at a time when everyone is off at a community picnic.

In the meantime, the secondary story of Rosemary Sydney, a spinster schoolteacher who boards with Flo, is being told. Rosemary, at once excited by Hal's vitality and repelled by his lack of breeding, denounces him in a moment of drunkenness, but is so startlingly awakened as a woman that she humbles herself and begs her long-time casual admirer, Howard Bevans, to marry her. Rosemary and Howard have also made love on the night of Madge's seduction, and Rosemary is determined that this last desperate trump of hers must win.

Win it does—in the last act, Rosemary and Howard leave on their honeymoon. Hal, on the run from the police Alan has set on him by claiming his car was stolen, has a final fervent embrace with Madge. He tells the bewildered, ashamed girl that he loves her, and that she loves him. Then he hops a freight for Tulsa. Madge, unable to help herself, packs a bag and goes off to follow him by bus.

Ralph Meeker, Janice Rule

Janic Rule, Peggy Conklin, Kim Stanley, Ralph Meeker

PICNIC

THE CREDITS

A Play in Three Acts by William Inge.
Produced by The Theatre Guild and Joshua Logan.
Staged by Joshua Logan.
Opened at the Music Box Theatre, February 19, 1953, and ran for 477 performances.

THE CAST

Helen Potts	Ruth McDevitt
Hal Carter	Ralph Meeker
Millie Owens	Kim Stanley
Bomber	Morris Miller
Madge Owens	Janice Rule
Flo Owens	Peggy Conklin
Rosemary Sydney	Eileen Heckart

Kim Stanley, Ralph Meeker

ALAN SEYMOUR	Paul Newman
IRMA KRONKITE	Reta Shaw
CHRISTINE SCHOENWALDER	Elizabeth Wilson
HOWARD BEVANS	Arthur O'Connell

The Action of the Play Takes Place in a Small Kansas Town in the Yard Shared by Flo Owens and Helen Potts.

ACT I

Early Morning. Labor Day.

ACT II

Late the Same Afternoon.

ACT III

SCENE 1. *Very Early the Following Morning.*
SCENE 2. *A Few Hours Later.*

HISTORY AND REVIEWS

"A memory of women, all sorts of women—beautiful, bitter, harsh, loving, young, old, frustrated, happy—sitting on a front porch on a summer evening. . . ."

Picnic posed a most interesting question about the relationship in any play between the author's contribution and the director's. Was William Inge's play turned into a big hit by Joshua Logan's snap-crackle-pop direction? Or did that directorial job (even granting its commercial effectiveness) tart up an essentially fragile piece of work?

Inge himself, in two separate newspaper stories, talked about the play as he had originally conceived it. The pre-Broadway tour covered Columbus, St. Louis, Cleveland and Boston, and while he was in St. Louis the playwright was interviewed by the *Post-Dispatch*:

"I started out calling the new play *Summer Romance*, which will give you something of an idea of what it is about. The play simply tells the story of what happens to a couple of households composed entirely of women leading a life of guarded femininity when an obstreperously virile youth arrives in their midst and proceeds to change in varying degrees the tenor of their various lives. *Picnic* would never win any prizes in a best-plot contest, but I hope and feel that the play is rich in character, mood and atmosphere."

A month later, writing in *The New York Times* just prior to *Picnic's* Broadway opening, Inge said:

"*Come Back, Little Sheba* was a melancholy play that dwelt almost entirely on the sad lives of Doc and Lola, its two main characters. After it had opened and I set to work again, I felt a desire to expand beyond their dark, somewhat gloomy household and write a play that took place in the sunshine, filling it with all the variety I could find of character, mood, pathos and humor. The result is *Picnic*. One of the many titles I considered for my new play was *Women in Summer*. No one else seemed to like the title much so I forgot it, but I rather liked it, because it recalled something to me: a memory of women, all sorts of women—beautiful, bitter, harsh, loving, young, old, frustrated, happy—sitting on a front porch on a summer evening. There was something in that atmosphere, something I wanted to recreate, and that is how *Picnic* got under way."

The script of *Picnic* was changed considerably in the course of its out-of-town performances. William F. McDermott, a prominent Cleveland critic, had gone down to Columbus to see an early performance, and had not much liked what he'd seen. Logan wrote to him after the New York opening, saying:

"The big problem of our play was to make the boy and girl's story worth listening to, and that's what I think we finally achieved before we opened in New York. But we did not get it until after our opening in Boston. Certainly I can understand your feeling at our Columbus opening."

Here is George Jean Nathan, writing in the *Journal-American* after *Picnic* had been open on Broadway for some three weeks, and was obviously an established success:

"Make no mistake about it, William Inge's *Picnic* is a beautifully cast, handsomely acted, in the main skilfully directed and very interesting show, but I should like to learn what the play was originally like before the business of converting it into the show got under way. I should like to know because of my large critical regard for its author's earlier play, *Come Back, Little Sheba*, which indicated that he had a lot of the independent dramatic artist in him, because in an interview with Elliot Norton, the estimable Boston critic, he allowed that all kinds of changes had been made in it following outside suggestions, and because it has been published that at one point he became so irritated by some things Joshua Logan, the director, had done to his work that he walked out of the theatre. The show, in sum, is, as I have said, a good one, but I wonder if it isn't a good show at the expense of a good play."

Some of the other notices:

Brooks Atkinson in *The New York Times*:

"Taking a group of commonplace people, Mr. Inge has made a rich and fundamental play out of

Ralph Meeker,
Paul Newman, Janice Rule

them that is tremendously moving in the last act. *Picnic* is a deadly serious play. Before it is over, the vagrant with the loud mouth and the unsavory past has altered the whole landscape. The acting is superb. As the cheap braggart, Ralph Meeker acts from the inside out. Janice Rule gives a lovely performance. As a tom-boy with brains and artistic gifts, Kim Stanley gives a penetrating performance. *Picnic* is an original, honest play with an awareness of people. Most of the characters in *Picnic* do not know what is happening to them. But Mr. Inge does, for he is an artist."

Walter Kerr in the *Herald Tribune*:

"Joshua Logan is one of our finest, most emphatic directors of stylized farce. And in the vast frame of musical comedy, where the bold stroke is altogether permissible, he can turn to sentiment with stunning effect. But why he should have been tempted to apply his firm, staccato and rigidly defined style to the summer-sunset mood of William Inge's *Picnic* is a mystery to me. *Picnic* is a whisper of a play. But for far too much of the evening what should have been sensitive is made strident. Jo Mielziner's setting —two back porches leaning lazily across a yard—has the precise feeling of gentle melancholy which Mr. Inge's play suggests. The back yard belongs to Kansas. But the performance is hopped-up Broadway."

John Chapman in the *Daily News*:

"William Inge has written another good play, and last evening The Theatre Guild and Joshua Logan gave it a top-grade production. *Picnic* is an absorbing comedy of sex as sex is admired in a small town somewhere in Kansas. Again, as in *Come Back, Little Sheba*, Inge declines to bring his play to a neat conclusion; he sends the audience home with a feeling that somehow, sometime, something more is going to happen—which makes the work all the more interesting to me. Joshua Logan has staged *Picnic* with thorough professionalism. When an intelligently observant play is written, is acted by real actors, and is directed by a man who knows his stage business, it means good theatre."

John McClain in the *Journal-American*:

"*Picnic* doesn't seem to me to pack the bite of Inge's *Come Back, Little Sheba*, yet it is performed and presented with such artistry that it measures up to a highly satisfactory evening. These are characters easily recognizable from anybody's youth, and if the author has not chosen to bring them to grips with any problems of cosmic importance, he can certainly be credited with making them powerfully human. *Picnic* is no great masterpiece, but it succeeds wonderfully well in bringing a small theme to a high level."

Richard Watts, Jr., in the *Evening Post*:

"Excellently acted and sympathetically staged by Joshua Logan, William Inge's new work revealed the power, insight, compassion, observation and gift for looking into the human heart that we had all expected in him, and I'll be astonished if it isn't a dramatic hit of vast proportions. Here is a dramatist who knows how to set down how people behave and think and talk, who can create the feeling of a small Kansas town, and is able to write dramatic scenes that have vitality, emotional power and heartbreak. There is a true sense of the sadness and wonder of life in this new dramatist. William Inge knows how to write."

Janice Rule, Ralph Meeker, Peggy Conklin, Eileen Heckart, Arthur O'Connell

Peggy Conklin, Eileen Heckart, Reta Shaw, Elizabeth Wilson

Inge went on from *Picnic* to write two subsequent successes, *Bus Stop* and *The Dark at the Top of the Stairs*, and in the case of *Bus Stop* the highly acclaimed director was Joshua Logan, which would seem to indicate that any possible differences between the two gentlemen had long since been melted away by that universal solvent, success. Indeed, the published version of *Picnic* was dedicated to Mr. Logan by Mr. Inge.

ALSO-RANS: *The Crucible, Camino Real, On Borrowed Time, The Climate of Eden, The Time of the Cuckoo*

SUMMATION

A good choice, although a case certainly could have been made for Arthur Miller's *The Crucible*; strong suggestions of anti-McCarthyism in the Miller play perhaps made it too "controversial" for the Pulitzer committee. *Picnic* also won the Critics' Circle Award. *Wonderful Town* was their choice as Best Musical.

Janice Rule, Ralph Meeker

David Wayne, John Forsythe

1953-54

THE TEAHOUSE OF THE AUGUST MOON is set on Okinawa, shortly after the end of World War II. The American Army, having won the war, is now going to convert the easygoing Okinawans to a different way of life—as the choleric Colonel Purdy says, "they're going to learn democracy if I have to shoot every one of them."

Young Captain Fisby is assigned to put Army Plan B into effect, with the aid of an Okinawan interpreter named Sakini, an engaging man-of-all-work who frequently breaks out of character to address the audience directly.

Fisby's mission involves building a school (pentagon-shaped, naturally), organizing an Okinawan Ladies' League for Democratic Action in Tobiki Village, and in general trying to force the Okinawans into the American mold, a task that proves to be hair-raisingly frustrating.

A geisha girl, Lotus Blossom, attaches herself to Fisby's headquarters; not only does she disrupt

Associate producer George Schaefer, producer Maurice Evans, director Robert Lewis, playright John Patrick

THE TEAHOUSE OF THE AUGUST MOON

the pattern of local village life (all of the recently appointed Okinawan officials begin catering to her), but under her benign influence Fisby himself goes native, happily exchanging his uniform for kimono and sandals.

The villagers, it turns out, are of no mind to build a schoolhouse with the lumber that the Americans have supplied. They choose instead to build a lovely teahouse, and to organize, with Fisby's help, a thriving sweet potato brandy industry. Brandy, Fisby feels, will sell much better than the cricket cages the natives had originally intended to manufacture in quantity.

Colonel Purdy arrives in Tobiki just after the fine new teahouse has been completed; apoplectic at this "misuse" of Army lumber, he orders the structure demolished. But then he hears that his superiors in Washington are boasting about Tobiki, and citing it as an example of American get-up-and-go. The Teahouse of the August Moon is quickly set up again, and a glorious party celebrates its rebirth.

THE CREDITS

A PLAY IN THREE ACTS BY JOHN PATRICK.
Adapted from the novel by Vern Sneider.
PRODUCED BY MAURICE EVANS.
STAGED BY ROBERT LEWIS.
OPENED AT THE MARTIN BECK THEATRE, OCTOBER 15, 1953, AND RAN FOR 1,027 PERFORMANCES

THE CAST

SAKINI	David Wayne
SERGEANT GREGOVICH	Harry Jackson
COL. WAINWRIGHT PURDY III	Paul Ford
CAPTAIN FISBY	John Forsythe
OLD WOMAN	Naoe Kondo
OLD WOMAN'S DAUGHTER	Mara Kim
THE DAUGHTER'S CHILDREN	Moy Moy Thom
	Joyce Chen
	Kenneth Wong
LADY ASTOR	Saki
ANCIENT MAN	Kame Ishikawa
MR. HOKAIDA	Chuck Morgan
MR. OMURA	Kuraji Seida
MR. SUMATA	Kaie Deei
MR. SUMATA'S FATHER	Kikuo Hiromura
MR. SEIKO	Haim Winant
MISS HIGA JIGA	Shizu Moriya
MR. KEORA	Yuki Shimoda

John Forsythe, Mariko Niki

MR. OSHIRA	William Hansen
VILLAGERS	Jerry Fujikawa
	Frank Ogawa
	Richard Akagi
	Lawrence Kim
	Norman Chi
LADIES' LEAGUE FOR DEMOCRATIC ACTION	Vivian Thom
	Naoe Kondo
	Mary Ann Reeve
	Mara Kim
LOTUS BLOSSOM	Mariko Niki
CAPTAIN MCLEAN	Larry Gates

ACT I

SCENE 1. *Okinawa. Colonel Purdy's Office, GHQ.*
SCENE 2. *Outside Captain Fisby's Quarters, GHQ.*
SCENE 3. *Tobiki Village.*

ACT II

SCENE 1. *Tobiki Village.*
SCENE 2. *Captain Fisby's Office, Tobiki.*
SCENE 3. *The Same.*
SCENE 4. *Tobiki Village.*

ACT III

SCENE 1. *The Teahouse of the August Moon.*
SCENE 2. *Captain Fisby's Office, Tobiki.*
SCENE 3. *The Teahouse of the August Moon.*

HISTORY AND REVIEWS

"A wise, gently satirical and beautifully understanding dramatic fantasy concerning the impact on each other of East and West. . . ."

The Teahouse of the August Moon (surely the most engagingly titled of all of the Pulitzer Prize plays) was a strange and enchanting blend of delicate fantasy and broad, almost slapstick humor, an oriental fairy tale written with a bold, bright crayon. It said a lot of pertinent satirical things about the sometimes peculiar ways in which democracy works, and in Sakini, the Okinawan man-of-all-work who was the play's commentator and leading character, it gave the theatre one of the most delightful creations in years, a realist, a rascal and a total charmer.

The Teahouse of the August Moon was originally written as a novel. Vern Sneider, its author, had served in the Pacific during World War II, and drew much of the material for his book from his own experiences as a Military Government area supervisor at Tobaru, an Okinawan village. In writing the novel, Sneider had much more on his mind than mere fun. In an article in *The New York Times*, he said:

"Should the occasion arise (and I hope that it doesn't), perhaps the *Teahouse* might be of benefit to some United States Military Government officer, somewhere, sometime. Perhaps it might show him

David Wayne, Mariko Niki, John Forsythe

that if he looks to the wants of the people under him, then tries to satisfy those wants, he will have very little need for barbed wire and guards armed with rifles.

"Perhaps it will show him, among other things, that what works in Pottawattamie, Ohio, often will not work in Tobiki Village, Okinawa; that Plan 'See' is much better than Plan B. That the culture and way of life of an occupied country is often very old, and, strangely enough, ideally suited to that country. And that there is more to be learned in this old world than will ever be taught in a pentagon-shaped schoolhouse."

John Patrick, who adapted *The Teahouse of the August Moon* for the stage, was 47 when the play was produced, and had already been represented on Broadway by *The Willow and I*, *The Hasty Heart*, *The Story of Mary Surratt*, *The Curious Savage* and *Lo and Behold*. He called his play "a mixed brew, like any oriental tea," gave Mr. Sneider due credit for providing "the original atmosphere," and said that he himself had added "a dash of *kabuki*, one of the chief theatre styles of Japan, which seasons the whole pot." Patrick had served in India and Burma during the war; the familiarity he thus gained with the oriental viewpoint proved invaluable when he came to adapt *Teahouse*.

Some of the notices:

Richard Watts, Jr., in the *Evening Post*:

"A warm, charming and thoroughly delightful comedy. Knowingly and colorfully staged and played to perfection by David Wayne, John Forsythe and a fine cast of Orientals and Occidentals, the result is a wise, gently satirical and beautifully understanding dramatic fantasy concerning the impact on each other of East and West. The new play offers the most complete joy the theatre has provided for many a month. Because David Wayne, as the captain's guide, philosopher and friend, who is also the interlocutor of the play, gives one of the most effortlessly charming performances I can recall seeing on a stage, it might be easy to overlook what a brilliant characterization he is also offering. Even without a word to say, he can be wise or sympathetic or mildly disapproving, and, when speech is added to what he has to do, he manages it with superb understanding and quiet subtlety. It is about as complete and masterly a portrayal as the stage could well provide, and it deserves to be accepted as a humorous classic of character acting. *The Teahouse of the August Moon* goes to show how richly entertaining and what a contribution to authentic brotherhood the theatre can be."

Brooks Atkinson in *The New York Times*:

"John Patrick has turned some portentous ideas into a delightful comedy in *The Teahouse of the August Moon*, which is light and sagacious. The form is inventive and familiar. The point of view is droll. And as the middleman between Okinawa and America, David Wayne gives a rich, humorous, forgiving performance that must have come straight out of heaven, it is so wise and pure. Paul Ford's plain, cornfed portrait of the incredulous colonel who cannot believe what he sees is immensely funny and immensely winning. Under Robert Lewis' direction, Mr. Patrick's play is completely captivating. Although East and West look at each other with considerable hostility, they can meet on friendly terms if they keep their sense of humor. Things that might easily make for anger become reasonable, friendly and sweetly comic in this ingratiating play."

John Chapman in the *Daily News*:

"John Patrick's *The Teahouse of the August Moon* is—and I choose the adjective most carefully—a wonderful comedy, and last evening it was given a most beguiling production. The play is in turn uproarious and touching. Robert Lewis, the director, has evoked fine performances from everybody in the company. The physical production, designed for both sets and costumes by Peter Larkin, is simple but stunning. There can't be any more enjoyable theatre than this comedy."

Walter Kerr in the *Herald Tribune*:

"*The Teahouse of the August Moon* is a brightly colored comic-strip with a bland, broad grin on its face and a healthy share of mockery in its heart. Mr. Patrick has taken a handful of amiable caricatures and pasted them all flat against an enchanting Oriental landscape. The whole thing quickly becomes something painted—in bold and childlike hues—and it moves across the stage like a miniature circus. I found myself intermittently disturbed by the Broadwayese which pops up in the native double-talk."

John McClain in the *Journal-American*:

"One of the most charming and hilarious productions to be unveiled in these parts since *South Pacific*."

The Teahouse of the August Moon quickly became an international success. As *Das Kleine Teehaus*, it played almost 2,000 performances in West Germany, in a translation by Oscar Karlweis, who appeared as Sakini in Vienna and Berlin. In Belgium it was known as *Lotus and Bulldozer*, "Bulldozer" being the Belgian nickname for the American G.I. Holland knew the play as *Teehuis voor Tobiki*, and in Mexico it became *La Casa de Tede de la Luna de Agosta*.

The Habimah Theatre in Tel Aviv played *Teahouse* in repertory more frequently than any other American play, and the Kabuki Theatre in Tokyo made a bi-lingual production out of it, with Americans playing themselves and Japanese playing Okinawans, both in their native tongues. In Japan it was called *The Teahouse of the Night of August 15th*; that date is the rough Japanese equivalent of Thanksgiving.

As a final fillip, *Teahouse* was presented on Okinawa itself in April and May of 1954, for nineteen wildly cheered performances. At the end of the engagement, Major General D. A. D. Ogden, Commanding General, Ryukyus Command, wrote to Sol Jacobson, the play's New York press agent:

"The final performance of *The Teahouse of the August Moon* on Okinawa was held 4 May 1954. The play was a 'natural' and I am sure that the *Teahouse* had its most appreciative audience when it appeared in the local Army and Air Force theatres. We were extremely fortunate in being able to cast a group of professional and semi-professional actors, both American and Okinawan, and to find a very talented youngster (Glenn Q. Pierce, Jr.) who directed the production for us. Many of the Okinawans in real life were essentially the same sort of characters that they represented in the play. The $4,200 profit has been turned over to the Ryukyuan–American Friendship Committee for the rehabilitation of educational facilities."

ALSO-RANS: *Tea and Sympathy, The Caine Mutiny Court-Martial, Take a Giant Step*

SUMMATION

A very good decision; *The Teahouse of the August Moon* was warm, witty, and well deserving of the prize. *Tea and Sympathy*, another good play, was perhaps counted out because of the frank sexuality of its ending. *The Caine Mutiny Court-Martial*, marvelously theatrical, was taken almost bodily from Herman Wouk's book, with little changed or added. The Critics' Circle awards went to *Teahouse* and *The Golden Apple*.

Wrestlers:
Chuck Morgan (bald head), *Haim Winant*

Playwright Tennessee Williams

(Opposite Page)
Barbara Bel Geddes, Ben Gazzara, Mildred Dunnock, Madeleine Sherwood, Pat Hingle, Fred Stewart, R. G. Armstrong

1954-55

AT BIG DADDY'S HOUSE in the Mississippi Delta, Brick (Big Daddy's younger son) is sunk in impotent, alcoholic apathy, a condition that leads his wife, Maggie, to describe herself as a "cat on a hot tin roof." Maggie's sexual frustration, which has kept her childless, is coupled with her fear that Brick's drunkenness and indolence will make Big Daddy choose to leave his considerable estate to Gooper, his older son. The question of the inheritance is imminent, for Big Daddy, although he does not know it, is dying of cancer.

Brick's alcoholism and rejection of Maggie are rooted in a homosexual attachment he once had to his best friend, Skipper. Although Brick desperately tried to convince himself that his affection for Skipper was pure friendship, Skipper knew better, and committed suicide after Brick had rejected Skipper's drunken confession of his own unnatural love.

Big Daddy taunts Brick with the Skipper episode, and Brick, striking back, tells his father about the cancer that is killing him.

Gooper prepares an outline of a trusteeship for Big Daddy's property, and shows it to Big Mama, who indignantly rejects it; she knows that Brick, for all his faults, is actually her husband's favorite son, and that Maggie's childlessness is the only stumbling block to Brick's inheriting the estate.

As the play ends Maggie is comforting Brick, and tells him she is even willing to get him drunk, if that is the only way he will agree to make love to her. Maggie feels that she *must* get pregnant if her marriage is to have any chance of becoming normal.

CAT ON A HOT TIN ROOF

THE CREDITS

A Drama in Three Acts by Tennessee Williams.
Produced by The Playwrights' Company.
Staged by Elia Kazan.
Opened at the Morosco Theatre, March 24, 1955, and ran for 694 performances.

THE CAST

Lacey	Maxwell Glanville
Sookey	Musa Williams
Margaret	Barbara Bel Geddes
Brick	Ben Gazzara
Mae (Sister Woman)	Madeleine Sherwood
Gooper (Brother Man)	Pat Hingle
Big Mama	Mildred Dunnock
Dixie	Pauline Hahn
Buster	Darryl Richard

SONNY	Seth Edwards
TRIXIE	Janice Dunn
BIG DADDY	Burl Ives
REVEREND TOOKER	Fred Stewart
DOCTOR BAUGH	R. G. Armstrong
DAISY	Eva Vaughan Smith
BRIGHTIE	Brownie McGhee
SMALL	Sonny Terry

The Action Takes Place in a Bed-Sitting Room and Section of the Gallery of a Plantation Home in the Mississippi Delta. The Time, an Evening in Summer; the Action Is Continuous, with Two Intermissions.

HISTORY AND REVIEWS

"The cloudy flickering interplay of live human beings in the thundercloud of a common crisis. . . ."

On December 21, 1901, in Clyde Fitch's *The City*, Tully Marshall looked hard at Walter Hampden and called him "a God-damned liar," right out loud. A gasp rose from the first-night audience. Diamond Jim Brady was one of the indignant patrons who stalked out of the theatre, affronted by this first use of such high-calibre profanity on the Broadway stage.

It is just as well that the sensitive and apoplectic Mr. Brady was unavailable on the night some fifty-odd years later when *Cat on a Hot Tin Roof* opened. He would have flown right through the ceiling, diamonds and all.

This Tennessee Williams play, which embedded the phrase "Big Daddy" in our language, spared absolutely nothing in its frankness, particularly in sexual matters, and it came in for some heavy criticism on that score. Two weeks after the play opened, in fact, Williams toned down one of Big Daddy's gamier speeches, presumably at the request of Edward T. McCaffrey, Commissioner of Licenses.

McCaffrey went to see the play because of a complaint by the Children's Aid Society. At a backstage conference, he was assured that the four child actors ("no-neck monsters" was the happy description Williams had for them in the play) were invariably safe in their dressing rooms while the saltier portions of the dialogue were sputtering on the stage. The Commissioner didn't leave it at that, however. He had no official censorial powers, but he managed to imply that he would be pleased if Big Daddy's "elephant" story (a smoking car anecdote, extraneous to the play's action) were to be deleted. Deleted it was, and never missed, either.

Jack Gaver, the United Press critic, had these comments on the play's language:

"There is one thing certain about *Cat on a Hot Tin Roof*. There is more and rougher dialogue of a sexual nature—a lot more and a lot rougher—than in any other American play ever produced on Broadway. Much of it is completely unnecessary. It could be eliminated for the most part without altering the story an iota or without destroying the realism that the author probably fancies he has obtained by using it. The impression is really one of mere exhibitionism."

Cat on a Hot Tin Roof had certain vague roots in an earlier Williams short story, *Three Players at a Summer Game*. In a pre-opening article in *The New York Times*, Williams wrote of what he was trying to do in his new play, in words as intimate as if he were addressing his readers over a friendly cup of coffee:

"The fact that I want you to observe what I do for your possible pleasure and to give you knowledge of things I feel I may know better than you, because my world is different from yours, as different as every man's world is from the world of others, is not enough excuse for a personal lyricism that has not yet mastered its necessary trick of rising above the singular to the plural concern, from personal to general import. But for years and years now, which may have passed like a dream because of this

Madeleine Sherwood, Barbara Bel Geddes

obsession, I have been trying to learn how to perform this trick and make it truthful, and sometimes I feel that I am able to do it. Meanwhile!—I want to go on talking to you as freely and intimately about what we live and die for as if I knew you better than anyone else whom you know."

Some of the notices:

Richard Watts, Jr., in the *Evening Post*:

"*Cat on a Hot Tin Roof* is a play of tremendous dramatic impact. There are many other things to be said of Tennessee Williams' tormented and tormenting new drama, with its emotional intensity, its almost sadistic probing into lost souls, its neurotic brooding, its insight into decadence, and its torrent of language both lyric and lewd. But the main impression that emerges from a first viewing of Elia Kazan's brilliant production is that of enormous theatrical power."

Brooks Atkinson in *The New York Times*:

"*Cat on a Hot Tin Roof* is a stunning drama, the work of a mature observer of men and women and a gifted craftsman. One of its great achievements is the honesty and simplicity of the craftsmanship. It seems not to have been written. It is the quintessence of life. It is the basic truth. Always a seeker after honesty in his writing, Mr. Williams has not only found a solid part of the truth but found the way to say it with complete honesty. It is not only part of the truth of life; it is the absolute truth of the theatre. As theatre, *Cat on a Hot Tin Roof* is superb. The acting is magnificent."

Walter Kerr in the *Herald Tribune*:

"*Cat on a Hot Tin Roof* is a beautifully written, perfectly directed, stunningly acted play of evasion: evasion on the part of its principal characters, evasion perhaps on the part of its playwright. Brilliant scenes, scenes of sudden lashing dramatic power, break open. Throughout the play images of searing intensity hold you fast to its elusive narrative. There is, however, a tantalizing reluctance—beneath all

Ben Gazzara, Barbara Bel Geddes

Barbara Bel Geddes

Ben Gazzara, Barbara Bel Geddes

Mildred Dunnock, Pat Hingle

the fire and all the apparent candor—to let the play blurt out its promised secret. This flaw should not keep you from seeing it. Tennessee Williams is the man of our time who comes closest to hurling the actual blood and bone of life onto the stage; he is also the man whose prose comes closest to being an incisive natural poetry. The production has no flaw. Apart from Barbara Bel Geddes' lashing and altogether luminous performance as the tenacious wife, and Ben Gazzara's steely-cold portrait of a man torn by divided loyalties and anguished self-doubt, there is a Rabelaisian contribution from Burl Ives that is apt to be the talk of the town. Mildred Dunnock is startlingly fine in an unfamiliar sort of role."

John Chapman in the *Daily News*:

"Tennessee Williams' *Cat on a Hot Tin Roof* is another of his perceptive and sympathetic dramas of frustration—but I think this time he has out-frustrated himself by failing to remain in command of his own play. After he's got it he doesn't know what to do with it. As a piece of theatre it has vivid characters and an occasional exciting scene and I sat intent through it all; but when it was over I felt frustrated myself—felt that some heart or point of purpose was missing. I also felt that the considerable amount of dirty talk in it was mere boyish bravado and rather pointless. There is a great deal of fine theatre in *Cat on a Hot Tin Roof*, but I wish there were more point and direction in the play."

George Jean Nathan in the *Journal-American*:

"I am no psychiatrist and don't know what Tennessee Williams, with his almost maniacal preoccupation with the more emphatic impulses and sensational aspects of sex, is trying to prove to himself. All I know is that, so far as we can gather from the evidence of his plays and stories, he seems to be trying awfully hard to conceal both from himself and from us his immaturity and torment by draping them with a literary or dramatic bravado, the impression of which on even the least initiated is of a youth with his foot on the bar rail loudly demanding in simulated boozy accents another lemonade."

Williams kept working on the play even after its Broadway opening. The "elephant" cut was quite minor, but he made a major change in the play's final lines, restoring a Barbara Bel Geddes speech which had been cut before the first performance; the intent seems to have been to end the play on more of an upbeat note. She speaks to Ben Gazzara, playing her impotent, drunken husband:

"Oh, you weak, beautiful people who give up so easily. You need somebody to hand your life back to you like something gold. And I can do it. I'm determined to do it. And there's nothing more determined than a cat on a hot tin roof, is there? Is there, baby?"

The play's international success made for some fascinating foreign titles. Scandinavia: *Kat Pa Hett Plattak*. Holland: *Kat Op Een Heet Zinken Dak*. Germany: *Katze Auf Dem Heissen Blechdach*. France: *Chat Sur Un Toit Chaud Der Fer Blanc*. Italy: *Gatto Sull'Infuocato Tetto Di Stagno*.

Williams, apparently nettled by the charges of obscurity that some critics had made, answered them in his introduction to the published version of the play:

"The bird that I hope to catch in the net of this play is not the solution of one man's psychological problem. I'm trying to catch the true quality of experience in a group of people, that cloudy, flickering, evanescent—fiercely charged!—interplay of live human beings in the thundercloud of a common crisis. Some mystery should be left in the revelation of character in a play, just as a great deal of mystery is always left in the revelation of character in life, even in one's own character to himself. This does not

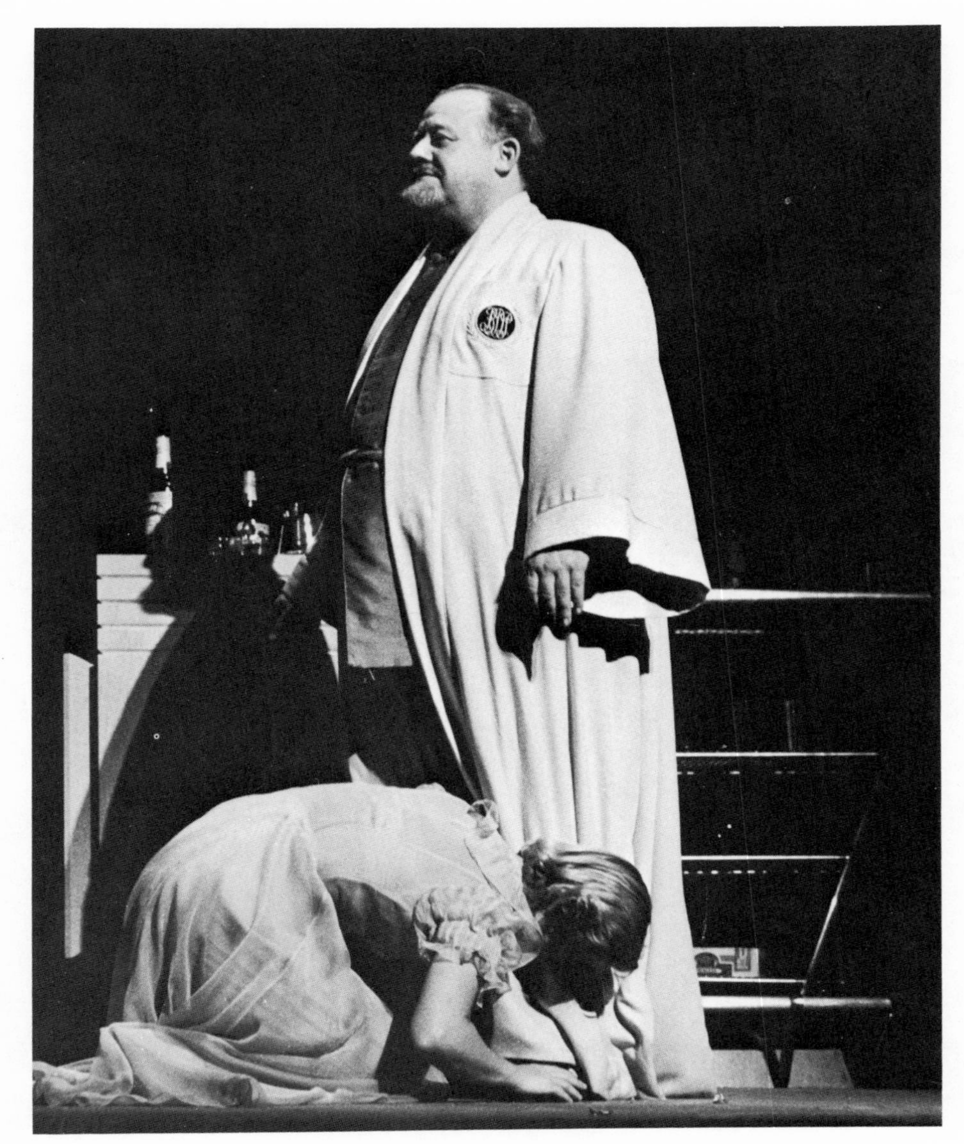

Barbara Bel Geddes, Burl Ives

absolve the playwright of his duty to observe and probe as deeply as he legitimately can, but it should steer him away from 'pat' conclusions, facile definitions, which can make a play just a play, not a snare for the truth of human experience."

ALSO-RANS: *The Flowering Peach, Bad Seed, Bus Stop, Inherit the Wind*

SUMMATION

Considering the tone of the play's language, a remarkable choice (see the 1924–25 sandbagging of *What Price Glory?*); considering everything else, a good selection, as a bow to *Cat's* smashing theatrical impact. The jurors were said to have recommended *The Flowering Peach*, but were overruled by the Advisory Board. *Bus Stop* would have been an equally solid choice; the William Inge play was barely nosed out by *Cat* (9 votes to 8) for the Critics' Circle Award. *The Saint of Bleecker Street* was the Critics' Circle choice as Best Musical.

Burl Ives, Ben Gazzara

Ben Gazzara, Burl Ives

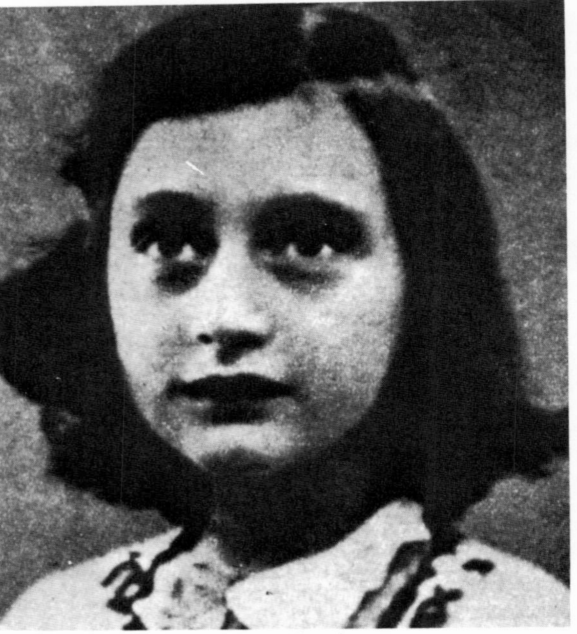
Anne Frank

1955-56 THE DIARY

WHILE THE PLAY HAS A Prologue and Epilogue, both set in 1945, the main action takes place between July of 1942 and August of 1944, in some rooms on the top floors of an Amsterdam office building and warehouse. The rooms are known familiarly to their occupants as the "Secret Annex," and they serve as a hiding place from the Gestapo.

Two Jewish families are living in the Annex, the Franks and the Van Daans; they are later joined by a fussy dentist, Mr. Dussel. Their food is smuggled to them by the building's owner, Mr. Kraler.

Mr. and Mrs. Frank have two daughters, Margot and Anne, while the Van Daans have a sixteen-year-old son, Peter. Anne is thirteen in 1942, a vivid, restless child who adapts with great difficulty to her strange new life, and spends much of her time writing in her diary. The Annex stowaways can make no noise during the daytime, not even turn on the water taps, for fear of alerting the workmen downstairs.

Cooped up together for more than two years, with the threat of discovery a constant terror (for discovery means almost certain death), the Franks and the Van Daans quite humanly get on each others' nerves, although there are saving moments of tenderness—a makeshift Chanukah celebration, a "date" that Anne and Peter arrange for themselves. Violence erupts briefly when Mr. Van Daan is caught stealing from the communal hoard of food.

After the Allies have invaded Europe, and rescue seems imminent, the existence of the Annex is discovered by the Gestapo, and although no Nazi troopers are ever seen, the audience hears the blood-chilling sound of the door being broken down. Mr. Frank survives the war, but in the Epilogue it is revealed that Anne has died in Belsen.

David Levin, Dennie Moore, Lou Jacobi, Gusti Huber, Joseph Schildkraut, Eva Rubinstein, Jack Gilford, Susan Strasberg

OF ANNE FRANK

THE CREDITS

A PLAY IN TWO ACTS BY FRANCES GOODRICH AND ALBERT HACKETT.
Based on the book *Anne Frank: The Diary of a Young Girl.*
PRODUCED BY KERMIT BLOOMGARDEN.
STAGED BY GARSON KANIN.
OPENED AT THE CORT THEATRE, OCTOBER 5, 1955, AND RAN FOR 717 PERFORMANCES.

THE CAST

MR. FRANK	Joseph Schildkraut
MIEP	Gloria Jones
MRS. VAN DAAN	Dennie Moore
MR. VAN DAAN	Lou Jacobi
PETER VAN DAAN	David Levin
MRS. FRANK	Gusti Huber
MARGOT FRANK	Eva Rubinstein
ANNE FRANK	Susan Strasberg
MR. KRALER	Clinton Sundberg
MR. DUSSEL	Jack Gilford

Joseph Schildkraut, Joan de Marrais, Otto Hulett (Chicago company)

The Time: During the Years of World War II and Immediately Thereafter. The Place: Amsterdam.

HISTORY AND REVIEWS

"A play that is—for all its pathos—as bright and shining as a banner. . . ."

"It is an odd idea for someone like me to keep a diary. It seems to me that neither I—nor, for that matter, anyone else—will be interested in the unbosomings of a 13-year-old schoolgirl."

Anne Frank set down those words in Amsterdam, in 1942, and had every reason to believe that they were true. Had she been told that her diary, published in the United States by Doubleday, would become one of the most famous books of the century, she would have laughed incredulously.

This unquenchable little girl laughed a great deal, all through the perilous years that she and her father and mother and sister, along with a few friends, spent in an Amsterdam attic, hiding from the Gestapo, not daring to make a sound by day for fear of giving away their hiding place. Anne laughed, cried, sulked, and was sometimes very humanly petty and childish. In *The Diary of a Young Girl* she wrote it all down, and her "unbosomings" deeply touched many thousands of people all over the world, years after she died of typhus in the concentration camp at Belsen in 1945.

Anne Frank and her family almost made it safely out of the attic; the Gestapo broke in only six weeks before the liberation of Amsterdam. The diary, stuffed into a briefcase that was overlooked by the Germans (one of her captors threw it carelessly on the floor), was found after her capture, by the Dutchwoman who had kept the Frank family alive in hiding. It was eventually published in twenty-six languages, and thirty countries have seen the moving play that Frances Goodrich and Albert Hackett (Mr. and Mrs. Hackett) adapted from it.

The Hacketts, determined that their adaptation should reflect as closely as possible the sweetness and integrity of the original book, wrote their way through fourteen stage versions of *The Diary* before they came up with the final one. The play was deliberately keyed low, with no theatrical tricks, and what it lost in glitter it gained in substance. In Europe, particularly in Germany, it moved audiences to complete stillness. Liesl Frank Mittler, a play agent who had arranged for its simultaneous opening in seven German cities in October of 1956, reported afterwards:

"At the end of the play, both Berlin and Düsseldorf audiences had the same reaction. The people left in silence, too moved to applaud, too gripped by the terrifying truth of the play's message."

The Hacketts visited Amsterdam in December of 1954, making the trip with Garson Kanin, the play's director. Otto Frank, Anne's father, had survived the war, and he took them to see the attic. He answered painful questions, to make the details of the play more authentic. "Did Anne miss dancing? Did she ever cry? Did she take an interest in her clothes?" A year later Mr. Frank declined an invitation to attend the play's New York opening, saying, in a note to the company:

"You will realize that for me this play is a part of my life, and the idea that my wife and children as well as I will be presented on the stage is painful to me. Therefore it is impossible for me to come and see it."

Some of the notices:

Walter Kerr in the *Herald Tribune*:

"Nearly all of the characters in *The Diary of Anne Frank*—they are Dutch Jews hiding out from Hitler in a dingy and overcrowded garret—are doomed to death. Yet the precise quality of the new play is the quality of glowing, ineradicable life in its warmth, its wonder, its spasms of anguish, and its wild and flaring humor. Frances Goodrich and Albert Hackett have fashioned a wonderfully sensitive and theatrically craftsmanlike narrative out of the real-life legacy left us by a spirited and straightforward Jewish girl. Boris Aronson's gabled setting from which the homeless look out on a thousand homes is brilliantly drawn, a stunning background for a play that is—for all its pathos—as bright and shining as a banner."

John Chapman in the *Daily News*:

"There is so much beauty, warm humor, gentle pity and cold horror in *The Diary of Anne Frank* that it is difficult to imagine how this play could be contained in one set on one stage. Last evening I felt that at any moment it might break out of its confines and run laughing and sobbing into 48th Street. This is a fine drama, beautifully acted, directed and mounted. Garson Kanin has staged the play impeccably; he has given it breadth and scope and at the same time a wonderful attention to detail."

Brooks Atkinson in *The New York Times*:

"They have made a lovely, tender drama out of *The Diary of Anne Frank*. Strange how the shining

Susan Strasberg

Tokyo: *Nina Mitsui*

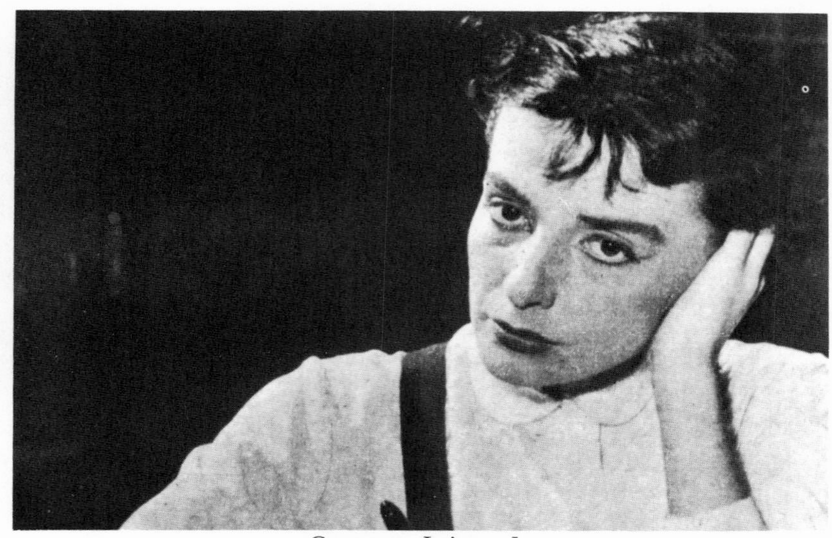
Germany: *Luitgart Im*

Sydney: *Elizabeth Waterhouse*

Barcelona: *Berta Riaza*

Rome: *Anna Maria Guarniera*

VARIOUS "ANNE FRANKS" AROUND THE WORLD

Toronto: *Abigail Kellogg*

Johannesburg: *Bodil Brink*

New York: *Susan Strasberg*

Germany: *Anya Romer*

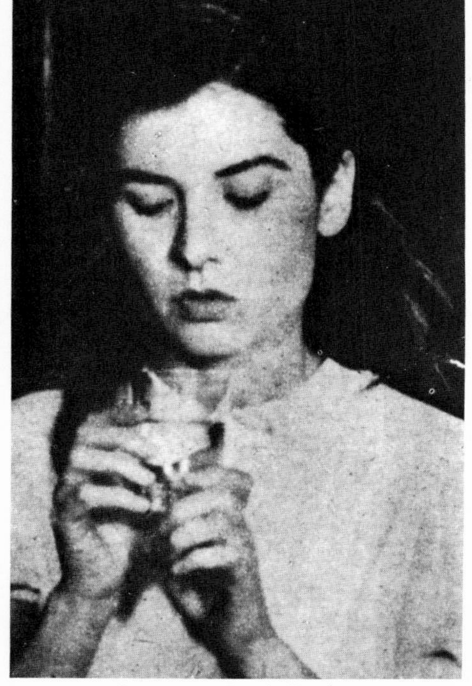
Germany: *Dorit Fischer*

Sweden: *Pia Skoglund*

spirit of a young girl now dead can filter down through the years and inspire a group of theatrical professionals in a foreign land. Among them, not the least and perhaps the finest is Susan Strasberg. By some magic that cannot be explained, she has caught the whole character of Anne in a flowing, spontaneous, radiant performance. As Papa Frank, Joseph Schildkraut plays with taste and kindness. From any practical point of view the job of making a play out of the diary of Anne Frank is impossible. Perhaps that is why Mr. and Mrs. Hackett have succeeded so well. They have not contrived anything; they have left the tool-kit outside the door of their workroom. Out of the truth of a human being has come a delicate, rueful, moving drama."

Richard Watts, Jr., in the *Evening Post*:

"There is a shattering sense of reality about *The Diary of Anne Frank*, which Frances Goodrich and Albert Hackett have dramatized from what must have been one of the most heartbreaking documents of the last war. By wisely shunning any trace of theatricality or emotional excess, the playwrights have made the only-too-true story deeply moving in its unadorned veracity, and, with young Susan Strasberg giving a lovely and sensitive portrayal of the title role, last night's opening provided a sense of truth that is unusual in playgoing. To call this a documentary play is perhaps to give a false indication that there is no emotion in it. The truth is that there is the deepest of feeling in it, but it is there by understatement, by implication, and in the quietest and therefore most convincing terms. There isn't a Nazi in it. There isn't a fabricated or highly-colored moment. Perhaps there is a minimum of art, but there is a maximum of honest compassion."

William Hawkins in the *World-Telegram and Sun*:

"*The Diary of Anne Frank* is theatre at its finest. The genius of this play is that there is nothing grim or sensational about it, and it makes no bid to rely on suspense for its interest. The climaxes are small, but the tension, in the will to survive, is enormous."

Once it was established on Broadway, *The Diary of Anne Frank* became the focus of a unique theatrical contretemps. Meyer Levin, author of such novels as *Compulsion* and *The Old Bunch*, and not to be written off as a mere publicity-seeker, claimed that the treatment of Anne's story by the Hacketts was "facile and glossy," and sought permission to have his own Anne Frank play produced. It, too, had

Gusti Huber

been adapted from the diary. Otto Frank had originally agreed that Levin should do the adaptation, but that agreement was voided when a vice-president at Doubleday insisted that the job called for a "big name writer." After producer Kermit Bloomgarden acquired the stage rights to the book, Levin was frozen out. Levin finally sued Bloomgarden and Mr. Frank, and was actually awarded $50,000 by a jury for alleged plagiarism, but the Supreme Court set the award aside.

It is interesting to note that in the Israel production of *The Diary of Anne Frank* there was a change in the play's last line. As originally written, Anne's father read a diary entry: "In spite of everything, I still believe that people are really good at heart." Then Mr. Frank said: "She puts me to shame." In Israel, the actor playing Anne's father shook his head doubtfully, and said: "I don't know. I don't know."

Director Garson Kanin summed up the play in this way, in an article printed in *The New York Times* just before the opening:

"This play makes use of elements having mainly to do with human courage, faith, hope, brotherhood, love and self-sacrifice. Anne Frank was certainly killed, but she was never defeated."

ALSO-RANS: *A View from the Bridge, The Ponder Heart, No Time for Sergeants, A Hatful of Rain, Middle of the Night*

SUMMATION

This was an obvious choice, and a good one; the play towered above most of its rivals. The judges did have to decide (as they had decided once before, with *There Shall Be No Night*) to give the Prize to a play that did not deal with some phase of American life. The closest competitor might have been *A View from the Bridge*, except for its overtones of incest and homosexuality. The Critics' Circle awards went to *Anne Frank* and *My Fair Lady*.

Susan Strasberg, Gusti Huber

Jason Robards, Jr.

1956-57

THE ENTIRE ACTION OF THE PLAY takes place in the New England summer home of the Tyrones, on an August day and night in 1912.

James Tyrone is an aging actor, an imposing-looking but miserly man. His wife, Mary, is gentle and nervous, and obviously in poor health. They have two sons: Jamie, a robust rakehell of 34, and Edmund, 23, thin and sick.

As the long day passes, and finally blends into the night, the members of this tortured family savage each other interminably, and the bitter truth about each one emerges. The elder Tyrone has long abandoned any thought of a decent acting career, and has contented himself with the money made from playing the same cheap, flashy role year after year. Years ago his stinginess led him to summon an inferior doctor when Mary was ill after Edmund's birth, and the morphine that the quack gave her turned her into an addict.

Fredric March, Florence Eldridge

LONG DAY'S JOURNEY INTO NIGHT

Fredric March

Mary is lost in a drug-fuddled world of her own. Her pathetic attempts to disguise her condition are futile; her husband and her sons are well aware of it. Jamie is revealed as a drunkard and womanizer; bitterly jealous of Edmund's talents, he seeks to hide this jealousy beneath an overlay of contempt and cynicism.

Edmund (O'Neill's self-portrait) discovers during the course of the play that he has consumption. James Tyrone is all for sending him to a cheap institution (a version of the same mistake he had made with Mary), and only reluctantly allows himself to be talked out of the plan.

At the end of the play all three men, much the worse for drink, are sitting in the gloom as Mary drifts in, wearing her faded wedding dress. She has lost all contact with reality, and is dreaming of her youth, when she married James Tyrone, and "was so happy for a time." Exhausted, the Tyrones are simply staring at each other as the final curtain falls.

Florence Eldridge, Fredric March

THE CREDITS

A Play in Four Acts by Eugene O'Neill.
Produced by Leigh Connell, Theodore Mann and José Quintero.
Staged by José Quintero.
Opened at the Helen Hayes Theatre, November 7, 1956, and ran for 390 performances.

THE CAST

James Tyrone	Fredric March
Mary Cavan Tyrone	Florence Eldridge
James Tyrone, Jr., *Their Elder Son*	Jason Robards, Jr.
Edmund Tyrone, *Their Younger Son*	Bradford Dillman
Cathleen, *Second Girl*	Katherine Ross

The Action Takes Place in the Living Room of the Tyrones' Summer Home.

ACT I

8:30 a.m. of a Day in August, 1912.

ACT II

scene 1. *Around 12:45 p.m.*
scene 2. *About a Half-Hour Later.*

ACT III

Around 6:30 That Evening.

ACT IV

Around Midnight.

HISTORY AND REVIEWS

"It restores the drama to literature and the theatre to art. . . ."

On November 29, 1945, Eugene O'Neill, a sick, weary and aging man, took the manuscript of a play to Random House. It had been finished for some time, since 1941, and it had been two years in the writing. Its title was *Long Day's Journey Into Night*; it was plainly autobiographical in nature; and, as years later its production was to demonstrate, it was almost surely the finest play ever written by an American.

The Gelbs, in *O'Neill*, quote Random House's Bennett Cerf:

"When O'Neill gave us the script of *Long Day's Journey*, he wanted us to seal it up. He insisted it be done with red sealing wax. We sent out for some, but when it arrived, none of us knew how to use it. We used up two boxes of matches and got wax all over our hands before we finally managed to seal the envelope that held the script. After the ceremony, we put it in our downstairs safe."

O'Neill then dictated a covering letter, which he and Cerf both signed:

"I am this day depositing with you, on condition that it not be opened by you until twenty-five years after my death, a sealed copy of the manuscript of an original play which I have written, entitled *Long Day's Journey Into Night*."

Never before had such mumbo-jumbo surrounded the script of any play, but O'Neill was not playing childish games. He had scraped *Long Day's Journey Into Night* right out of his bones, and had put himself and his family into it with deepest sympathy and understanding, but with absolutely naked candor. It had been a cruelly difficult play for him to write.

Bradford Dillman, Jason Robards, Jr., Florence Eldridge, Fredric March

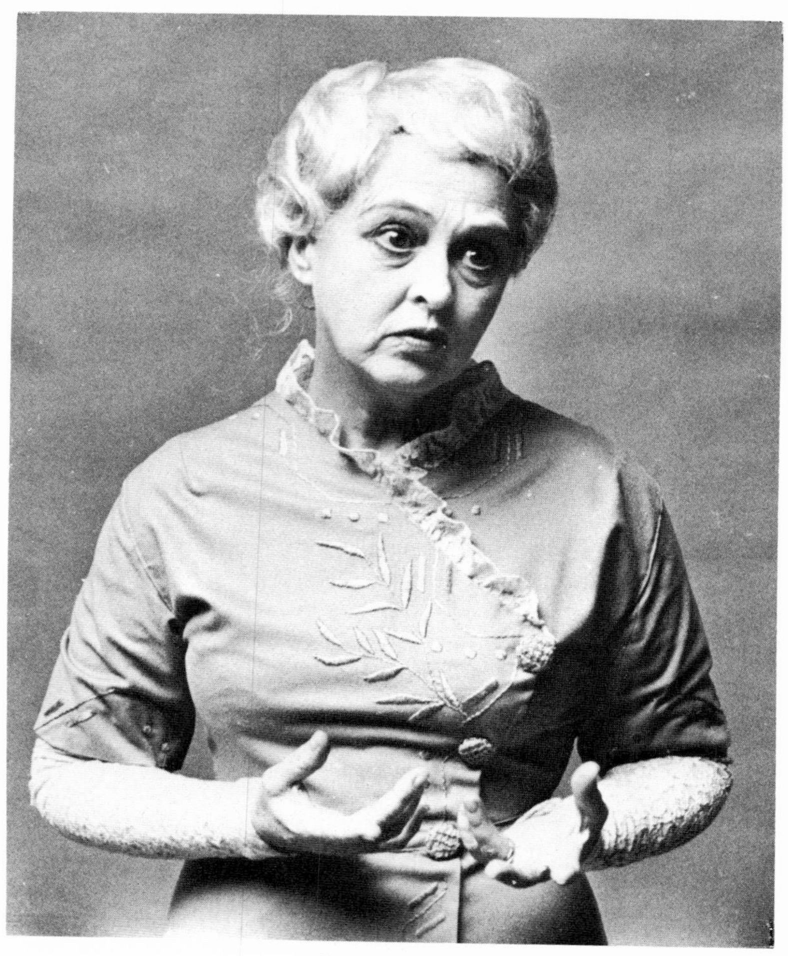

Florence Eldridge

Eugene O'Neill died on November 27, 1953, and some two years later his widow took the manuscript of *Long Day's Journey Into Night* away from Random House (Cerf refused to publish it, feeling bound by the original agreement) and turned it over to the Yale University Press. Almost simultaneously, she allowed the play to be given its first public performance, in Stockholm, where it was done with great success by the Royal Dramatic Theatre in February of 1956. Under the terms of O'Neill's will, Mrs. O'Neill was given full control of all of his plays, and consequently had every legal right to countermand O'Neill's twenty-five-year ban.

For a while Mrs. O'Neill considered denying the play an American production, at least for a few years, but relented in the light of the fine job that the Circle in the Square had done in its revival of *The Iceman Cometh*. She gave the Circle the American rights to *Long Day's Journey*, and the Circle lived up to its own side of the bargain by giving the play a flawless production.

Some of the notices:

Richard Watts, Jr., in the *Evening Post*:

"*Long Day's Journey Into Night* is a magnificent and shattering play. Eugene O'Neill's autobiographical drama broods with unsparing candor over some of the most pitiful and terrible personal concerns that a playwright ever tore out of his youthful memories and transforms them into a masterpiece of understanding, compassion and dark, tormented beauty. It seems to me that Fredric March gives the

Jason Robards, Jr.
Bradford Dillman

(Standing) *Fredric March*
(Seated) *Bradford Dillman, Jason Robards, Jr.*

finest and most penetrating performance of his career as the father, but he is no more impressive than Jason Robards, Jr., who demonstrates in the role of the older son that he is an actor of tremendous dynamic skill. This is a play that gives the entire season stature."

Brooks Atkinson in *The New York Times*:

"With the production of *Long Day's Journey Into Night* the American theatre acquires size and stature. The play is like a Dostoevsky novel in which Strindberg had written the dialogue. For this saga of the damned is horrifying and devastating in a classical tradition, and the performance under José Quintero's direction is inspired. *Long Day's Journey Into Night* could be pruned of some of its excesses and repetitions and static looks back to the past. But the faults come, not from tragic posturing, but from the abundance of a great theatre writer who had a spacious point of view. Fredric March gives a masterly performance that will stand as a milestone in the acting of an O'Neill play. This is a character portrait of grandeur. *Long Day's Journey Into Night* has been worth waiting for. It restores the drama to literature and the theatre to art."

John Chapman in the *Daily News*:

"The news this morning is that *Long Day's Journey Into Night* is a magnificent work, and last evening it was given a magnificent performance. It exploded like a dazzling skyrocket over the humdrum of Broadway theatricals. This is O'Neill's most beautiful play—perhaps the only beautiful one he ever wrote. And it is one of the great dramas of any time. Florence Eldridge reaches stunning heights in the art of acting. Last evening at the Helen Hayes was a great evening for the American theatre, and the first-night audience was spellbound and enraptured."

Walter Kerr in the *Herald Tribune*:

"Eugene O'Neill has held up his mother, his father and his brother at the arm's length of the stage, looked at everything that was ugly and misshapen and destroyed in them, and now the pain is gone. It is gone, too. Though the four-hour, endlessly savage examination of conscience on the stage of the Helen Hayes is deliberately, masochistically harrowing in the ferocity of its revelation, the agony that O'Neill felt whenever he contemplated his own beginnings is not passed on to his audience. It is in some curious and even exalting manner exorcized, washed away, leaving in its place an undefined dignity, an agreed-upon peace, a powerful sense of exhilarated completion. How has O'Neill kept self-pity and vulgarity and cheap bravado out of this prolonged, unasked-for, improbable inferno? Partly by the grim determination that made him a major dramatist; the insistence that the roaring fire he could build by grinding his own two hands together was the fire of truth. For anyone who cares about the American theatre, *Long Day's Journey Into Night* is, of course, an obligation. But it is more than that. It is a stunning theatrical experience."

ALSO-RANS: *Orpheus Descending, A Moon for the Misbegotten, A Clearing in the Woods, Auntie Mame*

SUMMATION

There could have been no other decision; *Long Day's Journey Into Night* completely overshadowed everything else produced this season (including O'Neill's own *A Moon for the Misbegotten*, an artistic and financial failure). The Critics' Circle awards went to *Long Day's Journey Into Night* and *The Most Happy Fella*, a musical version of *They Knew What They Wanted.*

(Opposite Page, Standing Left to Right) *Bradford Dillman, Jason Robards, Jr., Fredric March,*(Foreground) *Florence Eldridge*

Anthony Perkins

Frances Hyland, Anthony Perkins

1957-58

THE YEAR IS 1916, and the setting is Eliza Gant's boarding house—"Dixieland"—in Altamont, N.C. Eliza is a penny-pinching matriarch whose drunken husband, W. O. Gant, is a stonecutter. Their children are Ben, dying of tuberculosis; Helen, whom Eliza has turned into a slavey; Luke, away in the Navy; and seventeen-year-old Eugene, a giant, dreaming boy whose rebellion and eventual departure from Altamont is the hinge upon which the play turns.

Ben is involved romantically with Mrs. "Fatty" Pert, a plump boarder much older than he. Eugene too falls in love with an older girl, Laura James, who comes to board at Dixieland. Both romances are doomed. Ben's is sealed by his death; Eugene loses Laura when she slips away from Altamont to marry a man in Richmond after she reluctantly faces the fact that she needs someone steadier and older than Eugene.

Eliza attempts to sell her husband's marble yard, including the huge Carrara stone angel which symbolizes all of his lost dreams. Gant taunts Eliza by playing along with the sale, but when he tells her that he plans to use the money to set himself and Eugene free of her, she tears up the check.

In the play's final scene, Eugene tells his mother off for her years of throttling his ambitions, for her pettiness in making him work at menial jobs that have destroyed his self-respect. Ben has left him some money—he will use it to go to college. Eliza knows that she has finally lost, that she can keep Eugene at Dixieland no longer. "Try to be happy, child," she manages to say.

Arthur Hill, Anthony Perkins, Hugh Griffith, Jo Van Fleet

LOOK HOMEWARD, ANGEL

THE CREDITS

A Play in Three Acts by Ketti Frings.
Based on the novel by Thomas Wolfe.
Produced by Kermit Bloomgarden and Theatre 200, Inc.
Staged by George Roy Hill.
Opened at the Ethel Barrymore Theatre, November 28, 1957, and ran for 564 performances.

THE CAST

Ben Gant	Arthur Hill
Mrs. Marie "Fatty" Pert	Florence Sundstrom
Helen Gant Barton	Rosemary Murphy
Hugh Barton	Leonard Stone
Eliza Gant	Jo Van Fleet
Will Pentland	Tom Flatley Reynolds
Eugene Gant	Anthony Perkins

Anthony Perkins, Jo Van Fleet, Hugh Griffith

JAKE CLATT	Joseph Bernard
MRS. CLATT	Mary Farrell
FLORRY MANGLE	Elizabeth Lawrence
MRS. SNOWDEN	Julia Johnston
MR. FARRELL	Dwight Marfield
MISS BROWN	Susan Torrey
LAURA JAMES	Frances Hyland
W. O. GANT	Hugh Griffith
DR. MCGUIRE	Victor Kilian
TARKINTON	Jack Sheehan
MADAME ELIZABETH	Bibi Osterwald
LUKE GANT	Arthur Storch

The Action of the Play Takes Place in the Town of Altamont, in the State of North Carolina, in the Year 1916.

ACT I

SCENE 1. *A Fall Afternoon.*
SCENE 2. *That Evening.*

ACT II

SCENE 1. *One Week Later.*
SCENE 2. *Two Days Later.*

ACT III

Two Weeks Later.

HISTORY AND REVIEWS

"A rich, beautiful, moving and full-bodied play which is perfectly cast, stunningly acted, sensitively directed and admirably set. . . ."

Look Homeward, Angel gave Thomas Wolfe an ironic, posthumous triumph in the theatre, a medium he had been unable to conquer during his brief, turbulent life. Although he became world-famous through his sprawling autobiographical novels—*Look Homeward, Angel*; *The Web and the Rock*; *You Can't Go Home Again*—Wolfe had always been a frustrated dramatist. He studied playwriting at the University of North Carolina with Professor Frederick H. Koch, who organized the famous Carolina Playmakers during Wolfe's junior year. Later, when he was doing graduate work at Harvard, Wolfe was a member of Professor George Pierce Baker's "47 Workshop." One of Wolfe's major ambitions was to write a successful play.

Wolfe did write a drama called *Mannerhouse*, and submitted it to The Theatre Guild. The Guild was mildly interested, but asked him to cut it. Wolfe, a compulsive over-writer, simply couldn't do the job; whenever he chopped anything out he put back twice as much new material, so that the "cut" version of *Mannerhouse* turned out to be even longer than the original. It was never produced.

Look Homeward, Angel, the first and most striking of Wolfe's novels, was originally to have been called *O Lost!* It owed its publication to the unsparing efforts of Maxwell Perkins, the monumentally patient Scribner's editor who helped Wolfe pare his immense manuscript down to manageable size. The book was published in 1929, when its author was 28, and was transparently the story of Wolfe's early years; Wolfe called himself Eugene Gant, and changed his home town of Asheville, N.C., into Altamont.

When *Look Homeward, Angel* first appeared it enraged the good citizens of Asheville with its blunt, unsparing portrayal of the seamier side of Southern small-town life. Libraries in Asheville refused to stock the book, and Wolfe got letters warning him that it would be dangerous for him to consider setting foot in his old home town.

Jo Van Fleet, Anthony Perkins

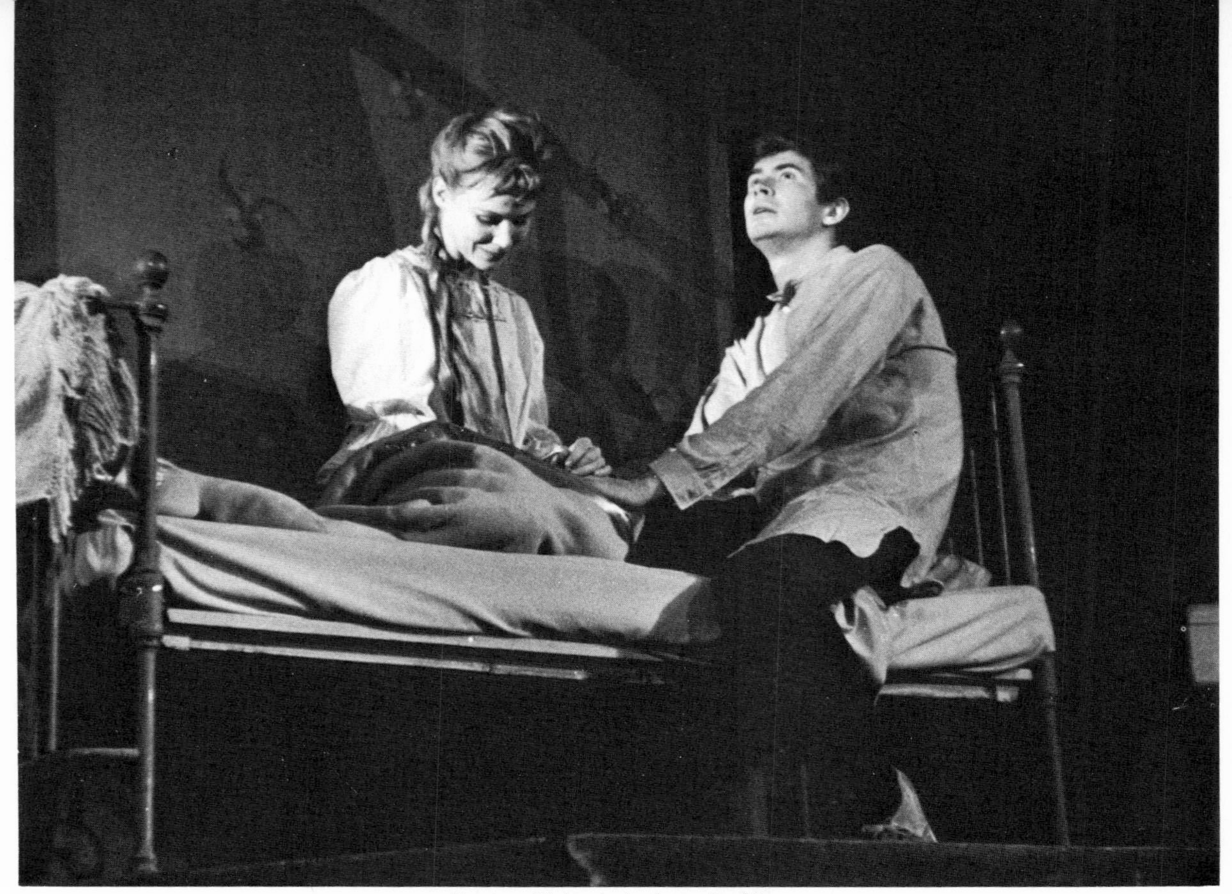

Frances Hyland, Anthony Perkins

Times have changed. These days the Asheville Chamber of Commerce prints a pamphlet promoting the city as a summer resort. The pamphlet's cover bears a drawing of Wolfe, with the legend: "Asheville's Famous Son—Thomas Wolfe."

Ketti Frings, who had the herculean task of jamming this steamer trunk of a book into the tight confines of the stage, had had one previous adaptation produced on Broadway, a whimsical failure called *Mr. Sycamore*. She was an established Hollywood script writer, and had done the screenplays for such films as *Come Back, Little Sheba*; *Guest in the House*; *About Mrs. Leslie* and *The Shrike*.

Miss Frings' original draft of *Look Homeward, Angel* contained both a prologue and an epilogue, with Wolfe (seen from the back only) as a shadowy interlocutor at the side of the stage, to introduce the actors. In her final version Miss Frings cut away all of this superfluous scaffolding, feeling that the play was strong enough to stand on its own. She also cut, as too sensual, the book's celebrated "jelly roll" sequence in which Eugene has his first furtive encounter with a prostitute.

In an interview with Henry Hewes in the *Saturday Review* of November 23, 1957, Miss Frings discussed her decision to limit the action of the play to a short period of time. To find the proper period, she looked for what she called "the point of non-blindedness," and discovered it in a single month of Eugene's seventeenth year.

"In a play," said Miss Frings, "the protagonist should have a blind spot about something. When that blind spot is removed for him, the play is over." She believed that Eugene's blind spot was his feeling that he was bound to respect and accept the ties of family love, at whatever cost to his personal feelings—his struggle against those ties drove the play to its conclusion, and to its hero's eventual liberation.

Some of the notices:

Walter Kerr in the *Herald Tribune*:

"The world of the Gants, as the late Thomas Wolfe lived it and wrote about it, was eternally two-faced. To a restless young writer doomed to simultaneous love and fury, it offered affection and solitary confinement in the same chilling breath. Here, on a gnarled and creaking Victorian porch, a man's heart could be warmed; it could also, in the same instant, be drained of every ounce of its blood. What makes the Ketti Frings adaptation of Mr. Wolfe's autobiographical novel so fascinating in the theatre is the perfect, perfectly sustained, tension with which it holds these violently opposed emotions in balance. You will hear, now and then, echoes of the effortful rhetoric that have disturbed even Thomas Wolfe's most ardent admirers. A few of the cliché-ridden catalogues creep in; there is pretentiousness here and there. But the essential, genuinely exciting theatricality of Miss Frings' play swallows these small burdens whole. *Look Homeward, Angel* looks at several sides of all the heartsick struggles it embraces. And it makes them live, very warmly, again."

John Chapman in the *Daily News*:

"From Thomas Wolfe's novel, *Look Homeward, Angel*, Ketti Frings has made a magnificent play which was given an almost miraculously beautiful performance last night. Here is a drama which ranks with, perhaps above, Arthur Miller's *Death of a Salesman* in strength and compassion. This is not merely an adaptation of a book, however profound the book may be; it is a work of splendid artistic creation on the part of Miss Frings."

Brooks Atkinson in *The New York Times*:

"What Thomas Wolfe could never do, Ketti Frings has done admirably. She has mined a solid drama out of the craggy abundance of *Look Homeward, Angel*. Obviously, a vast quantity of Wolfe's turbulent autobiography had to be omitted. But it is not to be missed. George Roy Hill, the director, has organized the play into a torrent of wild feelings. All the actors are superb in many styles and tempos —Hugh Griffith as the titanic father, Jo Van Fleet as the mother, Frances Hyland as Eugene's romantic ideal, Arthur Hill as the restless older brother. As Eugene, Anthony Perkins gives a brave and poignant performance."

John McClain in the *Journal-American*:

"*Look Homeward, Angel* is, quite simply, one of the best evenings I've ever had in the theatre.

Hugh Griffith,
Jo Van Fleet, Arthur Hill

Ketti Frings should receive the loudest praise, for she has most ingeniously telescoped a few chapters from the long autobiographical novel into an overpowering consideration of a young man's escape from adolescence."

Richard Watts, Jr., in the *Evening Post*:

"A rich, beautiful, moving and full-bodied play which is perfectly cast, stunningly acted, sensitively directed and admirably set. It just goes to show how stirring the theatre can be when all its elements are functioning imaginatively. *Look Homeward, Angel* is a dramatic event."

Wolfe's older sister, Mabel, his brother, Fred, and Mabel's husband, Ralph Wheaton, attended the Broadway opening and appeared to be not at all disconcerted by the fact that they were being portrayed on the stage.

"It was a tremendous emotional experience for all of us," said Mabel.

ALSO-RANS: *The Dark at the Top of the Stairs, Sunrise at Campobello, Two for the Seesaw, West Side Story, The Rope Dancers, The Music Man*

SUMMATION

A good decision; *Look Homeward, Angel* was skillful, sensitive, and marvelously theatrical without any sacrifice of integrity. *Sunrise at Campobello* was an effective, rather primitive study of Franklin D. Roosevelt's bout with polio. *West Side Story*, a strikingly original musical, owed too large a debt to *Romeo and Juliet* to be considered.

Frances Hyland, Hugh Griffith, Anthony Perkins

Pat Hingle, Nan Martin

Christopher Plummer

1958-59

THIS POETIC FANTASY is set in "a traveling circus which has been on the roads of the world for a long time." A balloon man, Mr. Zuss, and a popcorn vendor, Nickles, put on masks and serve as commentators on the play that unfolds. Mr. Zuss is God, Nickles is the Devil.

J. B. (Job) is the focus of their attention. As the play opens he is a happy man, serene in the company of his wife and children, healthy, rich. Nickles is convinced that once J. B. is deprived of these things, he will then curse God. Mr. Zuss, annoyed by what he thinks is the presumptuousness of this assumption, decides to put it to the test, and gives Nickles power over all that J. B. possesses.

J. B.'s children are killed, one by one; all of his money is taken away; he is stricken with torturingly painful disease. But his faith is not destroyed. All that he cries is: "Show me my guilt, O God!"

"Comforters" come to J. B. There are three of them, a psychiatrist, a Communist, and a cleric, but not one of them can supply an acceptable reason for God's silence in the face of J. B.'s woes. Finally Mr. Zuss, while never appearing to J. B., does restore his wife and his health, ironically reendowing him with the very mortality that had been his chief plague in the first place. J. B. never does curse God. As the play ends he has managed to hammer out a philosophy, if not a solution. To his patient wife Sarah he says:

"We *are*—and that is all our answer.
We are, and what we are can suffer . . .
But . . . what suffers, loves . . ."

(Left) *Christopher Plummer, Raymond Massey* (Standing), *Pat Hingle, Nan Martin*

Raymond Massey, Christopher Plummer

J. B.

THE CREDITS

A PLAY IN TWO ACTS BY ARCHIBALD MACLEISH.
PRODUCED BY ALFRED DE LIAGRE, JR.
STAGED BY ELIA KAZAN.
OPENED AT THE ANTA THEATRE, DECEMBER 11, 1958, AND RAN FOR 364 PERFORMANCES.

THE CAST

1ST ROUSTABOUT	Clifton James
2ND ROUSTABOUT	James Olson
NICKLES	Christopher Plummer
MR. ZUSS	Raymond Massey
PROMPTER	Ford Rainey
J. B.	Pat Hingle
SARAH	Nan Martin
DAVID	Arnold Merritt
MARY	Ciri Jacobsen

JONATHAN	Jeffrey Rowland
RUTH	Candy Moore
REBECCA	Merry Martin
THE GIRL	Janet Ward
MRS. BOTTICELLI	Helen Waters
MRS. LESURE	Fay Sappington
MRS. ADAMS	Judith Lowry
MRS. MURPHY	Laura Pierpont
JOLLY	Lane Bradbury
BILDAD	Bert Conway
ZOPHAR	Ivor Francis
ELIPHAZ	Andreas Voutsinas

The Scene is a Traveling Circus Which Has Been on the Roads of the World for a Long Time.

HISTORY AND REVIEWS

"A lovely work which sings of the unconquerable nobility of man's spirit. . . ."

With *J. B.*, God figured as a leading character in a Pulitzer Prize play for a second time, but that was about the only resemblance that the Archibald MacLeish play bore to *The Green Pastures*. Where *The Green Pastures* had been sweetly simple, *J. B.* was poetic and austere. Two plays could not have been cut from more different kinds of cloth.

"I badly needed an ancient structure," said MacLeish in a *New York Times* article before the opening, "on which to build the contemporary play that has haunted me for five years past, and the structure of the poem of Job is the only one I know of which our modern history will fit."

Some months later, in *Theatre Arts Magazine*, MacLeish discussed Job's willingness to accept a chance to take up his life again after he had suffered every possible anguish, and every possible loss:

"That willingness is as pure and naked an affirmation of the fundamental human thing—the fundamental human belief in life in spite of life, the fundamental human love of life *as* life and in spite of all the miseries of life—as I have ever found. The Book of Job is a *human triumph*. Its answer is not a dogma but an *act*—Job's *act*, Job's *doing*, Job's picking up his life again. And the myth of Job is a myth for our time because this is our answer also: the answer that moves so many of us who, without the formal beliefs that supported our ancestors, nevertheless pick up our lives again after these vast disasters and go on—go on *as men*."

MacLeish, sixty-six years old at the time of the opening of *J. B.* on Broadway, was a distinguished poet who had won two Pulitzer Prizes in that field, the first in 1932 for an epic poem called *Conquistador*, and the second in 1953 for his *Collected Verse*. His contributions to the theatre had been marginal—the libretto for *Union Pacific* in 1934, and a play called *Panic* the following year—but his poetry had made him famous, and since 1949 he had been serving as Boylston Professor of Rhetoric and Oratory at Harvard. In 1937 he had written a celebrated radio program, *The Fall of the City*, and he had also carved out a sizable government career as Librarian of Congress (1939–44), Associate Director of the Office of War Information, Assistant Secretary of State, and United States delegate to UNESCO.

Elia Kazan, Broadway's best-known director, who had staged four previous Pulitzer winners (*The Skin of Our Teeth*, *A Streetcar Named Desire*, *Death of a Salesman* and *Cat on a Hot Tin Roof*), agreed to direct *J. B.*, although it was utterly unlike any other play he had ever been involved with. Why did he take it on? "It was a rarity," said Kazan. "A real challenge. I had never done anything at all like it and didn't know if I could do it."

J. B. opened during a New York newspaper strike, and the reviews could not be printed until the

Lane Bradbury and Pat Hingle

strike was over, almost three weeks later. With a weaker play, the lack of immediate publicity could have been fatal; in the case of *J. B.*, it was no more than a minor annoyance.

Some of the notices:

Brooks Atkinson in *The New York Times*:

"Looking around at the wreckage and misery of the modern world, Archibald MacLeish has written a fresh and exalting morality that has great stature. In an inspired performance, it seemed to be one of the memorable works of the century as verse, as drama, and as spiritual inquiry. The performance is magnificent. As God and the Devil, respectively, Raymond Massey and Christopher Plummer preside over the central story with humor and imagination. As J. B., Pat Hingle gives an almost unbearably moving performance. In every respect, *J. B.* is theatre on its highest level."

Walter Kerr in the *Herald Tribune*:

"After every effort to find a meaning for so much pain has failed, Job gets to his feet, flexes his good right arm, and concludes: 'We are—and that is all our answer. We are—and what we are can suffer.' The words are clear, carved with dignity by the author; they are sometimes musical; and they are always words, the marching men of thought—something less than the fully-faced fleshes of men. We must settle for a dictionary of despair and reassertion, for a sober and handsome monument. As such a monument, *J. B.* is enormously impressive. The play's limitations are formal ones, deliberately elected by the author. If they keep the evening at some remove from wholly touching drama, they do nothing to rob it of its fascination as sheer theatre."

John McClain in the *Journal-American*:

"Scored by me as the best play of the season to date, perhaps of several seasons. It seemed to me it reached heights of poetry and performance seldom attempted in the history of the American theatre."

Richard Watts, Jr., in the *Evening Post*:

"Stunningly staged by Elia Kazan, with a splendidly imaginative setting by Boris Aronson, and notable performances by a fine cast, Mr. MacLeish's dramatic parable combines theatrical effectiveness with rueful lyric brooding on good and evil with impressive theatrical power. *J. B.* marks, I think, a considerable advance for its author as a writer for the theatre. He has always been a dramatic poet of power and eloquence, but here his dialogue, without sacrificing its dignity, has a clarity and forcefulness that work out admirably in theatrical terms. If it seems at its least impressive in its final scene, I suspect this is the inevitable fate of morality plays. The fact is that, no doubt due to something perverse in human nature, the theatre can dramatize the sadness, bitterness and desperation of mankind far more tellingly than it can explain the inscrutability of providence, and *J. B.* cannot escape it."

John Chapman in the *Daily News*:

"Not very often in my theatregoing have I been carried beyond the reach of my eyes and ears. *J. B.* is a lovely work which sings of the unconquerable nobility of man's spirit. This is a magnificent production of a truly splendid play. The setting by Boris Aronson goes beyond reality, which it should do in the ideal theatre. It is simple enough, as it stretches the canvas of its circus tent, but it seems to contain within it the whole and inspiring world of man."

Dealing as it did with the subtle and essentially mysterious dialogue which Man attempts to carry on with God, *J. B.* was bound to provoke a certain amount of theological discussion. After it had won the Pulitzer Prize, the play was the subject of a May 18, 1959, symposium in *Life*:

Reinhold Niebuhr, Professor at Union Theological Seminary:

"The puzzle of human existence is raised by the sharp contrast between man's greatness and his insignificance. As Job 7:17–18 puts it: 'What is Man, that Thou dost make so much of him, and that Thou dost set Thy mind upon him, dost visit him every morning, and test him every moment?' This is not only an even deeper problem than that of meaningless suffering but one more poignantly relevant to an atomic age which has the greatness to discover nuclear energy but lacks the wisdom to avoid the risk of nuclear war. MacLeish neglects this vital dimension of the original. He owes his dramatic success both to the honesty with which he states the problem and to the artistic ingenuity with which he fits his modern play into the old framework."

(Left) *Pat Hingle* (Right) *Christopher Plummer* (Standing) *Nan Martin*

Rabbi Louis Finkelstein, Chancellor of New York's Jewish Theological Seminary:

"The special appeal and effectiveness of *J. B.*, it seems to me, stems from the fact that ours is a Job-minded and Job-hearted generation. This is the unique discovery of MacLeish, the poet. In the character of J. B. he has created a symbol in which we see ourselves and our society, troubled and guilt-ridden."

Thurston N. Davis, S.J., editor of the Catholic weekly, *America*:

"Most of the people who see *J. B.* make the quite natural mistake of judging Archibald MacLeish's play to be about God. As a matter of fact, it isn't at all. *J. B.* is about Man—Man liberated from old theologies, Man obsessed with the notion that, as the final lines of the play have it,

'The candles in churches are out.
The lights have gone out in the sky.'

"If *J. B.* means anything, it is an urbane but shallow repudiation of religious faith."

ALSO-RANS: *A Raisin in the Sun, A Touch of the Poet, Sweet Bird of Youth, The Disenchanted, The Pleasure of His Company*

SUMMATION

An honorable choice; this was the first (and only) poetic play ever to win the Prize. *A Raisin in the Sun* (Critics' Circle Award) would have been a bolder and more contemporary selection, but there were no real complaints. *Sweet Bird of Youth* was far too gamy for consideration, and *A Touch of the Poet* found perennial winner O'Neill at less than his finest. *La Plume de ma Tante* was selected by the Critics' Circle as Best Musical.

(Center) *Pat Hingle*

Tom Bosley

Tom Bosley, Patricia Wilson

1959-60

FIORELLO! goes back to 1914 for its first act, when Fiorello H. LaGuardia was a perky and prosperous Greenwich Village lawyer. He runs successfully for Congress, goes overseas to become a flying hero in World War I, then comes home to plunge into New York City politics.

The first time he runs for Mayor he is overwhelmingly defeated by Tammany's James J. Walker, but as the musical ends, in 1933, he is preparing to run against Walker for a second time, and everybody knows how *that* election turned out.

In addition to his slam-bang politicking, Fiorello finds time for romance with two women: Thea, whom he marries, and who subsequently dies; and faithful Marie, who patiently waits for him for some fifteen years, and finally gets him.

The principal songs include "Little Tin Box," "Politics and Poker," "Till Tomorrow," "Gentleman Jimmy," "The Very Next Man," "When Did I Fall in Love?" and "The Name's LaGuardia."

(Left) *At rehearsal*: (L. to R.) *George Abbott, Jerome Weidman, Robert E. Griffith, Harold S. Prince, Sheldon Harnick, Jerry Bock* (At piano)

FIORELLO!

Tom Bosley

THE CREDITS

A MUSICAL IN TWO ACTS BY JEROME WEIDMAN AND GEORGE ABBOTT.
MUSIC BY JERRY BOCK. LYRICS BY SHELDON HARNICK.
PRODUCED BY ROBERT E. GRIFFITH AND HAROLD S. PRINCE.
STAGED BY GEORGE ABBOTT.
OPENED AT THE BROADHURST THEATRE, NOVEMBER 23, 1959, AND RAN FOR 796 PERFORMANCES.

THE CAST

ANNOUNCER	Del Horstmann
FIORELLO	Tom Bosley

Pat Stanley (Left) *leads a reprise of "Gentleman Jimmy"*

NEIL	Bob Holiday
MORRIS	Nathaniel Frey
MRS. POMERANTZ	Helen Verbit
MR. LOPEZ	H. F. Green
MR. ZAPPATELLA	David Collyer
DORA	Pat Stanley
MARIE	Patricia Wilson
BEN	Howard da Silva
ED PETERSON	Del Horstmann
2ND PLAYER	Stanley Simmonds
3RD PLAYER	Michael Quinn
4TH PLAYER	Ron Husman
5TH PLAYER	David London
6TH PLAYER	Julian Patrick
SEEDY MAN	Joseph Toner
1ST HECKLER	Bob Bernard
2ND HECKLER	Michael Scrittorale
3RD HECKLER	Jim Maher
4TH HECKLER	Joseph Toner
NINA	Pat Turner
FLOYD	Mark Dawson
SOPHIE	Lynn Ross
THEA	Ellen Hanley
SECRETARY	Mara Landi
SENATOR	Frederic Downs
COMMISSIONER	Michael Quinn

FRANKIE SCARPINI	Michael Scrittorale
MITZI	Eileen Rodgers
FLORENCE	Deedy Irwin
REPORTER	Julian Patrick
1ST MAN	Scott Hunter
2ND MAN	Michael Scrittorale
TOUGH MAN	David London
DERBY	Bob Bernard
FRANTIC	Stanley Simmonds
JUDGE CARTER	Joseph Toner

SINGERS: David Collyer, Barbara Gilbert, Del Horstmann, Deedy Irwin, Mara Landi, David London, Julian Patrick, Ginny Perlowin, Patsy Peterson, Silver Saundors, Ron Husman.

DANCERS: Charlene Carter, Bob Bernard, Elaine Cancilla, Ellen Harris, Patricia Harty, Scott Hunter, Bob La Crosse, Lynda Lynch, James Maher, Gregg Owen, Lowell Purvis, Dellas Rennie, Lynn Ross, Dan Siretta, Michael Scrittorale, Pat Turner.

ACT I

New York City, Shortly Before World War I.

ACT II

Ten Years Later.

HISTORY AND REVIEWS

"A song-and-dance jamboree with a curious streak of honest journalism, and a strong strain of rugged sobriety, about it. . . ."

Fiorello!, a musical inspection of the stormy life and times of New York's famous "Little Flower," Mayor Fiorello H. LaGuardia, was the second Pulitzer Prize production to deal in detail with the early career of a real-life political figure. Two more physically disparate politicians than Lincoln (of *Abe Lincoln in Illinois*) and LaGuardia could scarcely be found, but they did share a few important characteristics—both of them were incorruptably honest, and both were fighters.

On opening night, when the curtain went up on the first scene of *Fiorello!*, there was a chunky little figure sitting in front of a microphone, his glasses askew on his nose, reading the funny papers out loud in a squeaky, ridiculous, lovable voice. The audience burst into spontaneous applause. LaGuardia himself had been dead for more than a dozen years, but he was far from forgotten—and now, for a couple of hours, in the quite remarkable performance of Tom Bosley, he would live again.

Bosley made his Broadway debut as LaGuardia. When he first auditioned for the show, he somehow managed to get the impression that he was up for nothing more than the understudy to the lead. He had casually listened to a few of LaGuardia's recorded radio broadcasts, and had thumbed through a handful of old stills. Loose, nerveless, Bosley gave a reading so appealing that he landed the big part.

LaGuardia was a dream of a role for any actor, for the bantam Italian-American, cocky, ingratiating, bursting and bubbling with life, had been strictly a ham at heart. He loved to go to fires in his big black hat, and he loved those comics-reading sessions, when he brought the kids up to date on Dick Tracy and Joe Palooka and Little Orphan Annie. He also loved his work; he may well have been the most competent Mayor that New York City has ever had.

Before running for Mayor, LaGuardia spent ten straight years (1922–32) in the House of Representatives, where his flair for showmanship frequently came in handy. It was not enough for the young congressman to make a simple speech on the high cost of meat, for instance; he had to illustrate it dramatically. On the floor of the House, moaning about how much lamb chops cost, he fumbled through

"Politics and Poker"—Howard da Silva (Far Right)

his suit, and finally plucked a tiny chop out of his vest pocket. He wouldn't just talk about the air holes in a loaf of bread; he would squeeze the loaf itself until it collapsed like an accordion.

Fiorello! brought Jerome Weidman's talents to the stage for the first time; he collaborated with George Abbott on the musical's book. Some twenty-five years earlier, at the age of 22, Weidman had published his first novel, *I Can Get It for You Wholesale*, a sharp and knowing study of the garment industry, wise beyond its author's years, and an instant success. Weidman went on to a flourishing career as a short story writer and novelist, and once had this acid comment to make about some of his self-pitying contemporaries:

"I had the usual run of Typical American Boy jobs; soda jerk, delivery boy, newsboy, etc. None of these jobs taught me anything except, in later life, to distrust writers who say writing is drudgery. I can only assume that they never tried drudgery. I did, and it was appalling."

Fiorello! was the second Pulitzer Prize play to enlist George Abbott's services. He had been a young leading man back in the *Hell Bent fer Heaven* days; now, at the age of 72, ramrod-straight and curiously austere (although the theatre is a first-name business, nobody ever dreamed of calling him anything but "Mr. Abbott"), Abbott had come to be one of Broadway's very best directors of farce and musical comedy. The impeccably-paced *Fiorello!* revealed him at the peak of his powers. It also revealed that the celebrated Abbott austerity was something less than armor-plated. He sat with the rest of the company at the traditional party at Sardi's on opening night listening to the notices being read aloud, and he smiled when one reviewer called him "younger than springtime."

"I know I'm supposed to say I don't care about things like that," he said to a friend at his table. "But I do."

Some of the notices:

Brooks Atkinson in *The New York Times*:

"There are three ways in which *Fiorello!* is the ideal monument to our beloved Little Flower: it is exciting; it is enjoyable and it is decent. It recaptures a fabulous political firebrand and a breezy period in the life of New York. Jerome Weidman and George Abbott, old pros in excellent standing, have written the legend of LaGuardia's preliminary years in poster style—enjoying their hero as they go along. Jerry Bock has set it to a bouncy score. As the writer of lyrics, Sheldon Harnick is in an unfailingly humorous frame of mind. LaGuardia is extremely well played by Tom Bosley, who is short and a trifle portly, has a kindly face, abundant energy and an explosive personality. Under Mr. Abbott's invincible stage direction, the whole show comes to life with gusto."

Howard da Silva (Second from Right) *joins in rejoicing that "The Bum Won"*

Richard Watts, Jr., in the *Evening Post*:

"The new musical play is at its best when it is being a musical play. Its dramatic sections sometimes falter, and there are occasions when its narrative becomes tedious. Nor does it often quite live up to its opening few minutes. But its song and dance interludes are delightful. The show is a pleasant salute to a notable American."

John Chapman in the *Daily News*:

"Not since *Guys and Dolls* has there been a musical as down-to-the-sidewalks of New York as *Fiorello!* is. Not since *Of Thee I Sing* has there been a musical which achieves the sophisticated but cheerful attitude toward politics that *Fiorello!* does. It is indeed a well-built show, for Jerome Weidman and George Abbott have written the book and Abbott has staged *Fiorello!* with the clarity and swiftness that are his trademark and which few other big-show directors can achieve."

Walter Kerr in the *Herald Tribune*:

"Who is younger than springtime? George Abbott is younger than springtime. What the old master is up to at the moment is a song-and-dance jamboree with a curious streak of honest journalism, and a strong strain of rugged sobriety, about it. *Fiorello!* may, or may not, remind you of an exciting theatrical form once known as the Living Newspaper; in any case, it is apt to please the living daylights out of you. A crackerjack job. The thing is, when Mr. Abbott makes a musical, it's a beaut."

John McClain in the *Journal-American*:

"A warm, humorous and melodic panorama of the New York scene during the Tempestuous Twenties. The whole effort has a professional gloss and precision, and an odd lack of pretension, which are welcome in this era of over-or-under-simplification. *Fiorello!* is not a brash and busting big musical, and it doesn't try to be. It tells a heartening story well, and the music is in complete sympathy."

Fiorello! also won the Critics' Circle Award for Best Musical of the Year. The critics cited Lillian Hellman's *Toys in the Attic* as Best Play. John Mason Brown and John Gassner, the Pulitzer jurors, recommended *Toys in the Attic* and were shocked when the announcement of the *Fiorello!* award was made. They did not resign their posts, however, until three years later, when their recommendation of *Who's Afraid of Virginia Woolf* was disregarded.

ALSO-RANS: *Toys in the Attic, The Tenth Man, The Andersonville Trial, The Best Man, The Miracle Worker, The Sound of Music*

SUMMATION

A good decision, and a popular one, even though that perennial bridesmaid, Lillian Hellman, missed again. *The Miracle Worker*, a theatrically effective documentary about Helen Keller's childhood, was perhaps the strongest runner-up. As long as a musical was chosen, the meat-and-potatoes *Fiorello!* deservedly prevailed over the spun-sugar *The Sound of Music.*

"Home Again," from World War I (Left) *Ellen Hanley, Tom Bosley*

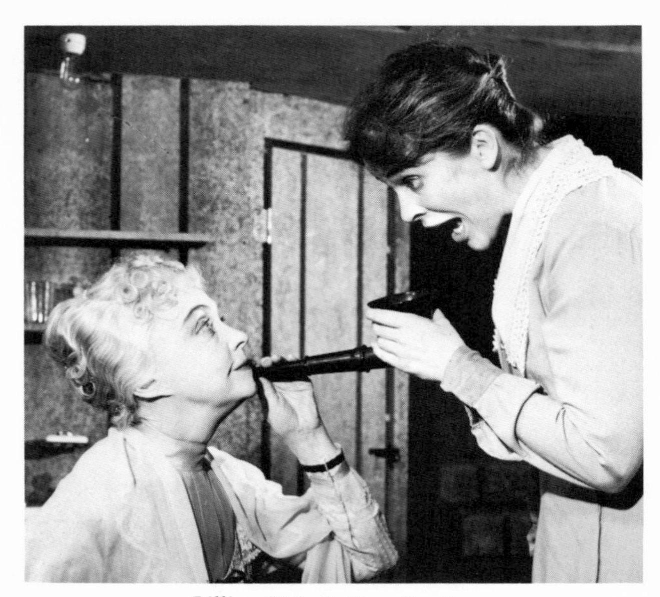

Lillian Gish, Colleen Dewhurst

John Megna, Tom Wheatley, Colleen Dewhurst

Arthur Hill, Colleen Dewhurst

1960-61

All the Way Home is set in Knoxville, Tennessee, and covers a period of four days in May, 1915. Jay and Mary Follet have a six-year-old son, Rufus, and it is the boy's first tremulous struggle to grow up, after the sudden accidental death of his father, that gives this low-key, almost plotless play much of its warmth and poignancy.

Rufus (a plainly autobiographical portrait of novelist James Agee) is shown in a variety of situations: cringing under the jokes of older boys, who taunt him for his "nigger" name; being taken to visit his 103-year-old great-great-grandmother; sharing chocolates with his beloved Aunt Hannah, as they go shopping to buy him a coveted cap.

Jay and Mary have made an obviously good marriage, warm and secure since Jay stopped the drinking that used to devil him. Jay is called out one midnight to drive to the bedside of his presumably dying father. On the way home, the steering mechanism of his car breaks down, and he is instantly killed when the car lurches off the road.

Mary is shattered, but manages to find the strength to go on living, and the courage to tell Rufus, for the first time, about the baby she is carrying.

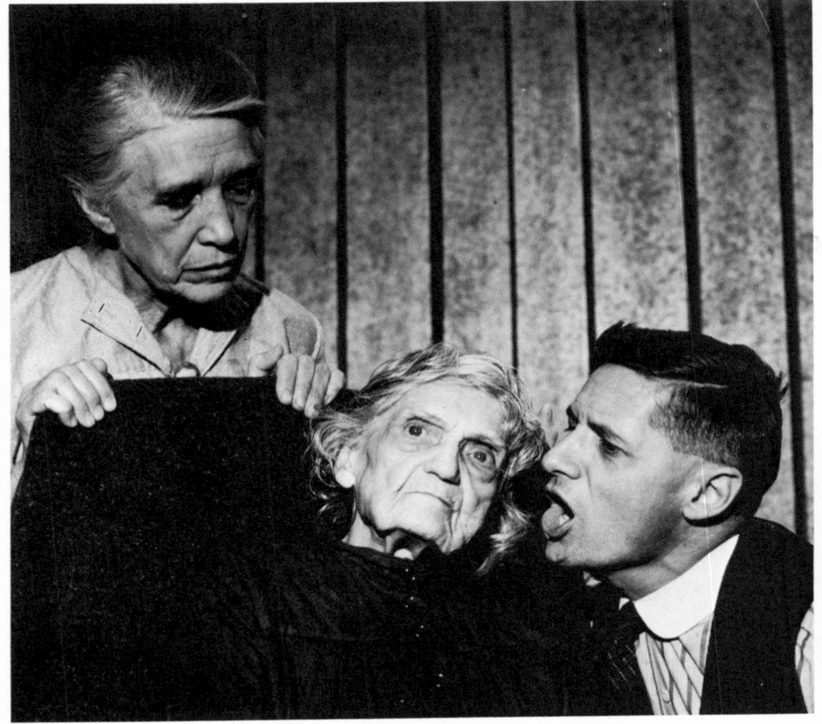

Dorrit Kelton, Lylah Tiffany, Arthur Hill

ALL THE WAY HOME

Christopher Month, Lenka Peterson, James Clifton

THE CREDITS

A Drama in Three Acts by Tad Mosel.
Based on James Agee's *A Death in the Family*.
Produced by Fred Coe, in association with Arthur Cantor.
Staged by Arthur Penn.
Opened at the Belasco Theatre, November 30, 1960, and ran for 334 performances.

THE CAST

Rufus	John Megna
Boys	Larry Provost
	Jeff Conaway
	Gary Morgan
	Robert Ader

JAY FOLLET	Arthur Hill
MARY FOLLET	Colleen Dewhurst
RALPH FOLLET	Clifton James
SALLY FOLLET	Lenka Peterson
JOHN HENRY FOLLET	Edwin Wolfe
JESSIE FOLLET	Georgia Simmons
JIM WILSON	Christopher Month
AUNT SADIE FOLLET	Dorrit Kelton
GREAT-GREAT-GRANMAW	Lylah Tiffany
CATHERINE LYNCH	Lillian Gish
AUNT HANNAH LYNCH	Aline MacMahon
JOEL LYNCH	Thomas Chalmers
ANDREW LYNCH	Tom Wheatley
FATHER JACKSON	Art Smith

The Action Takes Place In and Around Knoxville, Tennessee, in May of 1915.

ACT I

The First Day.

ACT II

The Second Day.

ACT III

Two Days Later.

HISTORY AND REVIEWS

"A simple and searching play about commonplace things like love and death and the need to go on living. . . ."

All the Way Home, adapted by Tad Mosel from *A Death in the Family*, a posthumous novel by James Agee, was one of those Cinderella plays that Broadway loves to sentimentalize into legends. The closing notice was posted for the first time the day after the opening, even though the reviews had ranged from respectful to ecstatic, and under normal circumstances *All the Way Home* would have vanished forever after a single week's run. That it eventually ran for well over nine months is a tribute to the tenacity of its producers, to the effectiveness of a hammer-and-tongs promotion campaign, and, of course, to the moving theatrical qualities of the play itself.

During its Broadway run *All the Way Home* lost about $115,000 of its original $150,000 investment, but the proceeds of the motion picture sale wiped out most of the remaining deficit, and eventually the small profits from stock rights may write off the rest.

All the Way Home began its precarious Perils-of-Pauline career when business perked up suddenly at the Saturday matinee and evening performances that were to have been its last ones on Broadway. The producers, Fred Coe and Arthur Cantor, decided to chance running it for at least one more week. Ed Sullivan mentioned the play very favorably on his television program that Sunday, and on Monday the New York newspapers appeared with ads trumpeting the news about "THE MIRACLE ON 44TH STREET!" At that time it would have seemed miracle enough had it run for a month, but producers

Coe and Cantor had cannily managed to open their play at a cost of only $105,000, leaving themselves $45,000 to maneuver with.

With this backlog, and with attendance sustaining a modest but acceptable level, *All the Way Home* lurched along for month after month, surviving half a dozen subsequent closing notices, its large band of devotees fierce and vocal in their support. The Critics' Circle Award gave it an extra shot of adrenalin at exactly the right moment, and so, of course, did the Pulitzer Prize. Those twin crowns helped tide the battered Cinderella over the summer of 1961, and it was a proud, if profitless, show that closed in September of that year.

James Agee, who died at the age of 45 in 1955, left behind him a series of brilliantly written autobiographical fragments that were stitched together after his death into *A Death in the Family*. The novel itself won a Pulitzer Prize in 1958, and when the play won the Pulitzer Prize for drama it marked only the second time that such a double victory had been scored; the first was *South Pacific*, ten years earlier.

As a young man Agee had worked as a harvest stiff in Kansas and Nebraska, and gained his first recognition as an author with a study of Southern sharecroppers called *Let Us Now Praise Famous Men*; he provided the searching and sensitive text, and Walker Evans took the equally memorable photographs. The book sold less than 600 copies the year it first appeared, but had a sturdy "underground" reputation, and was later reissued. Speaking of Agee, Evans said:

"Agee's rebellion was unquenchable, self-damaging, deeply principled, infinitely costly and ultimately priceless. Agee had an ingrained courtesy that emanated from him."

As a writer for various magazines, Agee was perhaps the finest motion picture reviewer this country has ever produced, and subsequently went out to Hollywood to write some excellent movies of his own, among them *The African Queen*, *Night of the Hunter* and *The Bride Comes to Yellow Sky*.

In 1958, with *A Death in the Family* on the best-seller lists, Fred Coe commissioned Tad Mosel to adapt it into a play. The two men had worked together in television, with Mosel contributing plays to *NBC/TV Playhouse*, *Omnibus* and *Studio One*. The 38-year-old Mosel had never written a Broadway play before.

Some of the notices:

Richard Watts, Jr., in the *Evening Post*:

"*All the Way Home* is a somber and beautiful play. It is an account of the effect on a family of the young father's accidental death, and it is concerned entirely with the capturing of a mood. But so sensitively is that mood caught and maintained, and so admirable is the casting and acting, that the result is remarkably true and moving in its brooding sadness. There couldn't easily be a more melancholy play, but the effect is not one of morbidness or striving for sentimental tearfulness. The mood is austere and reflective, and the spirit is philosophical and compassionate. Every performance deserves applause, and so does Arthur Penn's staging."

John Chapman in the *Daily News*:

"This minor-key drama was intended to 'get' me, but somehow I failed to respond as I should. I was led into the midst of two large Southern families and I should have become absorbed in their ordinary, unheroic lives; but instead of joining them I remained at a distance, wishing only that they would hurry up and get on with what they were doing. As a study of many characters *All the Way Home* is sensitive, honest and direct; but as a narrative for the stage, it lacks strength and unity."

Walter Kerr in the *Herald Tribune*:

"I don't know which I respect most, dramatist Tad Mosel's willingness to undertake the task of adapting James Agee's brilliant and difficult novel, or the theatrical daring he has displayed in adapting it. *All the Way Home* is a playwright's gamble, and it ends in one for the audience; is a central moment of truth worth an evening that wavers on the way to it and then wavers again as it is about to go home? I'd say that it was an experience for those theatregoers who also like risking something, and don't mind possible losses. Even in the losses, there is some courage and distinction."

John McClain in the *Journal-American*:

"It is at least a four-handkerchief tear-jerker with one good act, one quite good, but a final one which flounders and finally bogs down. The first act, in which the characters are skillfully and thoroughly developed, is first class. So is some of the second, but after the announcement of the tragedy, the play settles down to 10-proof anguish. There is nothing wrong with even stronger anguish, but when taken relentlessly over long periods of time it has a tendency to make the consumer resentful, and I'm afraid this is what happens here. The author's people are dimensional and honest and I liked them. Maybe that's why I became impatient that they had to suffer so much, all the (too) long way home."

Howard Taubman in *The New York Times*:

"*All the Way Home* is a simple and searching play about commonplace things like love and death and the need to go on living. Colleen Dewhurst plays Mary with delicacy and strength. Arthur Hill has firmness and tension as Jay. Alice MacMahon has a grand and touching dignity as Aunt Hannah. Lillian Gish is sweetly ineffectual as Mary's mother, and Thomas Chalmers is understanding as her father. Pint-sized John Megna does a wonderful job with the taxing role of Rufus. *All the Way Home* fills its simple story of good, weak men, women and children with a quiet compassion that one will remember long after some of the theatre's flashier sensations."

When *All the Way Home* was turned into a Paramount motion picture in 1962, a typical advertisement read, possibly inevitably:

"LOVE IS NOT A THING THAT GROWS ONLY IN THE DARK. That's what Mary Follet learns from marriage to Jay Follet. Mary Follet entered marriage a girl. She became a woman. A woman with a child. The child grew up to be James Agee, who wrote a Pulitzer Prize novel about Mary Follet's marriage. It is now a motion picture about all the kinds of love there are. . . ."

One can't help wondering what the cynical Mr. Agee, a free-swinger in his treatment of any kind of sentimental pap, would have had to say about that.

ALSO-RANS: *Period of Adjustment; Mary, Mary; A Far Country; Big Fish, Little Fish; The Wall; Advise and Consent*

SUMMATION

A good choice. *All the Way Home* was the best of a comparatively undistinguished lot. Jean Kerr's glossy but superficial *Mary, Mary* and Tennessee Williams' minor *Period of Adjustment* were never serious competitors. The Critics' Circle chose *Carnival* as Best Musical.

Lillian Gish, Colleen Dewhurst, Thomas Chalmers, Aline MacMahon, Tom Wheatley

(Left) *Choreographer Bob Fosse directing the "Coffee Break" number*

At rehearsal: Abe Burrows, Cy Feuer, Frank Loesser

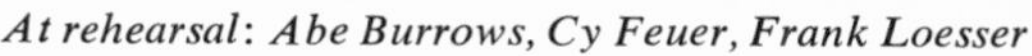

Rudy Vallee, Robert Morse

1961-62 HOW TO

J. Pierrepont Finch, a most ambitious young man, reads a book called *How to Succeed in Business Without Really Trying*, and assiduously applies its principles to his business career. He gets a job with J. B. Biggley's World Wide Wickets Company, and plays office politics with such superb *élan* that he moves swiftly and inevitably up the company ladder, from window washer to the mail room, and then through the advertising department right up to the very top, when he becomes Chairman of the Board.

En route Finch acquires a girl, Rosemary, but it is not to her that he sings the show's sweetest love song, "I Believe in You." No. Finch, peering soulfully into a mirror, sings the song to himself.

Other major songs include "Happy to Keep His Dinner Warm," "Coffee Break," "The Company Way," "A Secretary is Not a Toy," "Grand Old Ivy" and "Rosemary."

Robert Morse

(At Top) *Robert Morse*

SUCCEED IN BUSINESS WITHOUT REALLY TRYING

Rudy Vallee, Virginia Martin, Robert Morse

THE CREDITS

A Musical Comedy in Two Acts by Abe Burrows, Jack Weinstock and Willie Gilbert.

Based on the novel by Shepherd Mead.

Music and Lyrics by Frank Loesser.
Produced by Cy Feuer and Ernest Martin, in association with Frank Productions, Inc.

Staged by Abe Burrows.
Opened at the 46th St. Theatre, October 14, 1961, and ran for 1,417 performances.

Robert Morse

THE CAST

FINCH	Robert Morse
GATCH	Ray Mason
JENKINS	Robert Kaliban
TACKABERRY	David Collyer
PETERSON	Casper Roos
J. B. BIGGLEY	Rudy Vallee
ROSEMARY	Bonnie Scott
BRATT	Paul Reed
SMITTY	Claudette Sutherland
FRUMP	Charles Nelson Reilly
MISS JONES	Ruth Kobart
MR. TWIMBLE	Sammy Smith
HEDY	Virginia Martin
SCRUBWOMEN	Mara Landi Silver Saundors
MISS KRUMHOLTZ	Mara Landi
TOYNBEE	Ray Mason
OVINGTON	Lanier Davis
POLICEMAN	Bob Murdock
WOMPER	Sammy Smith

SINGERS: David Collyer, Lanier Davis, Robert Kaliban, Bob Murdock, Casper Roos, Charlotte Frazier, Mara Landi, Fairfax Mason, Silver Saundors, Maudeen Sullivan.

DANCERS: Nick Andrews, Tracy Everitt, Stuart Fleming, Richard Korthaze, Dale Moreda, Darrell Notara, Merritt Thompson, Carol Jane Abney, Madilyn Clark, Elaine Cancilla, Suzanna France, Donna McKechnie, Ellie Somers, Rosemary Yellen.

TIME: *The Present.*

PLACE: *The Park Avenue Offices of World Wide Wickets Co., Inc.*

HISTORY AND REVIEWS

"Crafty, conniving, sneaky, cynical, irreverent, impertinent, sly, malicious, and lovely, just lovely. . . ."

The French knew it as *Comment Reussir Dans Les Affaires Sans Vraiment Se Fatiguer*. The Japanese title was *Doryoku Shinaìde Shussei Suru Hoho*. In any language, *How to Succeed in Business Without Really Trying* was one of the longest titles ever squeezed onto a marquee, and one of the most maliciously entertaining shows in years.

Dr. Jack Weinstock and Willie Gilbert, a pair of television writers, and close friends outside of office hours (Weinstock once removed Gilbert's appendix, something Sir Arthur Sullivan never did for *his* Gilbert!), were the first men to see the theatrical possibilities in Shepherd Mead's 1952 book, *How to Succeed in Business Without Really Trying*, which had been subtitled: "The Dastard's Guide to Fame and Fortune." They wrote it as a straight comedy, and then were persuaded by producers Cy Feuer and Ernest Martin to join forces with Abe Burrows and Frank Loesser and turn their play into a musical.

Some years earlier, Burrows and Loesser had worked together on the delightful *Guys and Dolls*, a raffish song-and-dancer built around Damon Runyon's Broadway underworld. In his younger days, Burrows was famous for the songs of his own creation which he delighted to sing at parties: "Tokyo Rose," "I Am Strolling Down Memory Lane Without a Single Thing to Remember," "I Looked Under a Rock and Found a Rose," and "The Girl with the Three Blue Eyes" ("What makes her diff'rent?"). Loesser had first challenged Broadway with *Where's Charley?*, the show in which Ray Bolger sang "Once in Love with Amy."

"I never write the book *for* a musical comedy," said Burrows, shortly before the *How to Succeed* opening, in a *New York Times* interview with Maurice Zolotow. "A musical isn't a play with music glued on it. What I write is a musical comedy book. There's a lot of difference between a book for a musical comedy and a musical comedy book. When I hear a writer is writing a libretto before he even knows who the composer is I think the writer must be out of his mind. The composer and the book writer have to work together as a unity."

Like many funny men, Burrows is very serious about the business of making jokes. He spoke of his theatrical philosophy in an interview with Glenna Syse of the *Chicago Sun-Times*:

"The successful playwright is one whom the audience forgets. You should not be sitting there thinking of him. Howard Lindsay used to say, 'Don't let them catch you at it.' Illusion is the whole secret.

"When I give talks to drama students, to those who want to write plays, I always ask them, 'Where is the theatrical effect? Where is the audience going to laugh, where are they going to cry, where are they going to get hit in the stomach?' It's a calculated effect and the writer is there to make the effect.

"It's like meeting someone on the street who's in a hurry. You grab his lapel and say, 'I want to tell you a story.' It had better be a good one, because it's your responsibility that you've held him up. And it's the same in the theatre. You're responsible to that audience and you'd better know your theatrical effects."

How to Succeed provided its audiences with a superb example of counterpoint in the relationship of its two stars, the young Robert Morse and the veteran Rudy Vallee. The show was written with Morse

The dancing chorus goes all out in "The Yo Ho Ho"

Bonnie Scott,
Robert Morse, Rudy Vallee

specifically in mind; Burrows never considered any other actor for the role of Finch, the smiling young go-getter who slithers his way to the top of the corporate tree; Burrows had directed Morse in *Say, Darling* a couple of seasons earlier, and knew that the actor had just the quality he wanted. Vallee, thirty years older than the days when, armed with a megaphone and a boyish grin, he was the country's first crooner, was magnificently pompous as J. B. Biggley.

Some of the notices:

Richard Watts, Jr., in the *Evening Post*:

"*How to Succeed in Business Without Really Trying* is a brilliant musical comedy in which everything works out. In its first performance, its satire, humor, book, music, lyrics, cast, staging, choreography, setting and general gaiety of spirit combined in a smooth, fast pattern of expert showmanship to make the occasion a delightful event. It was a triumph for many talented people and cause for an ovation to Robert Morse in its vital central role. It is possible that Frank Loesser's score lacks any outstanding hit song, but it is invariably gay, charming and tuneful, and it has the enormous virtue of fitting in perfectly with the spirit and style of the book's satire. The new musical comedy is a smashing success."

John McClain in the *Journal-American*:

"The most inventive and stylized and altogether infectious new musical in recent recollection. It is gay, zingy, amoral, witty and shot with style. It comes very close to being a new form in musicals. It is difficult to imagine anybody but Robert Morse in the role of Pierrepont Finch. Another triumph of casting finds Rudy Vallee as J. B. Biggley. Abe Burrows must be responsible for moulding the whole mad, eye-filling conglomeration into an evening of excitement and delight. He was seen in the lobby on opening night wearing a gold vest and a tweed cap. Now he'll be able to afford a hat to match."

John Chapman in the *Daily News*:

"This splendidly sardonic account of Big Business is an example of perfect musical comedy construction, swift and sharp, jam-packed with characters and incident and clear-headed as it moves unerringly through an interesting and funny story. Frank Loesser is a perfect man for the songs; for he is a cynic without being tough. He has not put in a note of music or a syllable of lyric that doesn't carry the story along."

Walter Kerr in the *Herald Tribune*:

"*How to Succeed in Business Without Really Trying* is crafty, conniving, sneaky, cynical, irreverent, impertinent, sly, malicious, and lovely, just lovely. What most distinguishes a sassy, gay and exhilarating evening is—and you'll never believe this—the book. For the first time, really, an entire musical comedy has been fashioned along the deadpan, and deadly, lines of Mr. Burrows' celebrated piano parodies ("Good Luck, Boulder Dam"). This is a musical with a mind. A bland and caustic kidding of the American success story goes on all evening, without ever losing its frosty and lunatic altitude. Gags are subordinated to impish running commentary; Mr. Loesser's perky score is subordinated to the merry malice that is afoot; meaningful fantasy is given its head, and the point of view grins and glows with its own cocksure effrontery."

Howard Taubman in *The New York Times*:

"*How to Succeed in Business Without Really Trying* stings mischievously and laughs uproariously. It belongs to the bluechips among modern musicals. It arrives bearing precious gifts of an adult viewpoint and consistency of style. It never lets up; indeed, it becomes livelier and funnier as it moves up the ladder with Finch. Let Wall Street and Madison Avenue tremble as the rest of us rejoice."

The Pulitzer citation went jointly to Burrows and Loesser, citing them as "principal contributors" to *How to Succeed*, and ignoring the unfortunate Weinstock and Gilbert, who had only had the original idea of dramatizing Mead's book. Despite the acknowledged major contributions of the Messrs. Burrows and Loesser (there would never have been a real show without Burrows), it was an unwarranted slap at the first two collaborators.

ALSO-RANS: *The Night of the Iguana; Gideon; Oh Dad, Poor Dad, Mama's Hung You in the Closet and I'm Feelin' So Sad; A Thousand Clowns; Purlie Victorious*

SUMMATION

An excellent choice, for in all departments *How to Succeed* was the most purely professional show of the season. It also won the Critics' Circle Award for Best Musical. Kopit's *Oh Dad, Poor Dad* was a farce with delusions of grandeur. Williams' *The Night of the Iguana* (Critics' Circle Award) was flashily theatrical, but did not approach the emotional depths of his earlier *A Streetcar Named Desire*. According to rumor, Ossie Davis' *Purlie Victorious* was the closest contender.

(Center) *Robert Morse, Rudy Vallee*

1962-63

Uta Hagen and Arthur Hill in Who's Afraid of Virginia Woolf?

NO AWARD

One of the most searing and shattering plays of modern times, Edward Albee's *Who's Afraid of Virginia Woolf?*, was passed up by the Advisory Board this season in a spectacular display of foolishness and timidity that ranked with the *Old Maid/Children's Hour* fiasco of 1934–35. The ferocity of *Virginia Woolf*'s alcoholic battles, along with its outspoken language, undoubtedly served to disqualify it at Columbia, even though the two theatrical jurors, John Mason Brown and John Gassner, had unanimously recommended its selection. Both Brown and Gassner resigned their posts when their *Virginia Woolf* recommendation was turned down.

There were no other serious also-rans this season, in which two previous winners came up with poor plays: Tennessee Williams' *The Milk Train Doesn't Stop Here Any More*, and William Inge's *Natural Affection*. *Never Too Late* was the surprise comedy hit of the year, but never figured as a Pulitzer candidate.

The Critics' Circle chose *Virginia Woolf* as Best Play.

1963-64

Jason Robards, Jr., and Barbara Loden in After the Fall

NO AWARD

For a second year in a row no Prize was awarded. This season, however, there was no *Who's Afraid of Virginia Woolf?* to make observers feel that a genuinely striking drama had been slighted. The leading candidate for the Prize was probably Arthur Miller's *After the Fall*, but this *drame á clef* about an introspective man and his blonde movie star wife was almost unpleasant in its peepshow frankness, and may well have lost out on moral if not artistic grounds.

The other plays of the season were simply not Prize material. Neil Simon's riotously funny *Barefoot in the Park* was a superb commercial comedy, but lacked something of the warmth and heart that had distinguished such other comedy winners as *Harvey* and *You Can't Take It With You*. Edward Albee stumbled with an adaptation of Carson McCullers' *The Ballad of the Sad Café*, and Sidney Michaels' *Dylan* owed most of its success to the brilliance of putty-nosed Alec Guinness, making one of his rare American appearances. Paddy Chayefsky's *The Passion of Josef D* and Muriel Resnik's *Any Wednesday* were never really in the running. The Critics' Circle selections were *Luther* and *Hello, Dolly!*

Irene Dailey, Martin Sheen

(Right) *Irene Dailey, Jack Albertson*

Martin Sheen. Jack Albertson, Irene Dailey

1964-65

THE PLAY TAKES PLACE in the kitchen and living room of the Clearys' Bronx apartment. The time is May of 1946, and there are only three characters: John Cleary, his wife, Nettie, and their son, Timmy.

The play is a subtle examination of the stresses that lie beneath the surface of this apparently humdrum family, and of the hostility, sometimes verging on hatred, between father and son, and between husband and wife. There is little "plot" as such, the playwright being more concerned with character than with action.

Timmy Cleary comes home from a long hitch in World War II to an uneasy reunion with his parents. They fuss over him too much, and are obviously, for his sake, trying to hide the bad blood between them.

Timmy and his father go off to a ball game, and return with a bunch of roses for Nettie. John

Martin Sheen, Irene Dailey, Jack Albertson

Martin Sheen, Jack Albertson

THE SUBJECT WAS ROSES

Frank D. Gilroy

carries them, but Timmy suggested buying them. Nettie is delighted, and views the flowers as a token that her differences with John over his drinking, his coldness and his secrecy about money may yet be somehow resolved. Her delight evaporates when he brutally tells her, in the heat of one of their frequent quarrels, that the bouquet was all Timmy's idea.

The three of them squabble, make up, squabble again. Finally, sick of the whole situation, Timmy makes up his mind to leave home. John desperately wants the boy to stay, and humbles himself in the gravest way he can think of, by telling Timmy the exact amount of money he has. Timmy then relates a dream he has had, in which the boy found himself saying: "My father's dead, and he never said he loved me." Timmy, agonizingly vulnerable, now says to his father: "I love you, Pop." He decides to stay at home, but his father urges him to leave after all, realizing that Timmy's continued presence would only serve to heighten the tensions that have been building up in the apartment since his return.

Irene Dailey

THE CREDITS

A PLAY IN TWO ACTS BY FRANK D. GILROY.
PRODUCED BY EDGAR LANSBURY.
STAGED BY ULU GROSBARD.
OPENED AT THE ROYALE THEATRE, MAY 25, 1964, AND RAN FOR 832 PERFORMANCES.

THE CAST

JOHN CLEARY	Jack Albertson
NETTIE CLEARY	Irene Dailey
TIMMY CLEARY	Martin Sheen

SETTING: *A Middle Class Apartment.*
TIME: *May, 1946.*

ACT I

SCENE 1. *Saturday Morning.*
SCENE 2. *Saturday Afternoon.*
SCENE 3. *Saturday Midnight.*

ACT II

SCENE 1. *Sunday Morning.*
SCENE 2. *Sunday Evening.*
SCENE 3. *Sunday Midnight.*
SCENE 4. *Monday Morning.*

HISTORY AND REVIEWS

"With simplicity, humor and integrity he has looked into the hearts of three decent people. . . ."

The Subject Was Roses crept quietly onto Broadway in late May, a traditionally dreadful month for a serious drama to open in, particularly a three-character one without a single box-office name in its cast. It was produced by an unknown, directed by an unknown, and was the work of a playwright who had had only one other play done in New York. All of the signs pointed to a quick failure, and all of the signs were dead wrong.

Frank D. Gilroy's admittedly autobiographical play received notices that were for the most part excellent. The advance sale had been a pathetic $165.00, and despite the favorable reviews, business in the first few weeks was slim. Gradually, however, the public began to respond, and while business never reached capacity, it did increase to a point where the production was paying its operating expenses, and even making a few dollars each week. In the spring of 1965, when *Roses* had already been running for nearly a year, it won both the Pulitzer Prize and the Critics' Circle Award, producing an additional momentum which kept it alive for many months more.

Gilroy was 38 when *The Subject Was Roses* was produced. Born in the Bronx, he entered the Army at 18, after graduating from DeWitt Clinton High School. After the war he went to Dartmouth, graduating *magna cum laude*, and then spent a year at Yale Drama School.

Gilroy moved into television early, and very successfully; in the late 1940's and early 50's, many live television dramas were being done out of New York, and his scripts appeared on Playhouse 90, Kraft Theatre, Studio One, Omnibus and U.S. Steel. By 1957 he had saved enough money to take a few months off to write a play, *Who'll Save the Plowboy?* It was finally done off-Broadway by the Phoenix Theatre in the season of 1961–62, and won him an "Obie" as the best off--Broadway production of the year.

The first draft of *The Subject Was Roses* was written in 1961, and finally polished to Gilroy's satisfaction by April of 1962. It was two more years before it saw a stage. Gilroy told the whole story of its pre-production problems in a Random House book, *About Those Roses*, from which most of the following material has been excerpted.

As an example of the casting difficulties that were involved, take the list of men who were considered for the role of the father, and who for various reasons turned it down: Karl Malden, E. G. Marshall, Walter Matthau, Arthur Kennedy, Dan Dailey, Edmond O'Brien, Van Heflin, Art Carney, Dan Duryea, Eddie Albert, Robert Preston, Jason Robards, Jr. and David Wayne. Eventually, Gilroy happened to see Jack Albertson in a California revival of *Burlesque*, and from then on thought of no one else for the role —Albertson reminded the playwright so vividly of his own father that Gilroy insisted he was the only proper actor to play him.

The role of the mother was offered to such an assortment of actresses as Judy Holliday, Maureen Stapleton, Geraldine Page, Teresa Wright, Eileen Heckart, Colleen Dewhurst, Kim Hunter, Geraldine Fitzgerald and Shelley Winters, before it eventually went to Irene Dailey, an excellent but comparatively obscure actress who had made her chief reputation off-Broadway.

Fewer problems were presented by the role of the son. At one point Keir Dullea (of *David and Lisa*) felt he might want to play it, but in the end it was given to a young actor named Martin Sheen, who came to *Roses* fresh from *Never Live Over a Pretzel Factory*.

Two young producers, Leonard Soloway and Richard Altman, optioned the play, but reluctantly gave it up after a year; all of the male "names" they had approached had turned them down, and Gilroy by that time was becoming very stuffy in his insistence on Albertson. Early in the spring of 1964, Edgar Lansbury, an old television associate of Gilroy's, read the script and agreed to produce it. Ulu Grosbard, another old friend, was signed on as director.

The play's budget was set at $40,000. Gilroy himself agreed to raise $15,000 of it, and did so on the telephone, an indication that there might be another career open to him should he ever abandon playwriting. Lansbury got the rest, digging into his own pocket for the last $3,400 six days before the opening.

That *The Subject Was Roses* was produced on Broadway at all was a tribute to Gilroy's patience and his out-and-out stubbornness. At one point, for instance, he turned down a Lars Schmidt offer to do the play in Sweden, noting in his diary:

"It gives my ego a boost, but there is more to be lost than gained; if it's a flop, it will flag interest here—and I will never know why it flopped. The play as it stands is untested. I would surely alter it in production to arrive at a definite version—which I can't do in Sweden. The thing I would gain, if a hit there, it would heighten interest here. But then I wouldn't know why it was a hit."

Some of the notices:

Walter Kerr in the *Herald Tribune*:

"The play is a small one, often a quiet one. But Frank Gilroy's *The Subject Was Roses* is quite the most interesting new American play to be offered on Broadway this season. It is interesting because Mr. Gilroy is talented, not in the sense that he is promising but in the sense that he delivers absolutely everything that he intends to. Director Ulu Grosbard, also making his Broadway debut, has sensed precisely the level of bland, blanching, hard-edged whisper at which his author means to convey an ordinary family's secrets, and he has held the stage-tone in near-perfect suspension. Small in outline as this occasion is, recognition is due in every direction."

Richard Watts, Jr., in the *Evening Post*:

"Frank Gilroy once more demonstrates his talent for sternly naturalistic writing, rather more assured in his powers and with incidental moments of wry humor added, in a harsh and relentless story of the crisis confronting a disturbed Irish-American family. If *The Subject Was Roses* lacks some of the final pointed insight beyond naturalism, it is still realism of a high order. The three performances are notably fine. Irene Dailey is moving without ever being sentimental as the mother, Martin Sheen is admirably forceful as the son, and Jack Albertson brilliantly indicates the heart beneath the cantankerous speech of the father."

John McClain in the *Journal-American*:

"Frank Gilroy has a marvelous ear for dialogue, can create interesting and valid characters and maneuver them into compelling situations. What he can't do, apparently, is resolve the problems he sets for himself. An old axiom in the playwriting racket insists that characters in the successful drama must show progression or recession in the course of an evening and that, in my opinion, is what keeps *The Subject Was Roses* from being a much stronger play than it presently is. This may be an entirely valid slice of life, raw and uncompromising and often extremely moving, but it does not result in a very rewarding evening for the customers."

Howard Taubman in *The New York Times*:

"Frank Gilroy has made good on the promise of *Who'll Save the Plowboy?* His new play is not only an impressive stride forward but also an honest and touching work in its own right. Mr. Gilroy has not resorted to gimmicks, razzle-dazzle or advanced techniques to be in fashion. He has written a straightforward, realistic play that wears no airs. With simplicity, humor and integrity he has looked into the hearts of three decent people and discovered, by letting them discover, the feelings that divide and join them. Credit Ulu Grosbard's sensitive, unobtrusive direction and Edgar Lansbury's scrupulously commonplace set as well as Mr. Gilroy for the dignity and warmth of this modest, truthful play."

John Chapman in the *Daily News*:

"*The Subject Was Roses* is a low-key, kitchen-sink drama about a mother, father and war vet son who live in The Bronx and haven't got to know each other after all this time. Gilroy's intent has been a serious one, to write a play about three people, bound by the closest of human ties, who have remained strangers to each other—and to try to figure out why. His main trouble is, to me, that he has chosen three uninteresting characters to write about."

Gilroy's feelings about himself reflect the matter-of-fact manner of his plays. Three weeks after the opening, he was quoted in *Time* Magazine:

"I haven't set out to reverse any trends," said the playwright. "The stories I have told so far tell best in a realistic way. I have nothing against the avant-garde, I feel little tendencies in myself bubbling in that direction. I thought I had darned well better be able to present living persons on the stage before I tried to distill and abstract them."

ALSO-RANS: *Luv, Fiddler on the Roof, The Odd Couple, Slow Dance on the Killing Ground. Incident at Vichy, Tiny Alice*

SUMMATION

A good choice, and a just reward for a doggedly honest play. The wildly funny *Luv* was much too far out for the Pulitzer judges to consider, and *Tiny Alice* was much too murky. An excellent case could have been made for *Fiddler on the Roof*, but two of the last three Pulitzer selections had been musicals, which may have militated against it. *Fiddler* did win the Critics' Circle Best Musical award.

Richard Kiley and Irving Jacobson in Man of La Mancha

1965-66

NO AWARD

The two leading candidates ignored this season were *Man of La Mancha* and *Hogan's Goat*. *Hogan's Goat*, William Alfred's first play, was a poetical drama about an Irish political leader, and one of the biggest off-Broadway hits of the year. Dale Wasserman's *Man of La Mancha*, also off-Broadway, wove Don Quixote and the real-life Cervantes into a stunningly effective musical. Either of these productions would have been a worthy winner.

The rest of the season's plays were comparatively negligible, although *The Lion in Winter* struck some sparks with its conflict between Henry II and Eleanor of Acquitaine. *Generation* was a ho-hum comedy about conformity, and *The Impossible Years* was better fitted for a television screen than for a Broadway stage. Edward Albee came another cropper with *Malcolm*, and Alan Jay Lerner's ESP musical, *On a Clear Day You Can See Forever*, showed only flashes of the genius that had irradiated his earlier *My Fair Lady*.

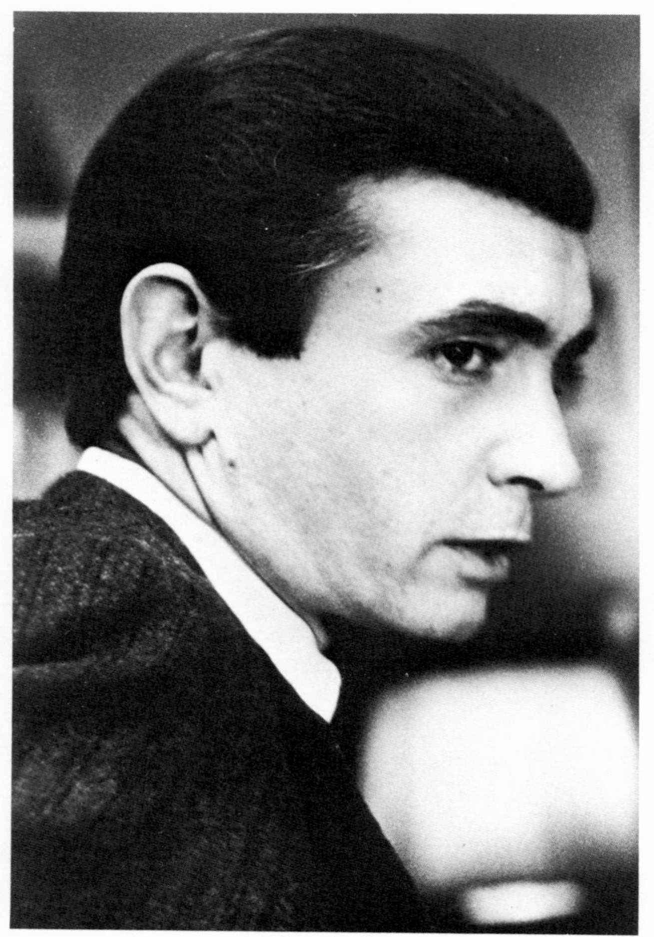

Edward Albee

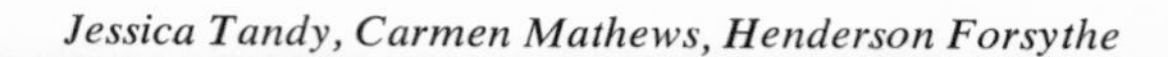

Jessica Tandy, Carmen Mathews, Henderson Forsythe

1966-67

TOBIAS AND AGNES are a well-off married couple in late middle age. Tobias has retired from business, and has made room in his house for Agnes' alcoholic sister, Claire. Claire is more or less in love with Tobias; Agnes, aware of this, hates her.

Harry and Edna, Tobias and Agnes' best friends, arrive at the house one evening, and it is soon apparent that they are not merely paying a visit, but have come expecting to stay. While they were sitting at home alone, a nameless fear had seized them both, and they felt they had to go *somewhere*. Bewildered, Tobias and Agnes put them up.

Soon the household is invaded by another visitor, Tobias and Agnes' daughter, Julia, who over the years has made a habit of running home after her various marriages have failed; this is her fourth trip. Julia bitterly resents the presence of Harry and Edna.

Tobias agonizes over the decision he has to make about Harry and Edna. They are obviously prepared to stay on indefinitely if he does not literally throw them out; on the other hand, if he forces them to go, is he not denying the validity of friendship's deepest claims, and lessening himself as a human being? In a hysterical, semi-poetic monologue Tobias analyzes the problem, and ends by pleading with Harry and Edna to stay, as much for his sake as their own. Unnerved by his outburst, they decide to leave immediately. The terrible question of ultimate responsibility is thus begged, and the forlorn little household teeters back to its "delicate balance."

(Left) *Marian Seldes, Hume Cronyn*

Jessica Tandy, Hume Cronyn

A DELICATE BALANCE

THE CREDITS

A PLAY BY EDWARD ALBEE.
PRODUCED BY RICHARD BARR AND CLINTON WILDER.
STAGED BY ALAN SCHNEIDER.
OPENED AT THE MARTIN BECK THEATRE, SEPTEMBER 22, 1966, AND RAN FOR 132 PERFORMANCES.

THE CAST

AGNES	Jessica Tandy
TOBIAS	Hume Cronyn
CLAIRE	Rosemary Murphy
HARRY	Henderson Forsythe
EDNA	Carmen Mathews
JULIA	Marian Seldes

Jessica Tandy, Rosemary Murphy, Carmen Mathews, Henderson Forsythe, Hume Cronyn

ACT I

Friday Night.

ACT II

SCENE 1. *Early the Following Evening.*
SCENE 2. *Later That Evening.*

ACT III

Early the Next Morning.

THE SCENE: *The Living Room of a Large and Well-Appointed Suburban House. Now.*

HISTORY AND REVIEWS

"This is Albee's best and most mature play, without any flashy fireworks. . . ."

Edward Albee was 38 when *A Delicate Balance* opened, the most discussed American playwright of his generation, a wary, youthful-looking cosmopolitan with two Picassos on the walls of his New York town house in Greenwich Village. Ten years earlier he had been occupying a cold water flat in that same Village, scratching out a living as a Western Union messenger, a waiter, a record salesman. He was drinking too much and writing poetry and unsuccessful novels.

"I felt as if a glass dome had been dropped over me," he once said about that early, difficult period. "Everything was terribly black."

Then one night he decided to begin a one-act play, *The Zoo Story*. He wrote it in three weeks. It was first produced in Germany, in 1959, and was done in New York the following year, at the Provincetown Playhouse. Other short off-Broadway plays—*The Death of Bessie Smith*, *The Sandbox*, *The American Dream*—gave him a rapidly growing reputation, and in 1962 the explosive *Who's Afraid of Virginia Woolf?* was the sensation of the Broadway season, only failing to win the Pulitzer Prize because of the peculiar timorousness of the Advisory Board.

Albee subsequently did two unsuccessful adaptations, of Carson McCullers' *The Ballad of the Sad Café* and James Purdy's *Malcolm*, and had little better luck with *Tiny Alice*, a rather incomprehensible excursion into metaphysics. *A Delicate Balance*, while nowhere near as great a commercial hit as *Virginia Woolf*, did put his career back on the rails.

Albee grew up in luxury in Larchmont, N. Y., as the adopted son of Reed Albee, co-owner of a large chain of vaudeville theatres. That odd Larchmont household was later to send vibrations through many of Albee's plays, particularly *The American Dream*. His father was small, eager to please, and so timid and retiring that he had a habit of jingling the coins in his pockets as a warning that he was about to enter a room. His mother, Frances, a large and dominating woman, frequently strode around the house wearing riding breeches and a derby, and carrying a crop.

In 1948, after a tentative, unavailing stab at college, Albee had a bitter fight with his mother, and left home. He supported himself haphazardly for ten years before *The Zoo Story* started him on his playwriting career.

Albee commented on *A Delicate Balance* during an interview with Tom Prideaux of *Life*: "A basic point of the play is that Tobias can no longer fill his life with the problem of making an important choice. He cries, 'Dilemma, come back!' But it is too late." And to Herbert Whittaker, of the Toronto *Globe & Mail*, he said: "*A Delicate Balance* is a social comedy. It has been interpreted as being about the responsibility of friendship. That's not the theme. It's about the difficulty of making a choice."

For Whittaker he also listed the modern plays that had not necessarily influenced him, but had made the greatest impressions on him: Beckett's *Endgame*, O'Neill's *The Iceman Cometh* and *Long Day's Journey Into Night*, and Williams' *Garden District*. "Influences?" he said to Whittaker. "If somebody said I was influenced by Noël Coward and Jean Genêt they would be closer to the truth."

Albee gave an interesting insight into his working methods in an article printed in the Chicago *Tribune* on February 23, 1964, just before *Virginia Woolf* opened in that city:

"It's dangerous for a writer to dwell too much on 'what he meant,' on the implications of what he has written. There's little enough spontaneity as it is, and if the writer doesn't dredge up pretty exclusively from his unconscious without superimposing anything more than formal control and intuitive reasoning, he's more likely to write a tract than a play, say. When a writer says that he gives his characters their heads and that he doesn't know exactly what they're going to say, he means that he is relying on both levels of his mind. What a writer 'means' by a play he writes is the total experience of the play on an audience, or, to put it more accurately, on the first audience—the audience of himself. And, too, it's a curious thing: I find for myself that maybe six months after I've completed a play I can no longer really recall either the experience of writing the play or the motivations for writing it."

Some of the notices:

John Chapman in the Sunday *News*:

"This is Albee's best and most mature play, without any flashy fireworks. It is an engaging, almost ingratiating play. In this drama, some of his characters come close to warm, human affection, which is unusual in this skilled but embittered playwright."

Richard Watts Jr. in the New York *Post*:

"*A Delicate Balance* has all the quality of brilliantly corroding and lacerating wit that has marked

Rosemary Murphy

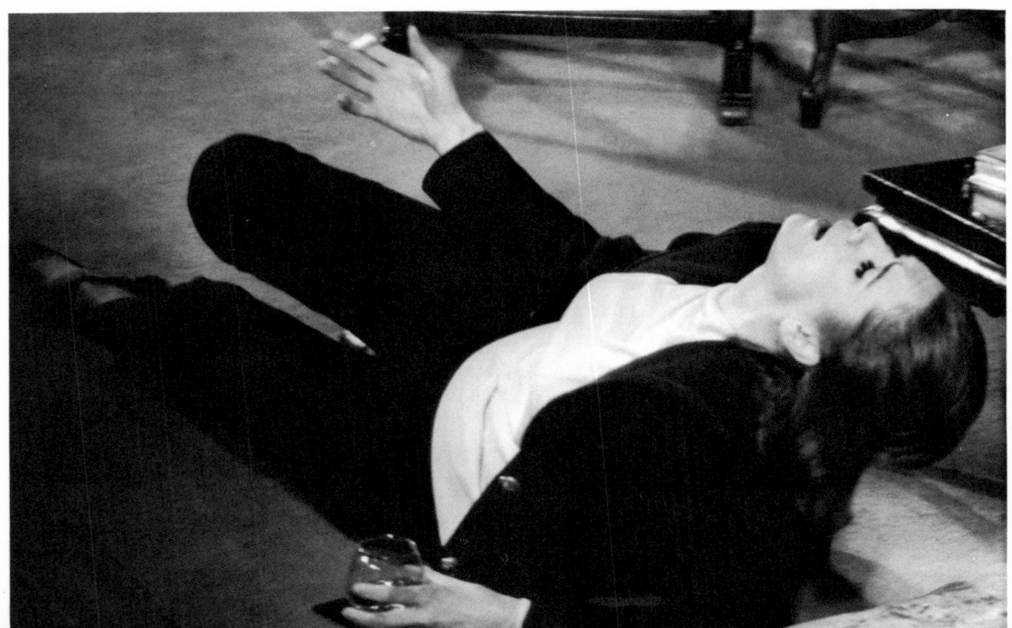

Edward Albee's previous work. But, amid the mutual exchange of biting insults in his dialogue, there is a sympathetic feeling for the embattled characters that represents an advance in the understanding of human inner-torment. It is splendidly acted. Hume Cronyn gives one of his finest performances as the husband, and Jessica Tandy is surprisingly sympathetic as the wife without striving for sympathy. Two unfailingly fine young actresses, Rosemary Murphy and Marian Seldes, are notably excellent as the cheerfully alcoholic sister and the restless, tormented daughter."

Walter Kerr in *The New York Times*:

"T. S. Eliot once said, 'I will show you fear in a handful of dust,' and then he did it. In *A Delicate Balance*, Edward Albee talks about it and talks about it and talks about it, sometimes wittily, sometimes ruefully, sometimes truthfully. But showing might have done better. *A Delicate Balance* is the sort of play that might be written if there were no theater. It exists outside itself, beside itself, aloof from itself, as detached from the hard floor of the Martin Beck, where it opened last night, as its alarmed characters are detached from themselves."

Harold Clurman in the *Nation*:

"Edward Albee's *A Delicate Balance* is a brilliant play. It is a further step in the author's progress and is superior to the more sensational *Who's Afraid of Virginia Woolf?* It deserves our close attention. There will be very few new American plays this season to warrant the same."

John McCarten in *The New Yorker*:

"On occasion, the author introduces a bit of acerbic wit into the proceedings, and every now and then he cuts loose with flights of poetically oriented rhetoric. On the whole, though, Mr. Albee, who is trying to show us some representatively hollow modern types, is not too successful in blending his various styles into a coherent pattern. He is not successful, either, in building *A Delicate Balance* to any sort of dramatic climax."

Albee did not take the Pulitzer Prize lying down. As soon as it was announced that he had won, he released the following statement to the press:

"There has been growing criticism over the years both of the Pulitzer Prize awards and of the methods employed in determining these awards. The criticism has not been limited to the award for drama, but perhaps it has been noisiest in that department.

"In 1963, some of us will recall, my play, *Who's Afraid of Virginia Woolf?*, was chosen by the nominating jury of John Mason Brown and the late John Gassner as the play most worthy of receiving the Pulitzer Prize that year. That nomination was passed on to the trustees who—several of them I regret to say without benefit of having either read or seen the play—voted by bare majority to reject the recommendation of the jury. That year, no Pulitzer Prize for drama was given, and both John Mason Brown and John Gassner resigned in protest.

"At that time I was asked how I felt about the trustees' rejection of *Who's Afraid of Virginia Woolf?* and about the jurors' resignation. I limited myself to saying that I felt no comment would be proper on an award that was not given.

"Now that I find myself, this year, recipient of the Pulitzer Prize for drama for my play, *A Delicate Balance*, I feel free to speak out—not about the 1963 non-award, in particular, but about the Pulitzer Prize in general.

"While it is true that the trustees of the Pulitzer Endowment are free to handle the recommendations of a jury in any manner they see fit, I would suggest that the Pulitzer Prize is in danger of losing its position of honor, and could, foreseeably, cease to be an honor at all.

"Certainly something should be done to counter the feeling in the arts that the Pulitzer Prize is not always given to the best work in any given year. Certainly something should be done to counter the feeling that the trustees will, from time to time, pass over a controversial work in favor of one more conventional, if of less value or, failing that option, choose to make no award at all. Certainly the resignations of John Mason Brown and John Gassner would suggest, if nothing else, that there is, now and again, a distance of mind between the trustees of the Pulitzer Prize and the men who are knowledgeable in the art fields they are chosen to represent.

"I think it would be well for the trustees of the Pulitzer Prize to wonder if they are always fulfilling the responsibility for which *they* have been chosen. And, certainly, I *do* think it is the responsibility of the trustees to familiarize themselves with whatever they happen to be voting on.

"I've given a good deal of thought to whether I should accept the Pulitzer Prize for drama this year, or whether I should refuse it. The Pulitzer Prize *has* been refused before . . . Saroyan refused it, if I'm not mistaken, and I believe Sinclair Lewis declined it at one time.

"I have decided to accept it . . . for three reasons: first, because if I were to refuse it out of hand I wouldn't feel as free to criticize it as I do accepting it; second, because I don't wish to embarrass the other recipients this year by seeming to suggest that they follow my lead; and, finally, because while the Pulitzer Prize is an honor in decline, it is still an honor, a considerable one.

"To conclude, it seems to me that no more proper use could be made of this year's drama prize money than to honor the late John Gassner, a critic and gentleman. I ask that this year's Pulitzer Prize drama jurors, Richard Watts, Elliot Norton and Maurice Valency join with John Mason Brown and me in establishing a fit memorial for John Gassner . . . perhaps the establishment of a larger fund in Mr. Gassner's name, a fund to assist young playwrights, say, or to train young people in the art and responsibility of drama criticism."

ALSO-RAN: *MacBird, The Star-Spangled Girl*

SUMMATION

A good choice, for *A Delicate Balance* was much the best American play of the season, and far outclassed a remarkably poor field. Barbara Garson's primitive and vitriolic *MacBird*, a huge off-Broadway hit, was the most controversial show of the year, but could never have been in the running for the Prize because of the *Macbeth* parallel. The Critics' Circle chose *The Homecoming* as Best Play and *Cabaret* as Best Musical.

Rosemary Murphy, Jessica Tandy, Hume Cronyn

INDEX